Georgia
Bird Watching

A Year-Round Guide

Published by Cool Springs Press, a Division of Thomas Nelson, Inc., P. O. Box 141000, Nashville, Tennessee, 37214.

Thompson, Bill, III.
    Georgia bird watching : a year-round guide / Bill Thompson, III, and the staff of Bird watcher's digest.
        p. cm.
    Includes bibliographical references and index.
    ISBN 1-59186-098-9 (pbk.)
    1. Bird watching--Georgia. 2. Birds--Georgia. I. Bird watcher's digest. II. Title.
QL684.G4T48 2004
598'.072'34758--dc22

                                        2004014159

First Printing 2004
Printed in the United States of America
10 9 8 7 6 5 4 3 2 1

Managing Editor: Billie Brownell
Interior Designer: Bill Kersey, Kersey Graphics
Production Artist: S.E. Anderson
Map and Icon Illustrator: Heather Lynch
Sighting Notes Illustrator: Julie Zickefoose

Visit the Thomas Nelson website at **www.ThomasNelson.com**, and the Cool Springs Press website at **www.coolspringspress.net**

Photography Credits

Arthur Morris/Birds as Art: Front cover featured photo (brown thrasher); front cover top photo (snowy egret); intro photo page 6 (brown thrasher); Pages 8; 9; 16; 17 (both photos); 18; 19; 20 (both photos); 21 (dark-eyed junco); 22 (anhinga); 23 (cerulean warbler); 24 (prothonotary warbler); 26 (rose-breasted grosbeak & wood stork)

Maslowski Photography: Front cover bottom photo (red-headed woodpecker); Pages 15; 25 (red-headed woodpecker); 28

Barth Schorre: Front cover middle photo (painted bunting); Pages 11; 24 (painted bunting)

Brian Small: Pages 22 (brown-headed nuthatch); 25 (red-cockaded woodpecker)

Tom Vezo: Pages 10; 21 (hooded merganser)

Brian Henry: Back cover bottom photo (eastern bluebird)

Charles Melton: Back cover top photo (scarlet tanager)

Gary Meszaros: Page 23 (common moorhen)

Georgia
Bird Watching
A Year-Round Guide

Bill Thompson, III
and the staff of

BirdWatcher's *Digest*

COOL SPRINGS PRESS
A Division of Thomas Nelson Publishers
Since 1798

www.thomasnelson.com

Dedication and Acknowledgements

Dedication

To my parents, Bill and Elsa Thompson, who were bird watching *way* before it was cool and who had the courage and optimism to launch *Bird Watcher's Digest* in the living room of our home back in 1978. Thank you, Mom and Dad, for opening the door to my lifelong passion for birds and bird watching.

To Julie, Phoebe, and Liam (my own little family) who make each day sweeter than the last.

And to my siblings, Andy and Laura, for always being there.

Acknowledgements

There is no such thing as "too many cooks spoiling the broth" when creating a book. From the outset I leaned on and drew upon the talents of publishing professionals and birding experts in creating this book. At *Bird Watcher's Digest*: Deborah Griffith (special editorial blue ribbon), Heather Lynch (maps and cover design kudos), Andy Thompson, Ann Kerenyi, Linda Brejwo, Nate Wooley, Elsa "Catbird" Thompson, Helen Neuberger, Susan Hill, and David Scheimann deserve my never-ending thanks for their help with this project and for covering for me at *BWD* so I could stay home and write.

Andy Thompson, Charles Kirkwood, and Russell Galen made early and important contributions to the launching of this book.

My deep gratitude to the folks at Cool Springs Press—especially Billie Brownell, Hank McBride, David Dunham, and Roger Waynick—for their enthusiasm, guidance, and support. Thanks also to the many people who helped in the development of this book "behind the scenes"—to Tama Fortner for her copyediting expertise, to Bill Kersey for his art direction, and to S.E. Anderson for pulling it all together.

Helping with the content creation were Norma Siebenheller, Howard Youth, and Julie Zickefoose—three peerless bird authors. Without them I'd still be laboring over a smoking-hot laptop.

Among the Georgia birders I know, one person is consistently singled out as being *the* resource for information about the state's birds—Giff Beaton. Giff is an airline pilot who has been photographing and observing birds for nearly 30 years. He is the author of several books and articles about birds. He and his wife Becky live in Marietta, Georgia.

Giff helped me not only with the text for this book—he wrote the "Welcome to Bird Watching in Georgia" chapter—but also with the list of commonly encountered birds. His knowledge extends far beyond the Georgia state boundaries, and I was fortunate to have his input. Thanks, Giff!

Creating a book requires a lot of "cooks" and I am grateful for everyone's contributions. Any errors, omissions, or factual errors contained herein are utterly inadvertent and remain the responsibility of the author (me).

Finally, thank *you* for reading this book. I hope our paths cross someday in a beautiful natural place where there are lots and lots of birds. What could be better?

—Bill Thompson, III

Table of Contents

Welcome to Bird Watching

in Georgia . . . Giff Beaton

Georgia has a long, rich history of bird watching and bird study. The first published reference to birds in Georgia is from 1557—an account of turkeys being provided to a Spanish expedition! The first real study of Georgia birds was made by Mark Catesby from 1722 to 1726, and published in his book The Natural History of Carolina, Florida and the Bahama Islands *in 1730. Many famous early naturalists of North America spent some time in or around Georgia in the late 1700s and early 1800s, including John Bartram, John Abbott, Alexander Wilson, Thomas Nuttall, John James Audubon, and several of the LeContes. Many important avian discoveries were made in the late 1800s by William Brewster and Willis Worthington; though this practice is no longer prevalent, they documented their bird sightings by collecting (shooting) the birds.*

The early and mid-1900s were marked by many local bird authorities and their discoveries. Some of the most notable of these were Eugene Odum and Thomas Burleigh in Athens (author of *Georgia Birds*, published in 1958 and still a useful and important work), E. E. Murphey and J. Fred Denton in Augusta, Ivan Tomkins in Savannah, Herbert Stoddard in Grady County, and Earle Greene and William Griffin in Atlanta. All of these men published important information about their areas or about Georgia as a whole. And this list of naturalists is by no means complete or even close to it!

The Georgia Ornithological Society (GOS) was founded in Atlanta in 1936, and it became a way for the many local bird clubs to connect with each other. The GOS began publishing the official journal of Georgia ornithology, *The Oriole*, which is still published today. The GOS also started publishing many regional bird publications, most of which are still highly useful, and in 1945 they published the *Birds of Georgia*. The sixth edition of this book came out recently and is now titled the *Annotated Checklist of Georgia Birds*. Any student of Georgia's birds should have a copy of this publication.

The sheer size of Georgia makes it difficult to see all of it (it's the largest state east of the Mississippi River), and it has among the highest number of ecoregions and attendant bird species of any eastern state. From the Mountains region in the Blue Ridge, through the rolling hills and large rivers of the Piedmont, and from the swamps of the Coastal Plain to the Atlantic coast, you can find many different bird species at any one time. Over the course of a year, or several years, you can see many more species, all within the confines of our state.

Key Species and Phenomena

In Georgia, there are species with very northern ranges in North America that are passing through as migrants, breeding in the Blue Ridge, or spending their winter in the state. Some of these include the ruffed grouse, golden-winged and cerulean warblers, red crossbill, and pine siskin. In the southern sections of Georgia, many species with more southern distribution can be found, especially in summer, such as the Mississippi and swallow-tailed kites, chuck-will's-widow, and Swainson's warbler. The Georgia coast always has some species of shorebirds, gulls, and terns—no matter what season—as well as offshore species. In short, Georgia is in a perfect position to see just about all the species that can be found in eastern North America!

Yellow-rumped warbler

Another reason that Georgia is great for birding is the thrill it offers warbler and other colorful land bird migrant lovers. Those eastern species that migrate south for the winter use several different paths for their flights south in fall and for their return in spring. The two most often used paths are called *trans-gulf* and *Florida/West Indies*. Those using the trans-gulf route in fall follow the Appalachian Mountains south, head right through west-central Georgia, and then take off from the Gulf Coast between Tallahassee and Houston to hit Central or South America for the winter. In spring, they funnel up Central America and take off from the Yucatan Peninsula, landing on the Gulf Coast in the same swath mentioned above to come right back up through west-central Georgia. At the same time, the Florida/West Indies migrants come down the Atlantic Coast in fall, follow along the Georgia coast, and continue south through Florida to the West Indies and beyond. In spring, they come back up the Florida peninsula. When they hit the Georgia border, they scatter inland as well as up the coast, heading to their breeding grounds. Lucky birders in Georgia get to see them going both ways!

There are a few things to keep in mind throughout the year in order to maximize the number of species of birds you can find and enjoy. Take advantage of the birds that are most common, when they are most common, and where they are most common. This sounds simple, and it is. Look at maps in bird books (such as this one) or bird guides, and figure out if the species you are looking for is a summer bird, a winter bird, or a during migration bird. For example, the common moorhen lives in Georgia all year, but it is much more common in summer. It is also much more common in the Coastal Plain, so look for it there in summer in a watery location.

If you want to see the winter wren—that little brown dynamo—look for it in winter in a wooded location near a stream in the Piedmont. The great crested flycatcher is only here in summer—look for it then, and remember that you will often hear its explosive *wheep!* call before you see it. A book such as *Birding Georgia*, which has bar graphs giving a pictorial representation of exactly when each species can be found in each part of the state, can really help you plan your trips to find species of interest.

Many birders think of warblers and tanagers when they think of migration, but all the species that come here for the winter are also migrants. Ducks, shorebirds, and sparrows are also migrants, and thousands of them may pass through during their migration. The beautiful and stately sandhill cranes—migrants as well—practically fly right down Interstate 75 for their brief winter stop. Once you see or hear a flock of these huge, gray birds bugling overhead, you'll never forget it!

Tips for Successful Birding

One of the great things about bird watching is that you can enjoy it anywhere, at any time—all you really need are a pair of binoculars and open eyes! However, there are quite a few things you can do to increase your enjoyment and success on bird trips, especially for trips away from your local area. Here are a few suggestions for optimizing your enjoyment of Georgia birds.

1. Be prepared for any type of weather! Always wear layers of clothing and some type of rain or sun protection, including a hat.

2. Try to do a little research about where you are going. This includes maps and directions, what birds to look for and where, and any tips for the specific place you are going. Check out bird-finding guides or site guides for this kind of information, much of which may be available online (especially maps). If you have certain birds that you hope to see, check bar graphs for the best time of year and location.

3. Depending on the season, be prepared for animals that might hamper your enjoyment of the outdoors. You are unlikely to ever see a poisonous snake, but always watch where you are walking and where you put your hands. Be especially watchful around water below the Fall Line for cottonmouths and around bunchgrass on barrier islands above the High Tide Line for eastern diamondback rattlesnakes. However, you are unlikely to see either species.

4. Take along repellant if you know that flies and mosquitoes find you tasty. This isn't much of a problem in winter, but in summer there can be some fearsome biting bugs in Georgia! You haven't lived until you have been on the coast when the sand gnats are out in force. Ticks are other pests to avoid. Follow standard tick-prevention techniques, such as wearing light-colored clothing, tucking your pants into your socks, and spraying tick repellant on your clothing.

5. Finally, you need to be careful about chiggers and fire ants. Chiggers aren't actually harmful, but they burrow under your skin and cause red itchy welts that may take several days to go away, so it's best to avoid them. They are found in grass—the taller the better—and if the grass is in a field with grazing animals, that is chigger nirvana. Stay away from the tall or taller grassy areas, and do not sit or lie down in grass. Other ground covers may have them also, such as pine needles, but grass is the worst. In avoiding fire ants, the thing to be aware of is how the ground feels. As you are walking along a field or pond edge, and the ground where your foot just landed feels soft, immediately look down and see if you just stepped in an anthill. If you did, move a few feet away quickly, because they will come streaming out of the hill to bite your legs in an attempt to drive away the "intruder" (your boot). One bite is no big deal, but if you just stand there, you might get dozens.

Spreading Your Wings: Birding Beyond This Book

This book is intended as a starting point for your enjoyment of Georgia's birds. In order to enhance your understanding and appreciation of Georgia's birds, there are many things you can do to "spread your wings" beyond the limits of this book. Most importantly, you will want to improve your bird-identification skills, as well as your bird-finding skills. The following are some tips for increasing your birding knowledge and abilities—as well as your enjoyment.

Identifying Birds

Almost all bird watchers eventually want to be able to identify the birds they see and hear. A great thing about birding is that there is so much diversity out there that you can spend your whole life studying birds and never get bored! While learning the birds of your area (or your state) might seem like a daunting prospect at first, there are many things you can do to simplify the process. There are two approaches to this, and you can choose either or both.

House wren

Chuck-will's-widow

Probably the easiest method is simply to be around other, more experienced, birders. They can help you learn to identify the birds you see. This could be a relative who has been birding longer, a local expert, or members of a local bird club or other nature group.

Alternatively, you can begin right in your own backyard. Many birders start by watching the birds in their yards and using a field guide to help them with identification.

Getting comfortable with Georgia's most common bird species will speed your learning process. For this reason, we have included in this book a profile of the 100 most common birds in Georgia. Check out their pictures and descriptions, and compare these with information in your field guide to see what might be in your yard. This list won't cover every bird you see, but it will have most of the ones you'll see when you are just starting out.

Finding Birds

One of the wonderful things about bird watching is that you can do it anywhere at any time! However, there are many places and many times that will greatly increase your success at finding particular birds or even entire groups of birds. First, you can see plenty of birds in your yard, especially if you put out feeders and landscape with plants that attract birds. Once you are ready to venture beyond your home turf, just about any park or other green space can be worth checking for birds. Local and state parks, wildlife management areas, many school campuses, and other areas can offer good birding opportunities. Again, a local bird club can help with this. They will already know many good spots in or near your area.

The next step is to get a book specifically designed for locating birds, such as *Birding Georgia*, which lists specific spots all over the state and tells you when to go and what you may find there. Bird-finding guides provide the "where" and "when" of bird distribution. If you are flipping through your field guide some day and spot a species you would really like to see, check the map to see if it occurs in Georgia, and then go to the bird-finding guide to learn when it will be available and where. It's that simple— although another joy of this hobby is that you do not ever know exactly what you may find when you venture afield!

You will also need a good map. The best map for Georgia is the *DeLorme Georgia Atlas and Gazeteer*, which is available all over the state at bookstores, gas stations, and office supply stores. It has a great amount of detail and will help you find any spot you are seeking. Other resources include state maps, city or county maps, and online maps from local Convention and Visitor's Bureaus (CVBs). These CVB sites often list hotels, restaurants, and other items of interest, as well. A great site to link to any statewide CVB is the official Georgia tourism site at www.georgia.org/tourism. A free guidebook is available by calling 1-800-VISITGA.

Ecoregions of Georgia

Georgia can be divided into different regions based on the geographic and physical characteristics of the land; these divisions are called ecoregions. They are useful in helping birders determine what types of birds to look for in a particular area. Basically, the land areas of Georgia can be split fairly easily into four main ecoregions: Mountains, Piedmont, Coastal Plain, and Coast. The ecoregions are shown on the Georgia map on page 27. An additional ecoregion is the offshore waters of the Atlantic Ocean for pelagic species—birds found only away from the coast.

The following pages will describe each region, tell where it is, identify some key features, and list some of the expected or typical birds for that region. Of course, many of the more common species are found statewide in every ecoregion, but some are very restricted or found more commonly in one region over another.

Mountains

The Mountains ecoregion is in the northern part of Georgia and may be most easily described by what it is not! This region encompasses everything north of the Piedmont (which is described in the next section). The Mountains ecoregion extends to the Tennessee and North Carolina borders to the north, to Alabama to the west, and to just a bit of South Carolina to the east, as this region angles up toward the northeast. The Mountains region is actually three smaller regions or provinces lumped together for their proximity and, in many cases, for their bird life.

The only real mountains in Georgia are in the far northeast section of the state; this is called the Blue Ridge province. It contains all of Georgia's highest mountains and has a distinctly northern flavor both to its bird life and its plant life, as well. The extreme northwest corner of the state is the Cumberland Plateau, the next highest part of Georgia, though not as high as the Blue Ridge; it lacks the true mountain component and does not have the northern bird and plant life. Sandwiched in between these two is the

Ridge and Valley province, a series of ridges with low valleys in between. Even though it is pretty far north in the state, it shares much of its bird life with the Piedmont region.

The Blue Ridge province is the highest section of Georgia by far, with elevations ranging from 1,600 to 4,700 feet. It's also the coolest part of the state, with January temperatures ranging from 30 to 50 degrees Fahrenheit, and July temperatures ranging from 65 to 90 degrees Fahrenheit. With all this elevation and cooler temperatures, you can find many interesting plant communities and bird species. Many of the highest mountains are actually *balds*, so named because they have just bare rock or stunted growth at the summit. The highest of these, such as Brasstown Bald and Rabun Bald, are the only places in the state to look for northern species, such as breeding common ravens, veeries, Canada warblers, and rose-breasted grosbeaks. The upper elevations of this entire province have other breeding species not found in other regions, such as ruffed grouse, dark-eyed juncos, and chestnut-sided, black-throated blue, Blackburnian, and worm-eating warblers. Unique sections such as Burrell's Ford have rare habitats for Georgia

Scarlet tanager

(such as old-growth white pine and hemlock), and species to look for there include breeding red-breasted nuthatches. Other typical plants for this province include large hardwoods, such as various oaks, evergreens, mountain laurels, and rhododendrons.

The next highest province is the Cumberland Plateau, which is a fairly small area in the extreme northwest corner of Georgia. Elevations range from 800 to 2,000 feet, and this area is part of a high plateau (as the name suggests) that extends into parts of Tennessee and Alabama. Lookout Mountain is the largest feature, and some of the same habitats as the lower sections of the Blue Ridge are found here, along with many of the same bird species except the ones identified for the balds. Other species found here are also found on many of the ridges in the Ridge and Valley province, such as blue-headed vireo, black-throated green warbler, and scarlet tanager.

In between these two provinces lies the Ridge and Valley, where elevations range from 700 to 1,600 feet. Most of the lower elevations are the valleys between the ridges, which are very Piedmont-like in their plant and bird life. The ridges and their higher elevations remain somewhat different from the Piedmont, though, with many of the same species listed for the Cumberland Plateau.

Piedmont

Just south of the Mountains ecoregion is the Piedmont, which is much more homogenous throughout. *Piedmont* is the name of a region in Italy that translates to "the foot of the mountain," which is a good description of the northern edge of the region. The southern edge is the Fall Line, a line roughly running from Columbus to Macon to Augusta across the center of the state. This line corresponds to a break from the relatively higher elevations of the Piedmont to the lower elevations of the Coastal Plain. Many rivers have waterfalls at this break. These waterfalls are where the term *Fall Line* comes from, even though many of those rivers are now dammed. These waterfalls provided a source of power to early settlers as well as an impediment

to proceeding farther upriver, and this is why many of Georgia's cities are situated right at the Fall Line. The western border for Georgia is the Alabama state line and the eastern border is the South Carolina state line. The Piedmont ranges in elevation from 500 to about 1,500 feet, with a few slightly higher sites, such as Kennesaw Mountain at 1,808 feet. Temperatures, like elevation, are intermediate between the Mountains and Coastal Plain regions. January temperatures average from 32 to 55 degrees Fahrenheit, and in July the average is 70 to 90 degrees Fahrenheit.

The Piedmont region's topography is more uniform than that of the mountains, with rolling terrain and a few isolated higher hills. Though many of these are called mountains, they are actually *monadnocks*, or isolated out-crops of hard rock (usually granite). Many of them, such as Kennesaw, are excellent migrant bird locations. The rivers in the Piedmont are generally larger and flatter than those in the mountains. The forested areas along rivers are excellent spots for not only migrants, but also many breeding species as well. Typical plants include many hardwoods as in the Mountains region, plus many evergreens in the form of pines. The types of trees or shrubs at a particular site may have strong implications for which birds you will find there.

Typical birds for the Piedmont vary. Breeding species include whip-poor-will, hairy wood-pecker, eastern phoebe, American robin, black-and-white warbler, and chipping, field, and song sparrows. Some of the winter species that are found easiest in the Piedmont include horned grebe, brown creeper, winter wren, and golden-crowned kinglet.

Coastal Plain

The next Georgia ecoregion to the south is the large Coastal Plain. It is bordered to the north by the Fall Line, and extends west to the Alabama border, south to the Florida border, and east to about Interstate 95. For the purposes of this book, the Coastal Plain can be considered as one entity stretching almost to the coast, to the approximate limits of tidal influence (about

30 miles). The Coastal Plain is flat, mostly sand or clay, and it was underwater for much of pre-history (the Fall Line was an ancient coastline). The elevation ranges from 70 to 500 feet, and the temperatures are just a couple of degrees warmer on average than the Piedmont.

Within the Coastal Plain are many types of habitat, including river hardwoods (called *riparian corridors* when they follow a river), pine forests, swamps, agricultural fields and pastures, and ponds and lakes. Most of the large hardwoods occur along the rivers, and many of the best birding spots in this region are found there also. You cannot go far in the Coastal Plain without finding pine trees, but the type of pine makes a big difference in the type of bird species you will see there. The red-cockaded woodpecker is a highly sought-after species. To find them, however, you need to look for their preferred pine species, which is longleaf in the south and loblolly toward the upper part of the Coastal Plain. Other typical species that favor pine—such as pine warbler and brown-headed nuthatch—are more wide-spread and less picky.

The river floodplain hardwood forests are good spots for migrant land birds and host typical breeding species, such as the Acadian flycatcher, northern parula, and Louisiana waterthrush. The cypress-tupelo swamp habitat is home to many water bird species and also land bird species, such as the prothonotary warbler. Water birds found in swamps and all nonflowing water habitats in the Coastal Plain include anhinga, great egret, and common moorhen. Fish crows are widespread in this region and have recently been moving into the Piedmont as well. Cattle egrets nest in water habitats, but they are usually seen foraging in grassy fields and pastures or along grassy road corridors.

Coast

The last main ecoregion in Georgia is the Coast—everything between the Coastal Plain and the Atlantic Ocean. This strip of land is roughly 30 miles wide and includes all of Georgia's barrier islands and mainland beaches. This region is flat, with a high elevation of about 70 feet, and has the same temperatures as the Coastal Plain. It often feels cooler due to the sea breeze, which is quite welcome on hot, summer days.

In addition to the beaches, other important habitat types in this region include coastal scrub, salt marsh, and the tidally influenced rivers. A very large percentage of this region is made up of salt marsh, much of which is inaccessible. Some species are common throughout this region, such as fish crow and boat-tailed grackle. Others are more discriminating and are found only in one type of habitat. For example, in the salt marsh, typical species include the clapper rail, marsh wren, and seaside sparrow. They are rarely found outside this habitat, but they can be fairly common within it.

Beaches are well known as bird hotspots and are great places to look for shorebirds, gulls, and terns. Year-round beach birds for Georgia include the American oystercatcher, laughing gull, royal tern, and black skimmer. Other common species are only here in one season. Winter species include most other shorebirds, such as the black-bellied plover, western sandpiper, and dunlin, along with higher numbers of gulls (including herring and ring-billed) and Forster's tern. Other species—such as Wilson's plover and Sandwich and least terns—are found mostly during summer. In winter, ducks such as buffle-head and red-breasted merganser are common here, and in summer it is home to the gorgeous painted bunting.

One last ecoregion to discuss is the "offshore" region off the coast, extending away from the land and out to the Gulf Stream almost 70 miles. Many birds found on the coast can be found out here, such as some of the gulls and terns, but there are also other species that never come to land at all in Georgia. These sea-going, or *pelagic*, species include summer species such as Audubon's shearwaters and sooty and bridled terns, or rare winter species such as Manx shear-waters and razorbills. One winter species that inhabits this region is the northern gannet; they can often be seen from shore, unlike the other species listed here, which can only be observed from a boat.

Georgia Bird Watching by Season

Spring

Bird watching is spectacular in Georgia in spring! The birds are in their spiffiest plumage, and they are singing their heads off. Spring generally runs from March to May, but in reality the first stirrings are in February. The beginning of March brings the first wave of migrants to the southern coast and the southeastern part of the state, with blue-gray gnatcatchers and northern parulas leading the way, followed closely by white-eyed vireos.

Yellow-throated warblers are suddenly singing everywhere in the southeast corner of the state, and they work their way north and west through the month of March. Louisiana waterthrushes can be found singing along small creeks and rivers by mid-March. The first swallows and purple martins show up in the south; in the northern part of the state blue-headed vireo numbers pick up and red-winged blackbirds return. Ruby-throated hummingbirds will hit the southwest and coast by the end of the month. Also along the coast and in the deep southeast, the numbers of green and tricolored herons begin to increase. By the end of March, whip-poor-wills are starting to sing all over the northern half of the state, swallows are moving north, and a few warblers have made it above the Fall Line, mostly black-and-white and black-throated green warblers.

Duck migration continues to pull the winter residents away. Numbers drop at winter waterfowl locations and ducks begin showing up in spots that are used most in migration. Lakes and deep ponds will have both dabblers (such as mallards and gadwalls) and divers (such as mergansers and buffleheads), and flooded fields and shallow ponds will have dabblers. Wintering ducks leave the most southern spots first, but as March continues even the northern duck spots show a drop in numbers. Most northern gannets depart from the coast, and inland numbers of land bird winter residents (such as golden-crowned kinglets and dark-eyed juncos) begin to decrease.

Even permanent residents get into the act, with breeding behavior and nest-building activity showing up in backyards and parks. Chickadees and titmice start singing across the state, and checking out nesting sites. American robins build nests everywhere above the Fall Line by the end of the month, and mourning doves work on their spindly stick nests. Great horned owls have already hatched their young, and the young birds will be leaving the nest this month. Barred owls are starting to nest, and screech-owls are thinking about it.

April is when migration really breaks loose! Land bird and other migrants pour into the state. Many species not thought of as migrants are also moving, such as the blue-winged teal. Other ducks continue north, including northern shovelers, ruddy ducks, and lesser scaup. Loons are mostly gone by the end of the month.

Nonbreeding sparrows are mostly gone by the end of April, including the Savannah, swamp, and white-throated sparrows that were so common a month ago. Those sparrows that breed in northern Georgia withdraw from their wintering areas in the south. Almost all of the wintering bird species that nest farther north in North America—including yellow-bellied sapsucker, winter wren, and brown creeper—are gone by the end of April. In the Coastal Plain, the summer resident water birds—anhinga, white ibis, and cattle egret—arrive in large numbers. Wood storks begin nest building, and ospreys return to build their stick nests on platforms near water all across the state. The first few chimney swifts also make it to Georgia. Chuck-will's-widows—and their incessant nighttime calling—arrive in April.

April also brings lots of shorebird movement. Winter residents on the coast continue to depart for their northern breeding grounds, and some species (such as dunlin) are mostly gone by the end of the month. Other species are just arriving, such as lesser yellowlegs and solitary and spotted sandpipers. These three species can often be seen along the edges of small ponds and in wet fields across the state, south of the mountains. Greater yellowlegs and pectoral sandpipers are increasing in numbers. Back on the coast, black-bellied and piping plovers leave and are replaced by migrating semipalmated plovers and summer-resident Wilson's plovers.

Two shorebirds popular with birders—the red knot and whimbrel—increase their numbers in mid-April through mid-May; they can be seen on the beaches and mudflats respectively. The full-scale departure of gulls is underway, especially among the great black-backed, herring, and ring-billed gulls. A few will remain all summer, but only laughing gulls breed here. Summer terns begin to arrive, including Sandwich terns and migrant common terns.

As the trees leaf out, the bright colors and exuberant songs of arriving land birds work their way north throughout Georgia. There is about a two-week delay between birds arriving in the southernmost parts of the state and their arrival in the northernmost parts. First to arrive are the species that breed here, including great crested flycatcher, red-eyed vireo, wood thrush, prothonotary and hooded warbler, summer tanager, and indigo bunting. Ruby-throated hummingbirds arrive in northern Georgia around mid-April.

Every spring about 35 warbler species appear in Georgia, and most are here by April 20. Inland, look for Cape May and blackpoll warblers; this is the only season they can be found inland. Hot on the heels of these small birds are the hawks, also migrating north. American kestrels, merlins, and peregrine falcons can be seen heading north along the coast, along with kites and sharp-shinned and Cooper's hawks. Some of these species are seen inland, as well, along with the inland-migrating broad-winged hawk.

Migration continues through May, but the actual species change and overall numbers drop drastically after the first 10 days. Most permanent residents have already made their nests, laid eggs, and in many cases are feeding their young. By the end of May, many land bird species (especially in the south) will be working on a second brood.

In the first week of May, many birds are just passing through northern Georgia, and many species are just arriving in the mountains. A surprisingly large number of species don't appear anywhere in Georgia until May. These "just passing through" species include both gull-billed and least terns. Statewide, many species show up in smaller numbers in late April, but most arrive in May. Among these are yellow-billed cuckoo and most flycatchers, including eastern wood-pewee and blue grosbeak. Least and willow flycatchers are also late migrants. Highly sought-after species, such as the Connecticut warbler, occur only in May; a few other warblers (such as the yellow-breasted chat) are also among the latest arriving species. Possibly the latest migrant is the white-rumped sandpiper, which only appears in late May or early June.

Summer

As far as changes in bird life go, June is a pretty slow month, but that doesn't mean things are boring. All the birds are still in their best spring plumage and are busy raising their broods. The business of feeding themselves and their chicks takes a lot of energy, so birds are sometimes less wary during this time of year and easier to see. Many of the males are still singing, which makes it easier to find them. All of the great natural areas of Georgia are worth visiting at this time of year because you can see lots of interesting species, and it isn't too hot yet to enjoy being outdoors.

One interesting phenomenon to be aware of is that many species that breed far north of here have predictable numbers of individuals that spend all summer here. These birds are called nonbreeders, and many of them are in their first summer; they will catch up with the rest of the members of their species the next summer. The most obvious examples are the shorebirds and gulls.

July is the height of summer's heat, yet many species start their southward migrations during this month. As early as the first 10 days of the month, the first southbound migrant cerulean warblers and Louisiana waterthrushes will be detected. Swallows and martins also get an early start. Martins leave their breeding areas in early July, and start to head south. Instead of continuing south out of Georgia, they gather in huge communal roosts at night—sometimes many thousands of birds in one roost—and fan out during the day to forage. During the second half of July, look for barn and bank swallows anywhere, and look for large flocks of tree swallows along the coast. And by the end of July, there are hummingbirds everywhere! If you have feeders up, you can watch their little turf battles all day long.

Many other species will be found away from their breeding areas, but not really migrating. This phenomenon is called *post-breeding dispersal*, and it refers to the young birds of the summer and the adults that have finished breeding that simply wander around a bit, seemingly aimlessly, but aren't really heading south yet. One group that is well known for post-breeding dispersal is the long-legged waders, which show up in large numbers well north of their breeding areas in early fall. Little blue herons and great egrets appear across the lower Piedmont; in the Coastal Plain, snowy egrets and white ibises will be present. Some years, quite a few wood storks wander north.

Many shorebirds start their southbound migration in July, and the ones that you see in Georgia

Sanderling

Orchard oriole

oriole is another very early migrant to look for in fall, and ruby-throated hummingbird numbers are at their peak all month.

There are also a few other highlights to watch for in August. The black tern—which will no longer be in black breeding plumage but already in paler winter or nonbreeding plumage—is one species that passes through in August, both inland and more commonly along the coast. Mississippi and swallow-tailed kites find fertile fields of their insect prey during August, and they congregate in large numbers—sometimes up to 50 of each species! These congregations are usually in the eastern Coastal Plain, but small groups may be found much farther north. It is an amazing and beautiful sight to see two dozen or so of these graceful birds wheeling around the sky, chasing beetles and dragonflies. Another interesting insect-eater that congregates during August is the common nighthawk, which starts gathering and migrating in the last two weeks of the month. Any source of bright light, from buildings to billboards, can have a few of these nocturnal birds cruising around after dusk, usually uttering their distinctive *peent* calls.

in July have already come very far from their breeding areas. Species to look for anywhere in the state in the second half of the month include both yellowlegs and solitary, spotted, and least sandpipers. On the coast, other species—such as whimbrels, red knots, and sanderlings—start arriving in July.

One other thing to watch (or listen) for in July is the amount of birdsong. Many land birds continue singing, though at a much reduced rate, but some species stop singing altogether and become very difficult to find at all. Examples of these species would include whip-poor-will, chuck-will's-widow, yellow-billed cuckoo, and great crested flycatcher.

August is another month that most folks would consider summer, but as far as a great many species of birds are concerned, August is really fall. About half of the warblers and vireos that migrate through Georgia begin to appear in decent numbers by the end of August. For some species—such as the cerulean and worm-eating warblers and the Louisiana waterthrush—this month is their peak time of passage through Georgia! Along the coast, you're likely to see yellow and prairie warblers. August is peak for some of the swallows as well, including purple martins and bank swallows—if you don't see them in August, they will all be gone for the year. Orchard

Yellow-billed cuckoo

Autumn

September is the beginning of fall in Georgia, even though it can still be quite hot! Just about every species that was migrating through in spring is now migrating back southward again, although many have changed into much duller winter plumage. Almost none of these migrants are still singing, much to the chagrin of birders trying to find them, though many still give characteristic calls. All of the land birds that leave North America in winter are moving in large numbers, including most members of the flycatcher, vireo, warbler, and tanager families. Those few species that winter in Georgia, such as blue-headed vireos and orange-crowned warblers, typically do not show up until the end of September or later.

Fall migration is more spread out and more protracted than spring, and fall migrants often stop to linger for a few days in an area of good foraging. The bulk of the land bird migrants are still following two major paths through Georgia, the path from the Blue Ridge in the northwest diagonally southwest to the Gulf Coast or right down the coast. Once they leave the mountains, migrants follow the rivers and creeks, and birding areas that include these natural migration pathways often offer better birding.

One of the differences between spring and fall migration is that these paths change a little: Many species experience an eastward shift in their path in fall and are found on the coast in larger numbers. Good examples of this include Cape May, yellow, and prairie warblers, all found in much larger numbers on the coast in fall. A few species take this concept to extremes and fly south, mostly offshore, in fall. The most well-known example of this is the blackpoll warbler. As far as timing goes, the early part of the month is the last good chance for several species, such as blue-winged, golden-winged, and Canada warblers. Yellow and prairie warblers, which started early, are almost finished. The thrushes and flycatchers also occur in greater numbers on the coast in fall, although most of them are still found on inland migration paths.

Other groups, such as the hawks and other daytime (or diurnal) raptors, are migrating by now as well. The largest numbers are along the

Red-tailed hawk

coast, where from the second half of September into October, a bird watcher can see several hawk species and all three Georgia falcons (kestrel, merlin, and peregrine) in one day. On warm, sunny days with good tailwinds, there can be hundreds of hawks flying south along the beaches. Inland can also be good for hawk migration, especially from the end of September through October under the same weather conditions. The first really strong cold front from the west or northwest will usually spur many lingering hawks southward, and if you can get to a high spot in northwest Georgia a day or two after the front passes, you may see many migrating hawks. Observers have often seen several hundred broad-winged hawks in a day under these conditions in late September.

September is also a great month for shorebird migration because numbers of most species continue to increase both inland and along the coast. Many birds are found inland at sod farms and in just about any shallow pond in a farm field. Right after a heavy rain is a good time to search for these migrants, which will migrate in good weather but be forced to land during rain.

Change is the name of the game along the coast in October, both in shorebird numbers and in species, and especially in the gulls and terns. The typical winter gulls, such as ring-billed and herring gulls, are starting to arrive toward the end of the month. From late August through October is the best time to see one of the rarest gulls here, the lesser black-backed gull. Look for this gull on any of the beaches along the coast. Most of the breeding tern species are leaving. By the beginning of the month, almost all of the least and gull-billed terns are gone, and the numbers of black terns are dwindling.

Although October is still a great month for migration among all groups and across the state, the makeup of some of the migrants changes and the numbers really start tapering off by mid-month. Many of the early land bird migrants are completely finished, including most of the swal-

White-throated sparrow

lows and several warblers (see Summer), and only a few true migrants are still coming in. After the second week of October, only the coast still has large numbers of land bird migrants. The good news is that the migrants are being partly supplanted by incoming winter residents, both inland and on the coast.

Inland, above the Fall Line, migrant warblers really fall off about mid-October. However, a few species are at their highest numbers in October, mostly well inland, such as the Tennessee and bay-breasted warblers. Most of the species that are occurring in larger numbers inland are the winter residents that are just arriving. Just about all of the sparrows start to appear in larger numbers during October, including such backyard favorites as song and white-throated sparrows and, later in the month, dark-eyed juncos. Farther afield you can look for incoming white-crowned, vesper, and Savannah sparrows. Other arriving winter residents include blue-headed vireos, the first winter wrens, yellow-bellied sapsuckers, and kinglets. The ruby-crowned kinglets arrive first, starting in late September. Golden-crowned kinglets do not start really trickling in until mid-month and are most commonly found in pine trees.

Winter

November signals the beginning of winter, and it is a mirror image of the late winter and early spring exodus of March. A few land bird migrants are still filtering through in the first week or two, but the bulk of the birds arriving or seen are either permanent or winter residents. All the wintering sparrows are now here in good numbers. Along with the arriving backyard sparrows (such as the white-throated sparrow and dark-eyed junco, the latter mostly north of the Fall Line), check out short-grass fields or spent agricultural fields for Savannah and vesper sparrows (the latter mostly in the south) or wet habitats for swamp sparrows. Look also for the more scarce white-crowned sparrows in the northern part of the state in shrubs and hedgerows, or along the immediate coast as migrants. Other winter residents you might find in these fields are horned larks or American pipits. Some of the sparrows that spend the summer mostly in the northern half of Georgia—such as song and chipping sparrows—now move back into the southern parts. Many of these same fields will also host large flocks of blackbirds, and in the southern and western parts of the state, check for Brewer's blackbird in these flocks. In the northern half of the state, you can search wet forests and fields for rusty blackbirds.

Many waterfowl are moving into the state in higher numbers, and by the end of the month

Chipping sparrow

even the hardiest northern species such as the common goldeneye (mostly inland at large lakes, especially West Point) and black scoter (found along the coast, with a few seen inland) are arriving on their wintering grounds. Many small ponds across the state now have a couple of hooded mergansers or maybe a small flock, and you should check larger ponds or lakes for other arriving ducks. The "dabbling" ducks again are mostly found in shallow weedy ponds or fields. The most common of these are both species of teal (blue-winged will be anywhere as migrants, but only in the Deep South in midwinter, whereas green-winged will be scattered around the state south of the mountains), mallards, northern shovelers, gadwall, and American wigeon. The greatest numbers of these will move through as migrants and be found more readily during midwinter in the southern parts of the state. More rare, but worth

Mallard

looking for, are northern pintail and American black ducks; the latter are primarily in the northern half of the state. Species that dive for food (divers) are now showing up as well. Most common by far are ring-necked ducks, but lesser scaup are also fairly widespread, especially in larger bodies of water (also check for ruddy ducks and bufflehead on these lakes). This is the best time to see flocks of migrating red-breasted mergansers inland into early December, but they are more common along the coast with buffleheads. At the largest lakes, look for horned grebes and common loons, species that prefer deep water. Eared grebes are also increasing throughout the northern parts of the state and along the coast, but they are still fairly rare.

A few shorebirds can still be found inland, though the majority of them are now along the coast. Dependable lingering shorebirds away from the coast are yellowlegs and least sandpiper (found in decent numbers below the Fall Line all winter) and a few lingering migrant dunlin.

Starting at the end of November and continuing into December is the obvious migration of sandhill cranes. These magnificent birds more or less follow Interstate 75 through Georgia both ways; in fall, they are heading for their wintering grounds in southeastern Georgia and northern Florida to enjoy their short winter stay. On any clear day, especially one with south winds, look for loose flocks of these great birds meandering south or southeast. Listen for their prehistoric-sounding calls of *garoo, garoo!* If you are really lucky, you may find cranes on the ground somewhere at an overnight roost. They fly during daylight hours when the sun provides warm-air thermals to help them climb.

Crane migration continues into December, and about the only other new birds are the latest of the hardy ducks. If there is bitterly cold weather to the north of Georgia, we might get an influx of species trying to escape the cold, especially gulls or waterfowl, and some of the rarest species in these groups only occur under such conditions. The other major news in December is the many Christmas Bird Counts, or CBCs, (www.gos.org/cbc.html) held toward the end of

Hooded merganser

the month and into early January. These all-day bird counts are held in the same spot every year and offer new bird watchers a chance to get out in the field with some more experienced locals.

There is not a lot of bird action in January. In early January, it's often possible to see a few flocks of sandhill cranes. By the end of the month the trickle of spring migrants increases, and just about all of them are starting their very long journey north to their breeding grounds.

In February, the first hints of impending spring are the movements of waterfowl across the state, especially toward the end of the month. While the earliest migrant ducks start heading north, another sign of spring is the dusk and dawn courtship flights of the American woodcock. These well-camouflaged birds of wet forests and fields are sprinkled across the state, higher in numbers above the Fall Line. Throughout the month, you can see their whistling display flight and hear their *peent* flight calls (sounding very similar to a common nighthawk).

Dark-eyed junco

Georgia's Ten Must-See Birds

Anhinga
Anhinga anhinga

The anhinga is a fairly large (35-inch) diving bird that looks a little like a skinny cormorant. It is long and slender, with a long sharp bill it uses to spear fish underwater. Another name for this bird is "snake bird," because it frequently swims with just its head above water, looking like a snake.

Like hawks, anhingas also soar on thermals in midday. They can quickly be separated from hawks by their slender profile, with a long skinny neck and head in front and a long tail behind. No other dark soaring birds have this profile. Males are mostly dark, with white feathers on the upper wings, and females are dark below, with brown heads and necks. They can often be seen spreading their wings to dry in the sun prior to making another dive for fish. After many repeated dives, their feathers get waterlogged, so they need to dry them periodically.

This species can be found at most wetlands below the Fall Line, especially in summer when they are most numerous. They don't need much water to dive in, but do need a little open water to maneuver. Easy places to see anhingas include Harris Neck and Eufaula national wildlife refuges, and the Altamaha Wildlife Management Area.

Brown-headed Nuthatch
Sitta pusilla

This tiny bird with the large personality is another favorite of bird watchers everywhere in the South, and if you live or travel anywhere near mature pines, you are likely to run into a group of these inquisitive little birds. They are less than 5 inches long and often stay high up in pine trees, so you frequently must locate them by their chatter and squeaky "bathtub toy" noises. They are usually in groups of three to five, so once you see one, keep watching for the others. When you see one, notice its grayish back, white belly, and brown head with a stubby bill for prying food out of pinecones and bark. They are often seen hitching their way down pine trunks in search of insects and seeds.

This is one of the easiest species to find—just look anywhere with large pines! In many cases this may be your yard, because this is the species that often is found at seed and suet feeders. Brown-headed nuthatches live in Georgia year-round. About the only place you can't find them is up in the Blue Ridge Mountains, where they are rare at higher elevations.

Cerulean Warbler
Dendroica cerulea

The cerulean is a beautiful little blue warbler, less than 5 inches long, and one of the migrant species that seems to be declining at a great rate. The color of the male is a gorgeous light blue (yes, it's cerulean blue!) with a bright white underside broken only by a thin blue "necklace." The females are similar, but are a more blue-green and often have a yellowish tinge below. Both sexes have the typical short, thin warbler bill and are also quite short-tailed even for warblers.

In Georgia, cerulean warblers breed only in a couple of spots up in the Blue Ridge, with most numbers along Ivy Log Gap. They may be difficult to find there, because they tend to stay in the treetops and are present only in small numbers. However, most members of this species migrate right through the western half of Georgia, and probably the best single spot to see this bird in the east is at Kennesaw Mountain in late April or in August during the peak of their seasonal migration. Unfortunately, this warbler is one of the neotropical migrants that is declining, so many conservation organizations are studying them intensely to see if there is anything that can be done to reverse this trend. The data from Kennesaw Mountain birders is being used to help this study.

Common Moorhen
Gallinula chloropus

The common moorhen is a small, ducklike bird, about 14 inches long, found in many marshes and swamp habitats throughout the southern half of Georgia. They are most numerous in summer but occur year-round, especially along the coast. The most obvious feature is the bright red bill with a yellow tip, on a bird that is mostly gray with a white line along its sides. Common moorhens are usually found in groups, paddling in and out of reeds and marsh grasses while squabbling among themselves. If you see one on land or sitting up on a log, notice its huge yellow legs and feet. In summer, family groups of one or two adults and several young birds are often seen. The immatures will be light gray overall with a yellowish bill.

Areas with ponds or marsh habitats along the coast or in the Coastal Plain host many of these birds all summer. Some of the easiest places to see them include Phinizy Swamp, the Bradley Unit of Eufaula National Wildlife Refuge, Harris Neck National Wildlife Refuge, and the Altamaha Wildlife Management Area. They can also be found in these same places in winter, but in fewer numbers.

Painted Bunting

Passerina ciris

It's hard to describe the sheer beauty of this songbird. As a start, the old name for this species was the French word nonpareil *for its singular beauty. The male is amazing, with a blue head, red underparts, and greenish back. And it's not just blue and red, but yellow and green! The female is a greenish yellow. Both sexes are the same size—just under 6 inches long—with a stubby finch bill. They sound similar to their inland and equally striking relative the indigo bunting. Females can look similar to indigo females, but the painted female is quite greenish compared with the browner female indigo. Keep in mind also that painted buntings are found mostly along the coast and sparingly in the Coastal Plain, usually near large rivers. Remember, too, that first spring males may still be mostly greenish, but will sing just like full adult males.*

Painted buntings are most common along the coast, on any barrier island, or along the immediate coast in maritime scrub habitat. Good places to look include Harris Neck National Wildlife Refuge, all the islands, and the Altamaha Wildlife Management Area. They also breed in small numbers right along some of the major rivers, such as the Savannah and the Altamaha (including the feeder rivers the Ocmulgee and Oconee), all the way up to Augusta and Macon.

Prothonotary Warbler

Protonotaria citrea

The prothonotary is a gorgeous, 6-inch, yellow bird with gray wings, a white lower belly, and a long bill for a warbler. Females are almost as bright as males, but with a greener hue to the top of the head and neck. In spring, males have black bills, but in late summer, their bills fade to bone-color like the females. Their insistent sweet-sweet-sweet-sweet call can be heard throughout the southern half of the state in swampy woods and along rivers in the Piedmont. This is the only cavity-nesting warbler in the East, and it will nest in boxes if they are placed in the right swamp habitat. When seen through the darkness of a southern cypress swamp, they can be amazingly bright as they fly back and forth. Old-timers call this bright bird the swamp canary.

Great places to see the prothonotary warbler include any location with access to swampy ponds or river backwaters, such as the Bradley Unit of the Eufaula National Wildlife Refuge or Harris Neck National Wildlife Refuge. A few breed at the Newman Wetlands Center. Many other places also have large populations, such as the Okefenokee National Wildlife Refuge, which is full of them in spring and summer (the only times this species is in Georgia).

Red-cockaded Woodpecker
Picoides borealis

This rare woodpecker is found only in the South year-round, and in Georgia it is found only in large pine and wiregrass forests. It is just slightly smaller than the hairy woodpecker, with a similar pattern of black and white barring, but it also has a large white cheek patch that covers almost the whole side of its head. The "cockade" for which it is named is nearly impossible to see. The red-cockaded lives in family groups called clusters and requires mature pines with red-heart disease to make its nest and roosting cavity. These holes are easy to recognize because they make them in living trees, and there is usually a large, obvious flow of sap from the hole down the front of the tree.

Red-cockaded woodpeckers are now restricted to areas that have populations of the large pines they require, along with periodic controlled burning to maintain the correct wiregrass habitat. The only public areas with good numbers in Georgia are Piedmont National Wildlife Refuge and the Okefenokee National Wildlife Refuge. All large Army bases in Georgia also have decent populations.

There are still several other areas with small numbers of red-cockaded woodpeckers, especially in the southwestern part of the state, but the smaller areas of habitat are gradually losing their populations. Efforts are underway to transplant some of the smallest clusters into areas with good habitat before they vanish.

Red-headed Woodpecker
Melanerpes erythrocephalus

This striking bird is a favorite across the state, and if you live near any kind of woods, you might find them in your yard at least part of the year. They are present throughout the state, except for the higher elevations in the mountains. With a bright all-red head, black body, and large white patches on the wings, they are not likely to be confused with any other species. The red-bellied woodpecker can have red on the back half of the head, but not the black and white colors on the body. Both woodpeckers are just under 10 inches long, and both come to feeders readily. The red-headed woodpecker can sometimes be seen flycatching from the tops of trees.

Red-headed woodpeckers are fairly common throughout the state all year except in the mountains, and they are especially common in thinned woods or partial clearcuts. They also favor beaver swamps with a few isolated trees. They can be found just about anywhere with dead or dying standing trees. They can also be observed in rural areas or subdivisions with just a few scattered trees. In more northern parts of the state, they are only present for part of the year.

Rose-breasted Grosbeak
Pheucticus ludovicianus

The rose-breasted grosbeak is a striking 8-inch-long bird that can sometimes be seen at feeders, although usually only during spring migration in late April and early May. The spring male is unmistakable, with his black head and back, white belly and marks on the wings, and splash of rose on the breast. The female looks similar to a huge purple finch, with a brown back, streaked underparts, a white line above the eye, and—like the male—a large, seed-eating bill. In fall, the male may look more like the female, with just a hint of the rose on the breast.

Rose-breasted grosbeaks can be seen during spring or fall migration, either in your backyard at feeders or at other migration bird-watching spots. They can also be found in their small breeding range in Georgia during the summer. Brasstown Bald and the other highest peaks in Georgia make up their breeding range from May to August. One way to find them is by listening for their distinctive call note, which has been likened to the squeak of gym shoes on a wooden gym floor.

Wood Stork
Mycteria americana

The wood stork is a huge, prehistoric-looking, black-and-white wading bird. Once you have seen one, you will not mistake it for anything else! It stands about 40 inches tall and has a huge 61-inch wingspan, but its most obvious feature is its dark featherless head. This species shares this last feature with its close relatives the vultures, although it does not seem to share much else with them. When the wood stork is soaring, as it commonly does, the black wing tips really stand out against the rest of the white body. It is interesting to watch the wood stork's feeding behavior as it swings its large bill around feeling for food underwater.

Like other waders, wood storks are most easily found feeding in shallow ponds and pools, and in Georgia they are most common along the coast. Several spots along the coast have good numbers in summer, though wood storks do shift their breeding sites from year to year in response to water levels. The most reliable site is Harris Neck National Wildlife Refuge, where the water levels are specifically maintained for this species, but the storks can be seen feeding or soaring anywhere along the coast. A few colonies are spread throughout the Coastal Plain, and in late summer a few individuals wander around the state, sometimes reaching as far north as Atlanta.

Georgia's Ten Best Bird-Watching Spots

Georgia Ecoregions

- **COASTAL PLAIN**
- **PIEDMONT**
- **MOUNTAINS**
- **COAST**

Key Code

1. Brasstown Bald
2. Kennesaw Mountain
3. E. L. Huie Land Application Facility
4. Piedmont NWR
5. Phinizy Swamp Nature Park
6. Bradley Unit of the Eufaula NWR
7. Harris Neck NWR
8. Altamaha WMA
9. St. Simons Island
10. Jekyll Island

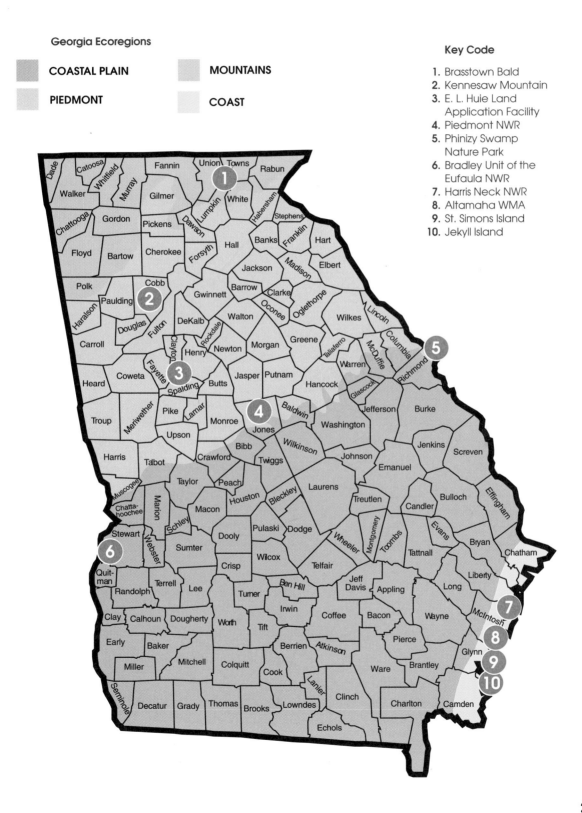

Boardwalk and Spanish Moss

⑧

Altamaha Wildlife Management Area

(Ansley Hodges M.A.R.S.H. Project)
(912) 262-3173
http://georgiawildlife.dnr.state.ga.us

Located just south of Darien and just east of Interstate 95, Altamaha Wildlife Management Area is one of the best year-round birding sites in Georgia. There are many impoundments here, managed primarily for waterfowl in winter, but they are also good for many species of waders and other water birds. Species to watch for are all the herons and egrets, glossy ibis, and common moorhen. Ducks to look for in winter include both blue and green-winged teals, northern shoveler, and mottled duck. Summer species include least bittern, purple gallinule, and painted bunting.

⑥

Bradley Unit of the Eufaula National Wildlife Refuge

509 Old Highway 165
Eufaula, AL 36027
(334) 687-4065
http://eufaula.fws.gov

This refuge is located on the Chattahoochee River just north of Georgetown at Lake Walter F. George. The several impoundments in the Bradley Unit have many species of waterfowl (including greater white-fronted geese) and sparrows (including the hard-to-find Le Conte's) around them in winter, and they host many species of breeding water birds in summer. Spring and fall are good for land birds in the woods and shorebirds in the flooded fields and also along the impoundment edges. Anhingas can be found here year-round.

Brasstown Bald

Brasstown Bald Visitors Information Center
(706) 896-2556
Blairsville Ranger Office
1881 Highway 515
Blairsville, GA 30512
(706) 745-6928
http://ngeorgia.com/travel/brasstown.html

Brasstown Bald is Georgia's tallest mountain and has a good paved access road and a visitor's center just a few miles east of Blairsville off the GA 180 spur. The best time to visit is late spring or summer. Species to look for here include ruffed grouse, common raven, veery, Canada warbler, and rose-breasted grosbeak. Drive to the parking lot, and walk the edges of the lot or the trails up to the visitor center. If you have more time, try the many trails away from the parking lot, which also offer good birding.

E. L. Huie Land Application Facility
(770) 603-5606
http://www.atlantaaudubon.org/pages/
sites.htm#huie

This series of wastewater treatment ponds and nearby wetland center is located just south of Atlanta off U.S. 41 in Jonesboro. The ponds are great for ducks in winter or shorebirds during migration; the wetland center is good for warblers in spring and fall and sparrows in winter. There are scheduled guided walks offered.

Harris Neck National Wildlife Refuge

Route 2, Box 2147, Townsend, GA 31331
(912) 832-4608
http://harrisneck.fws.gov

Located just east of Interstate 95, about 30 miles south of Savannah, Harris Neck National Wildlife Refuge is another superb year-round birding site. It offers many impoundments and a driving tour loop with other great habitats. This site is home to the largest colony of wood storks in Georgia, and they—and many other ducks and waders—can be found in the impoundments here (storks and purple gallinule in summer, ducks in winter, and waders year-round). Many bird species can be observed in the scrubby fields of this former military field, including large numbers of painted buntings in summer. The auto tour goes through some great maritime forest with a variety of breeding species in summer and land bird migrants in spring and fall.

Jekyll Island

Convention and Visitors Bureau
P.O. Box 13186, Jekyll Island, GA 31527
(877) 453-5955
http://www.jekyllisland.com/index2.phtml

Jekyll Island is the next island south from St. Simons along the Georgia coast. It offers not only excellent beaches (especially the southern tip), but also some good forest habitat and a good spot for winter ducks on the northern tip (for greater scaup and black scoter). There are small picnic areas and parks all over this island, and all of them can be good during spring and fall migration. The beaches are good birding all year long as well. The scrub area and beach at the southern tip may be the best single birding spot in Georgia. While driving the causeway onto the island, stop at the visitor center to scan the mudflat behind it at low tide—another good shorebird spot.

② Kennesaw Mountain

900 Kennesaw Mountain Drive
Kennesaw, GA 30152
(770) 427-4686
http://www.nps.gov/kemo/

A National Battlefield Park just northeast of Atlanta off Interstate 75, Kennesaw Mountain is Georgia's single best location for migrating land birds. During peak migration in late April and through most of September, it is not uncommon to see 15 to 20 warbler species in a single day. Vireos, thrushes, and tanagers can be seen here as well. Most bird watchers walk up the paved road to the top or drive to the top and walk around there. The migration seasons run from mid-April to mid-May (spring) and mid-August to mid-October (fall). There are also several guided walks here each season.

⑤ Phinizy Swamp Nature Park

540B Telfair Street
Augusta, GA 30901-2310
(706) 828-2109
http://www.phinizyswamp.org/index.html

Located right near the Augusta airport, Phinizy Swamp Nature Park has hundreds of acres of wastewater treatment impoundments and an education center. This spot offers superb birding year-round, with many guided bird walks offered. In winter, the spotlight is on ducks; in summer, birds to look for include common moorhen, purple gallinule, and least bittern. In late summer and early fall, there are lots of waders here, such as the great egret and little blue heron. Several rail species winter here, including Virginia, king, and sora.

④ Piedmont National Wildlife Refuge

718 Juliette Road
Round Oak, GA 31038
(478) 986-5441
http://piedmont.fws.gov

The Piedmont National Wildlife Refuge is located about 20 miles east of Interstate 75 in Forsyth, just north of Macon. This refuge is best known for resident red-cockaded woodpeckers and nesting Bachman's sparrows, both of which are most easily seen in spring and early summer. There are miles of dirt roads through loblolly pine forests to explore, as well as several lakes and other habitats. In summer, many notable species found here include Acadian flycatchers and prairie, hooded, and Kentucky warblers. In winter, many sparrow species can be observed in the fields, and a few ducks can be found in the lakes.

⑨ St. Simons Island

http://www.gacoast.com/navigator/ssi.html

St. Simons Island is immediately east of Brunswick on Georgia's Atlantic Coast, and has great beaches for birding all year-round. Gould's Inlet on the southeast corner of the island has the best beach viewing in Georgia for shorebirds, gulls, and terns; it is best at a high or falling tide. Toward low tide this is a good spot for reddish egret. In summer, look for Wilson's plover and least tern; in winter, look for many shorebirds, including piping plover and marbled godwit. During migration, this is a good place to see red knot and whimbrel.

Resources for Georgia Bird Watchers

Birding Clubs and Societies

Albany Audubon Society
P.O. Box 705
Albany, GA 31702
www.angelfire.com/ga3/albanyaudubon/

Atlanta Audubon Society
Box 29189
Atlanta, GA 30359
(770) 913-0511
www.atlantaaudubon.org

Augusta-Aiken Audubon Society
4542 Silver Bluff Road
Jackson, SC 29831
http://home.comcast.net/~ehoward24/

Coastal Georgia Audubon Society
P.O. Box 21726
St. Simons Island, GA 31522
www.geocities.com/coastalgas

Georgia Ornithological Society
http://www.gos.org/
The GOS site is the most comprehensive, statewide resource and has links to many of the smaller local parks and nature centers.

Ocmulgee Audubon Society
11420 Forest Hill Court
Milledgeville, GA 31061
www.wesleyancollege.edu/OAS/

Oconee Rivers Audubon Society
P.O. Box 48132
Athens, GA 30604-8132
http://alpha.rmy.emory.edu/~ORAS/

Ogeechee Audubon Society
P.O. Box 13806
Savannah, GA 31416-0806
http://www.ogeecheeaudubon.org

Books and Publications

Beaton, G. 2000. *Birding Georgia*. Falcon for Globe Pequot Press.
This is a guide to many of the best birding spots in the state, with very detailed directions and maps for birding each spot. There are also bar graphs to see which birds can be seen in the state at different times of the year.

Beaton, G., Sykes, P., & Parrish, J. 2003. *Annotated Checklist of Georgia Birds*. Georgia Ornithological Society.
This book lists all the species that have occurred in the state, and gives a summary of their status and distribution.

Burleigh, T. D. 1958. *Georgia Birds*. Norman, OK: University of Oklahoma Press.
This book by Thomas Burleigh is long out of print, but remains the most detailed book about Georgia and its bird life. You can find copies at used book dealers, but they are getting scarce and expensive as time goes on.

Georgia Atlas and Gazetteer, published by DeLorme.
By far the best map of the state, it has 72 large pages, and it is the best way to find all types of parks and wildlife management areas.

Georgia State Travel and Tourism
800-VISITGA
http://www.georgia.org/tourism/
all_of_georgia/home.asp

Important Bird Areas Website

www.atlantaaudubon.org/pages/
conservation.htm

Rare Bird Alerts, Discussion Lists, and Festivals

Georgia Birders Online

http://listserv.uga.edu/archives/gabo-l.html
This is the site of the state birding discussion list. Rare Bird Alert transcriptions are posted here.

Georgia's Colonial Coast Birding and Nature Festival

www.coastalgeorgiabirding.org/

Pinewoods Bird Festival

www.pinewoodsbirdfestival.com/

Wildlife Refuges, Parks, and Preserves

America's National Wildlife Refuge System

800-344-WILD
http://refuges.fws.gov/
This site contains information and links to Georgia's national wildlife refuges, including Bond Swamp, Eufaula (headquarters are in Alabama), Harris Neck, Okefenokee, Piedmont, and Savannah (headquarters are in South Carolina).

Chattahoochee-Oconee National Forests

1755 Cleveland Highway
Gainesville, GA 30501
(770) 297-3000
www.fs.fed.us/conf/

Colonial Coast Birding Trail

http://georgiawildlife.dnr.state.ga.us/content/
displaycontent.asp?txtDocument=85
Several of the best birding locations along the coast are part of the Colonial Coast Birding Trail, and this site offers information on these areas.

Georgia Department of Natural Resources

2 Martin Luther King, Jr. Drive
S. E., Suite 1252 East Tower
Atlanta, GA 30334
(404) 656-3500
www.gadnr.org/
This is the website for wildlife management area and public fishing area information, although this site does not offer many wildlife management area maps. The *DeLorme Atlas* remains the best location for researching those sites.

Georgia State Parks

2 Martin Luther King, Jr. Drive
Suite 1352 East
Atlanta, GA 30334
800-864-7275
http://www.gastateparks.org/
Georgia has many parks and wildlife management areas with good birding, including public fishing areas. There are almost 50 state parks and 80 wildlife management areas!

National Park Service

http://data2.itc.nps.gov/parksearch/
geosearch.cfm
This website contains information and links to Georgia's national parks and monuments, including the Chattahoochee River National Recreation Area, Chickamauga and Chattanooga National Military Park, Cumberland Island National Seashore, Kennesaw Mountain National Battlefield Park, and Fort Pulaski and Ocmulgee National Monuments.

Getting Started in Bird Watching

Bird watching, or birding, is one of North America's fastest-growing and most popular hobbies. According to a recent survey by the U.S. Fish & Wildlife Service, there are as many as 44 million bird watchers in the United States. Back in 1978, when my family began publishing Bird Watcher's Digest in our living room, bird watching was still considered a bit odd. The image many people associated with bird watching was Miss Jane Hathaway of The Beverly Hillbillies. Fortunately, that stereotype is long gone now, and our culture has come to embrace bird watching as an enriching, exciting pursuit—one that can be done with little expense and enjoyed almost anywhere at any time.

Why Do We Watch Birds?

Birds have inspired humans for thousands of years. Birds can fly—something we humans have mastered only in the past 100 years. Birds have brilliant plumage, and some even change their colors seasonally. Birds are master musicians, singing beautiful and complex songs. They possess impressive physical abilities—hovering, flying at high speeds, and withstanding extreme weather conditions, as well as the rigors of long migration flights. Birds also have behaviors to which we can relate, such as intense courtship displays, devotion to their mates, and the enormous investment of effort spent in raising their young. Sound familiar? In short, birds are a vivid expression of life, and we admire them because they inspire us. This makes us want to know them better and to bring them closer to us. We accomplish this by attracting them to our backyards and gardens, and by using optics to see them more clearly in an "up close and personal" way.

Early Bird Study

Before the advent of modern optics that help us view birds more closely, humans used a shotgun approach to bird watching. Literally. Famed ornithologist and bird artist John James Audubon was the first European to document many of the North American bird species in the early 1800s. He did so by shooting every unfamiliar bird he encountered. Having a bird in the hand allowed him to study it closely and draw it accurately. This was an excellent method of learning a lot about birds quickly, but it was rather hard on the birds. This method of bird study continued largely unchecked until the

Millions of Americans enjoy bird watching.

early 1900s, when the effects of market hunting on birds became unhappily apparent. In 1934, a young bird enthusiast and artist named Roger Tory Peterson published *A Field Guide to the Birds*, with a system of arrows showing key field marks on the plumage of each species. This enabled a person to identify a bird from a distance, with or without the aid of magnifying optics. Modern bird watching was born, and it was no longer necessary to shoot birds in order to positively identify them. The era of shotgun ornithology was over.

Modern Bird Watching

Bird watching today is about seeing or hearing birds and then using these clues to positively identify them. To reach this identification, we use two important tools of the bird-watching trade: binoculars and a field guide. The binoculars (or perhaps a *spotting scope*, which is a telescope especially designed for nature watching) help you to get a closer, clearer look at the bird. The field guide helps you interpret what you see so that you can identify the bird species.

I like to say that we live in the golden era of bird watching. When I started birding more than 35 years ago, feeders, seed, birdhouses, and other supplies were hard to come by—we had to make our own. Now they are available in almost any store. We can buy a field guide or a book like the one you're holding in any bookstore. We can try out optics at camera stores, outdoor suppliers, and at birding festivals. We can learn about birds in special bird courses, on the Internet, in magazines, or from CD-ROMs, DVDs, and videos. We can join a local or state bird club and meet new bird-watching friends. We can take birding tours to far-off places.

Select binoculars that feel good in your hands and are easy to use.

There's never been a better time to become a bird watcher. So let's get started!

Basic Gear

If you're just starting out as a birder, you may need to acquire the basic tools—binoculars and a field guide.

Binoculars

You may be able to borrow optics from a friend or family member, but if your interest takes off, you'll certainly want to have your own binoculars to use anytime you wish. Fortunately, a decent pair of binoculars can be purchased for less than $100, and some really nice binoculars can be found used on the Internet or through a local bird club for just a bit more. The magnification powers that are commonly used for bird watching are 7x, 8x, and 10x. This is always the first number listed in the binoculars' description, as in 8x40. The second number refers to the size of the objective lens (the big end) of the binocular. The bigger the second number, the brighter the view presented to your eye. In general, for bird-watching binoculars the first number should be between 7x and 10x, and the second number should be between 30 and 45.

Try to find binoculars that are easy and comfortable to use. Make sure they focus easily, giving you a clear image, and that they are comfortable to hold (not too large or heavy) and fit your eye spacing. Every set of eyes is different, so don't settle for binoculars that just don't feel right. The perfect pair of binoculars for you should feel like a natural extension of your hands and eyes. Over time you will become adept at using your optics and, with a little practice, you'll be operating them like a pro.

Field Guide

When choosing a field guide, you'll need to decide what type of birding you'll be doing and where you plan to do it. If nearly all of your bird watching will be done at home, you might want to get a basic field guide to the backyard birds of your region, or at least a field guide that limits its scope to your half of the continent. Many field guides are offered in eastern (east of the Rocky Mountains) and western (from the

A field guide is one of birding's essential tools.

Rockies west) versions. These geographically limited formats include only those birds that are commonly found in that part of the continent, rather than continent-wide guides that include more than 800 North American bird species. Choose a field guide that is appropriate for you, and you'll save a lot of searching time—time that can be better spent looking at birds!

It Starts at Home

Most bird watchers like to start out at home, and this usually means getting to know the birds in your backyard. A great way to enhance the diversity of birds in your yard is to set up a simple feeding station. Even a single feeder with the proper food can bring half a dozen or more unfamiliar bird species into your yard. And it's these encounters with new and interesting birds that make bird watching so enjoyable.

Start your feeding station with a feeder geared to the birds that are already in your backyard or garden. For most of us this will mean a tube or hopper feeder filled with sunflower seeds. Place the feeder in a location that offers you a clear view of bird activity, but also offers the birds some nearby cover in the form of a hedge, shrubs, or brush pile into which the birds can fly when a predator approaches. I always set our feeding stations up opposite our kitchen or living room windows because these are the rooms in which we spend most of our daylight hours,

and because these rooms have the best windows for bird watching. We'll discuss bird feeding and attracting in greater detail in the next section.

Once you've got a basic feeder set up outside, you'll need to get yourself set up inside your house. You've probably already selected the best location for viewing your feeder. Next you should select a safe place to store your binoculars and field guide—somewhere that is easily accessible to you when you suddenly spot a new bird in your backyard. At our house we keep binoculars hanging on pegs right next to our kitchen windows. This keeps them handy for use in checking the feeders or for heading out for a walk around our farm.

Keeping Your Bird List

Most bird watchers enjoy keeping a list of their sightings. This can take the form of a written list, notations inside your field guide next to each species' account, or in a special journal meant for just such a purpose. There are even software programs available to help you keep your list on your computer. In birding, the most common list is the *life list*. A life list is a list of all the birds you've seen at least once in your life. Let's say you noticed a bright, black-and-orange bird in your backyard willow tree one morning, then keyed it out in your field guide to be a male Baltimore oriole. This is a species you'd never seen before, and now you can put it on your life list. List keeping can be done at any level of involvement, so keep the list or lists that you enjoy. I like to keep a property list of all the species we've seen at least once on our 80-acre farm. Currently, that list is at 180 species, but I'm always watching for something new to show up. I also update my North American life list a couple of times a year, after I've seen a new bird species.

Bird Watching Afield

Sooner or later you may want to expand your bird-watching horizons beyond your backyard bird feeders. Birding afield—away from your own home—can be a wonderfully exhilarating experience. Many beginning bird watchers are shy about venturing forth, afraid that their inexperience will prove embarrassing, but there's really no reason to feel this way. The best way to begin

Ten Tips for Beginning Bird Watchers

1. Get a decent pair of binoculars, ones that are easy for you to use and hold steady.

2. Find a field guide to the birds of your region (many guides are divided into eastern and western editions). Guides that cover all the birds of North America contain many birds species uncommon or entirely absent from your area. You can always upgrade to a continent-wide guide later.

3. Set up a basic feeding station in your yard or garden.

4. Start with your backyard birds. They are the easiest to see, and you can become familiar with them fairly quickly.

5. Practice your identification skills. Starting with a common bird species, note the most obvious visual features of the bird (color, size, shape, and patterns in the plumage). These features are known as field marks and will be helpful clues to the bird's identity.

6. Notice the bird's behavior. Many birds can be identified by their behavior—woodpeckers peck on wood, kingfishers dive for small fish, and swallows are known for their graceful flight.

7. Listen to the bird's sounds. Bird song is a vital component to birding. Learning bird songs and sounds takes a bit of practice, but many birds make it pretty easy for us. For example, chickadees and whip-poor-wills (among others) call out their names. The Resources section of this book contains a listing of tools to help you to learn bird songs.

8. Look at the bird, not at the book. When you see an unfamiliar bird, avoid the temptation to put down your binoculars and begin searching for the bird in your field guide. Instead, watch the bird carefully for as long as it is present—or until you feel certain that you have noted its most important field marks. Then look at your field guide. Birds have wings, and they tend to use them. Your field guide will still be with you long after the bird has gone, so take advantage of every moment to watch an unfamiliar bird while it is present.

9. Take notes. No one can be expected to remember every field mark and description of a bird. But you can help your memory and accelerate your learning by taking notes on the birds you see. These notes can be written in a small pocket notebook, in the margins of your field guide, or even in the back of this book.

10. Venture beyond the backyard and find other bird watchers in your area. The bird watching you'll experience beyond your backyard will be enriching, especially if it leads not only to new birds, but also to new birding friends. Ask a local nature center or wildlife refuge about bird clubs in your region. Your state ornithological organization or natural resources division may also be helpful. Bird watching with other birders can be the most enjoyable of all.

birding away from the backyard is to connect with other local bird watchers via your local bird club. Most parts of North America have local or regional bird clubs, and most of these clubs offer regular field trips. Bird watchers are among the friendliest people on the planet, and every bird club is happy to welcome new prospective members. If you don't know how to find a local bird club, ask your friends and neighbors if they know any bird watchers, check the telephone directory, search the Internet, or ask at your area parks, nature centers, and wild bird stores.

Getting out in the field with more experienced bird watchers is the fastest way to improve your skills. Don't be afraid to ask questions ("How did you know that was an indigo bunting?"). Don't worry if you begin to feel overwhelmed by the volume of new information—all new bird watchers experience this. When it happens, relax and take some time to simply watch. In time you'll be identifying birds and looking forward to new challenges and new birds.

Feeding and Housing

Birds need four basic things to live: food, water for drinking and bathing, a safe place to roost, and a safe place to nest. These vital elements are actually quite easy for you to offer to birds, even if your back-yard is small.

Food

Bird feeding is a good place to start your bird-attracting efforts. It's wise to begin with a single feeder, such as a hopper feeder or tube feeder filled with black-oil sunflower seeds. The black-oil sunflower seed is the most common type of sunflower seed available, because it's the seed type that most of our feeder birds can readily eat. Think of it as the hamburger of the bird world. The black-oil sunflower seed has a thin shell (easy for seed-eating birds to crack) and a large, meaty seed kernel inside. As you can see from the seed preference chart on page 147, many backyard bird species eat sunflower seeds.

Other excellent foods for birds include: mixed seed (a blend that normally includes millet,

Pictured from the top down:
Black-oil sunflower seed, peanuts, mixed seed, and cracked corn.

milo, cracked corn, and other seeds), sunflower bits (shells removed), peanuts (best offered unsalted and without the shell), suet or suet cakes, cracked corn, thistle seed (also known as Niger or nyjer seed), safflower seed, nectar (for hummingbirds), mealworms, fruits, and berries. Bird feeding varies from region to region—don't be afraid to experiment with new feeders or food. Birds will vote with their bills and stomachs and will let you know their preferences

Eating the food at feeders is not the only way birds find sustenance. A backyard or garden that includes natural food sources for birds—such as seed-producing flowering plants and fruit-bearing trees and shrubs—will further enhance its attractiveness to birds. In fact, it's often the natural features of a backyard habitat that attract the birds' attention rather than the bird feeders. Read the Bird-Friendly Plants section on page 162 for more specific suggestions.

Feeder Types

It's important to match the foods and feeders to each other, as well as to the birds you wish to attract. Sunflower seed works in a wide variety of feeders, including tube, hopper, platform, and satellite or excluder feeders (that permit small birds to feed, but exclude larger birds), as well as for ground feeding. Mixed seed does not work as well in tube or hopper feeders for a couple of reasons. First of all, the birds that prefer mixed seed tend to be ground feeders, so it's less natural for them to go to an elevated feeder for food. Secondly, elevated feeder designs (such as tubes or hoppers) are built to dole out seed as it is eaten and the smaller size of most mixed seed kernels causes excess spillage. Mixed seed works best when offered on a platform feeder or when scattered on the ground.

A fruit feeder.

take a few days or even a few weeks before they recognize your offering as a source of food. Sooner or later, a curious chickadee, finch, or sparrow will key into the food source, and the word will spread along the local bird "grapevine."

Housing for Birds

Almost every bird species builds or uses some type of nest to produce and rear its young. However, only a small fraction of our birds use nest boxes provided by humans. Birds that use next boxes or birdhouses are called *cavity nesters*, because they prefer to nest inside an enclosed space, such as hole excavated in a tree, as many woodpeckers do. Nest boxes simulate a natural cavity, but they have the added advantage (for humans) of our being able to place them in a convenient spot. To the birds' advantage, we can protect the nest box from predators, bad weather, and other problems.

When purchasing your feeders and foods, make sure they will work effectively with each other. Specialty foods such as suet, peanuts, thistle (Niger), mealworms, fruit, and nectar require specific feeders for the best results for you and the birds. The Food and Feeder Chart on page 147 is a great place to start.

Being a landlord to the birds is a thrilling experience. You are treated to an intimate peek inside the lives of your "tenants" and rewarded with the presence of their offspring, if nesting is successful. To help ensure the nesting success of your birds you need to provide the proper housing in an appropriate setting, and you should monitor the housing during the nesting season.

Your Feeding Station

Place your feeding station in a spot that is useful and attractive to you and the birds. When we moved into our farmhouse, we looked out all the windows before choosing a spot for our feeding station. You may want to do the same thing. After all, the whole point of bird feeding is to be able to see and enjoy the birds. From the birds' perspective, your feeders should be placed adjacent to cover—a place they can leave from and retreat to safely and quickly if a predator appears. This cover can be a woodland edge, brushy area or brush pile, hedges or shrubs, or even a weedy fencerow. If your yard is mostly lawn, consider creating a small island of cover near your feeding station. This will greatly enhance the feeders' appeal to birds.

Be patient. You've spent the money and effort to put up feeders, but don't expect immediate dividends. Birds are creatures of habit, and it may

The Right Housing

Two factors are key to providing the right nest box for your birds: the size of the housing and

Male northern cardinals at a sunflower feeder.

Exterior latex stain helps prolong the life of a birdhouse and protects the birds inside.

the size of the entry hole. Not all cavity nesters are picky about the interior dimensions of the cavity, except when it is excessively big or small. But the size of the entry hole is important because it can effectively limit the entrance of large, aggressive nest competitors, predators, and inclement weather. For example, an entry hole with a diameter of 1½ inches on a bluebird nest box will permit entry by bluebirds and many smaller birds, including chickadees, titmice, nuthatches, wrens, and tree swallows. But this same size keeps European starlings out and prevents them from usurping the box.

Use the Nest Box Chart (page 148) to help you determine the appropriate nest box details for your backyard birds. Whether you build your own birdhouses or buy them at your local wild bird products supplier, see page 40 for a few tips for "landlords" that you will want to consider.

An Appropriate Setting

Place your nest boxes where they will be most likely to be found and used by birds. Bluebirds and swallows prefer nest sites in the middle of large, open, grassy areas. Wrens, chickadees, nuthatches, flycatchers, woodpeckers, and other woodland birds prefer sites that are in or adjacent to woodlands. Robins, phoebes, Carolina wrens, barn swallows, and purple martins prefer to nest near human

dwellings, perhaps for the protection from predators that we provide.

Monitoring Your Nest Boxes

By taking a weekly peek inside your nest boxes, you will stay abreast of your tenants' activities, and you'll be able to help them raise their families successfully. During most of the year, your birdhouses will appear to be empty. This does not mean that the boxes are going unused. In fact, many birds use nest boxes during the win-

An example of a pole-mounted predator baffle.

Nest Box Tips for Landlords

- Do build or buy sturdily constructed nest boxes that are built from untreated wood (or another weatherproof material) with walls that are at least ³/₄ inch thick. See page 157 for a simple bird house plan.
- Do not stain or paint the interior of the box. Stain or paint on the box exterior will help the box last longer. Light colors reflect sunlight and keep box interiors from getting too hot.
- Perches by the entry hole are unnecessary and may actually encourage competitors and predators.
- The box roof should be slanted and extend out several inches over the entry hole to keep out the weather.
- Nest boxes should have an access door for monitoring. Access doors that swing upward to open on the side or front of the box are easiest to use and safest for birds.
- The box should have holes for ventilation at the top of the vertical walls. Drainage holes in the floor will permit excess moisture to escape.
- Mount boxes on poles away from nearby trees and structures.
- Place a pole-mounted predator baffle beneath the nest box to keep snakes and mammals from gaining access to the nest.

ter months as nighttime roosts. A loose feather, insect parts, berry seeds, or a few droppings are classic evidence of roosting activity.

During breeding season, your regular visits will help you know when nest building begins and when eggs are laid, and will give you an idea about how soon the eggs will hatch and the babies leave the nest. Bird nests are vulnerable

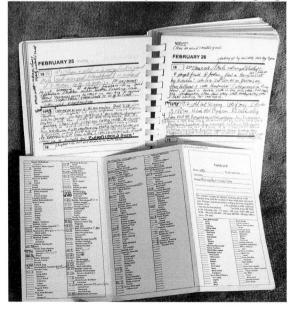

Top: A daily bird notes diary. Bottom: A checklist for sightings.

to a variety of dangers, including harsh weather and predators such as cats, raccoons, snakes, and even birds, as well as nest-site competitors. These dangers are greatly reduced when nest boxes are monitored because the birds' landlord (you) can take steps to protect the nest.

On my trips to check each of our 10 nest boxes, I keep a small notebook with me to record my observations. Each nest box has its own name and number in my notebook, along with the date of each visit and a note about what I've found. When nesting starts in a box I note the date, what materials are used to construct the nest, and the date that the first egg was laid. Once the clutch is complete and the female begins incubating the eggs, I can estimate the hatching date. This usually takes about 14 days. Another 14 to 21 days later, I know the young birds will be ready to leave the nest.

Peeking Inside

When checking a nest box, approach quietly. During the breeding season, you may scare the female off the nest temporarily when you open the box. Don't worry. If you keep your visit brief, she'll be back to the nest soon. I visit nest boxes

Checking the nest box.

in the late morning on sunny days, when the adult birds are likely to be away finding food. I open the box, quickly count the eggs or young, close the box and move away before pausing to record my notes. It's a myth that opening a nest box or checking the young will cause the adults to abandon the nest. In fact, over time many cavity-nesting birds that use nest boxes grow quite accustomed to regular visits.

One final note on nest monitoring. As fledging time approaches for the young birds—normally about two weeks after the eggs hatch—you should curtail your box visits to avoid causing a premature nest departure.

When Things Go Wrong

You open your nest box, and you find broken or missing eggs and the nest in disarray. What happened? The bad news is: A predator has raided your nest, and, in the natural order of things, the eggs or nestlings have been eaten. The good news: There are steps that you can take to avoid such an event in the future.

It's important to protect your nest boxes so predators cannot easily access them. For many landlords the best option is to mount the housing on galvanized metal poles with pole-mounted predator baffles installed beneath the boxes. An added advantage to pole-mounting (as opposed to mounting on a fencepost or tree) is

that the housing can be moved to a new location fairly easily.

Follow the steps outlined on page 148 for nest box placement, mounting, and baffling. You may also wish to consult one of the publications listed in the Resources section for specific strategies for dealing with nest box predators and pests.

Creating Bird Habitat

To make your backyard or garden a haven for birds, all you need to do is think like a bird. Look around your yard. Where is the food, the water? Where are the places to hide from predators or to shelter in bad weather? Is nesting habitat available?

An ideal bird habitat can be created in a tiny, urban garden just as it can be created in a large, rural setting. Birds love varied habitats; so when you are planning your yard, landscape, or gardens, resist the urge to plant matching plants in straight lines. Instead, let your imagination go wild—literally. Give the edges of beds or gardens natural curves. Scatter trees, shrubs, and vines in clumps or islands around the area you are designing. On the edges of your property, try to create natural transitions from the grass of your yard to the tops of your trees with short- and medium-height plants that provide food and shelter for birds.

Edible Habitat

Birds have evolved over millions of years right alongside the native plants with which they share the planet. These same native plants can work for you in your bird-friendly habitat plan. Your local nursery, nature center, or native plant society should be able to recommend plant species that are native to your region. Native plants not only provide food in the form of fruits and nuts, but birds may also eat the plants' buds, leaves, nectar, and sap, as well as the insects that live on the plants. When choosing your native plants, select a wide variety of species, sizes, shapes, and seasonality. Planting only one or two plant species will minimize the number of birds your habitat will attract. Consult the Bird-Friendly Plants chart on page 162 for suggested plant families.

Water

Birds need water all year long for drinking and bathing. The best way to offer water to birds is in a shallow birdbath with about 2 inches of water in it. I've always had good luck attracting birds to water in my yard when the bath was on or near the ground and when the water had some motion to it.

The sight and sound of moving water are highly attractive to birds. You can add motion to any birdbath or water feature with a mister, dripper, or a recirculating pump. Misters and drippers attach to your garden hose and let out a small amount of water that disturbs the surface of the bath; these ripples are eye-catchingly attractive to birds. Recirculating pumps, which require electricity, recycle the water from the main bath through a pump and filter, and then back to the bath. If you live in an area where water freezes in winter, add a small, electric birdbath heater to keep the water open and available to birds.

If you already have a water garden or water feature, consider making part of it accessible to birds. This can be accomplished by placing a flat rock shelf on or near the water's surface, or by allowing recirculating water to trickle over an exposed flat rock. Our backyard water garden is ringed with goldfinches almost every day all year-round. They use a large, flat piece of slate that gets splashed by our small waterfall as a place to grab a quick drink.

A male scarlet tanager bathes in a water feature.

Water is a universal attractant for birds—species that might otherwise never visit your yard, feeders, or birdhouses will visit a clean and alluring birdbath or water feature.

Shelter

When they need to rest, hide from danger, or get out of the weather, birds seek deep cover in the form of thick vegetation, vine tangles, dense evergreens, or brushy areas. These bits of habitat may not be first on a landscaper's list of backyard beautifying accents, but to a bird they are vital havens. Even a brush pile in a corner of your property can offer enough shelter during a storm to help sparrows, cardinals, and other backyard birds survive.

Look at your bird habitat, and observe where the birds go just before a storm or at dusk. These are the places in which they shelter themselves. Consider adding more habitat, and your yard will be even more attractive to birds.

Places to Nest

The majority of North American birds do not use nest boxes. Most build their nests in places that are hidden from view—in trees, bushes, or in secluded spots on or near the ground. Birds—such as phoebes, barn swallows, and Carolina wrens—are bold enough to build nests on porch ledges, in garages, and in barns. House finches and mourning doves are known for building their nests in hanging flower baskets, but these sites won't satisfy most of our birds.

The places where birds choose to nest are similar to the places they choose to roost and shelter—in thick vegetation and deep cover out of view of passing predators. In providing a nesting habitat for birds, the key is diversity. As you read through the species profiles in this book, notice the habitat features that each species prefers. Then factor this information into your habitat plans.

Helping Other Nesting Birds

There are many things you can do to help non-cavity nesters—all those birds that build

Allow lawn edges to grow wild.

open-cup nests and will never use one of our nest boxes. The most important thing is to offer variety in your landscaping or backyard habitat. A backyard that is mostly lawn with a tree or two staked out in the middle will not be nearly as appealing as a yard featuring a variety of plant types, including grasses, perennial plants, shrubs, bushes, trees, and other natural elements. The more your landscape looks like nature, the more attractive it will be for birds.

Places for You

As you plan for your bird-friendly habitat, you'll also want to incorporate elements that you can use and enjoy, such as a water garden, benches, shady relaxation spots, and perhaps a location for your feeding station. Remember, the whole point of attracting birds to your property is so that you can enjoy them while they enjoy your offerings. Plan with your favorite viewing spots in mind, and you'll be rewarded with year-round free (and natural) entertainment.

Tips for Helping Nesting Birds

- Consider letting a portion of your yard grow up into a weedy patch for sparrows, finches, and towhees to enjoy.
- Offer a basket of nesting material, such as 2- to 3-inch pieces of natural fibers (yarn, pet or human hair, stiff dry grasses, and the like).
- Keep pets, especially cats, from roaming freely in your yard during nesting season.
- Try to limit or eliminate the use of lawn and garden chemicals in and around the parts of your property being used by nesting birds.
- Trim hedges, shrubs, and trees in early spring before nesting season, or in late fall, after nesting season. This way you'll avoid disturbing nesting birds, which are often so secretive that you are unaware of the nest until you stumble onto it.

How to Use This Book

Hello! *and welcome to the fun, friendly, and exciting word of bird watching. Birding is America's fastest-growing hobby and requires little more than some basic tools—binoculars and a field guide—and an interest in the fascinating world of birds. The primary purpose of this book is to start you down the path to a greater understanding and enjoyment of this engaging pastime. To that end, we've chosen the content carefully to provide you, the reader, with the ideal blend of information and detail on many of the most commonly encountered birds of your state. If we've done our job right, this will* not *be the last bird book you buy.*

At the heart of this book is a set of profiles of your state's 100 most commonly encountered birds. These are the birds that you're most likely to see and hear regularly. *But remember*—birds have wings and they tend to use them, so you'll certainly see and hear many other species as your bird-watching experience grows. For this reason we suggest that you augment this book with a good field guide to help you identify those unfamiliar species you encounter.

Each species profile features a beautiful photograph of the bird, typically an adult male in breeding plumage since this is the most identifiable version of many birds. Please note that adult females, winter-plumage adults, and young birds can look very different. We describe these plumage differences in the profile, but space constraints prevent us from showing images of all these variations. Once again, a good field guide (see the Resources section on page 166 for suggestions) will be useful in identifying any mystery birds you encounter.

We cover all the interesting and useful natural history information about each of the 100 birds—appearance, sounds, behavior, nesting, feeding, range, and migration—and we even tell you where to go and what to do in order to encounter a particular bird in the "Backyard and Beyond" section.

The profiles in the main body of the book are organized *taxonomically*—this means that related species are grouped by bird family using the same general order that ornithologists use to list and classify birds. See the facing page to find a convenient alphabetic listing. In the 100 species profiles, we've used a series of symbols to provide instant insight into the lives of these birds. Here is a key to what each of these icons represents:

 Will use a birdhouse for nesting or roosting.

 Can be attracted to bird feeders.

 Will visit birdbaths or water features for bathing and drinking.

 Has a song or call and can be identified by its vocalizations or sounds.

 A migrant species, seen primarily during spring or fall migration.

Also, turn to pages 7 through 32 to read more about the natural history and ecology of your state and its bird life. We focus on bird watching by season—the specific birds you're likely to encounter and how to attract them—by feeding and by offering the appropriate bird-friendly habitat. This section also describes the many migrants that pass through in spring and fall. As an extra bonus, we briefly describe the "Ten Must-See Birds" for your state. We also include a summary of the "Ten Best Bird-Watching Spots."

At the end of this book you will find a resources list for bird watching (feeding and planting charts, answers to frequently asked questions, birdhouse plans, bird books, field and audio guides, and more) to help you enjoy this hobby more.

Happy bird watching!

—*Bill Thompson, III*

100 Most Commonly Encountered Birds

Pied-billed Grebe

Podilymbus podiceps

- Spring/Summer
- Year-Round
- Winter

Most North American grebes either breed far to the north or in the West, but the stocky little pied-billed grebe also breeds through much of the South. You can find this frequent diver in varied wetlands, including ponds, lakes, and marshes that have a thick cover of cattails or other vegetation. Pied-billed grebes most often are seen singly or in twos or threes. They don't often vocalize, except during breeding season when they call out a series of penetrating, barking notes.

All About

In general, pied-billed grebes occur in sheltered, lush wetlands. The other grebes that show up during winter migrations in the South are normally seen in bays or on large rivers or other open water. This bird is smallish but has a big head, stocky neck, and a thick bill that differs from the more pointed bills of horned and eared grebes. During breeding season, the bill (which is pale in winter) becomes distinctively adorned with a thick, black band that wraps around an otherwise horn-colored bill. Breeding pied-billed grebes also have black throats, but at other times their soft-brown necks and bodies contrast with whitish throats and puffy whitish undertails. The Southeast's other grebes have much sharper contrasting patterns on their heads and necks, and they are not as compact.

Habitat & Range

Pied-billed grebes nest in well-vegetated lakes, ponds, and pockets of marsh. You may find them in brackish water in winter, but they prefer freshwater habitats. The numbers of pied-billed grebes swell in the South during winter and migration, when many northern nesters abandon their frigid habitats for warmer, more productive wintering areas.

Feeding

Pied-billed grebes are frequently seen diving for food or diving to evade predators or observers. Their wide-lobed feet push them beneath the water's surface in search of small fish, amphibians, and a wide variety of aquatic invertebrates, including crayfish and insects. They also eat some plant matter.

Nesting

Mates call to each other as part of their courtship. Together, they build a nest that is basically a mound of matted vegetation. This mound is fastened to nearby plants and may float or rise from the shallows. The female lays four to six eggs, with the pair sharing the three-week incubation period. Both parents feed the young, which can fly by two months of age.

Backyard & Beyond

Scan marsh edges and ponds to find pied-billed grebes; they are rarely spotted in flight. They have a tendency to appear as if by magic and to disappear just as fast, often leaving a ring of ripples on the water's surface as the only evidence of their presence.

Brown Pelican

Pelecanus occidentalis

○ Spring/Summer
○ Year-Round
○ Winter

At 4 feet long and with a 7-foot wingspan, the brown pelican is one of our largest and most distinctive birds. Brown pelicans are back from the brink after conservation measures were strengthened and a ban on the pesticide DDT, which caused widespread breeding failure among these birds in the 1960s and 1970s, was instituted. The United States' first national wildlife refuge was established in Florida to protect a beleaguered brown pelican colony.

All About

The brown pelican's profile and marine habitat make identification easy. These massive birds have pencil lead-gray bodies and blackish flight feathers. North America's other pelican, the larger American white pelican, winters in parts of the South in freshwater or brackish habitats, but it is white with black flight feathers and a bright orange bill. During nesting season, the brown pelican sports a chocolate-brown hind neck; at other times, it is white necked. Yellow adorns the bird's crown at all seasons, but is a richer color during breeding season.

Habitat & Range

Brown pelicans are a familiar sight, flapping low over southeastern bays or cruising over the surf at the beach. In recent years, their range has expanded northward, with birds nesting in Maryland and up to New York. While they feed in public places, they require protected nesting areas. During the DDT era, brown pelican colonies failed and steeply declined, but numbers are recovering to former levels. Disturbance at breeding sites by boaters and beachcombers still causes problems at some nesting islands.

Feeding

Sardines, anchovies, menhaden, and other fish catch brown pelicans' attention, sending them from horizontal flapping and gliding to angled plunges into the water. As a brown pelican hits the surface and briefly sinks, its bill opens and its pouch fills with up to $2^{1}/_{2}$ gallons of water. The bird quickly strains out the water from its bill and swallows any captured fish. In some coastal states, brown pelicans loiter around docks and tussle over discarded fish scraps.

Nesting

Brown pelicans breed in colonies, setting up stick nests in trees such as mangroves, or nesting on scrapes in soil or on lumps of vegetation on islands. The female usually lays three white eggs, which both she and her mate incubate for about a month. Parents also share feeding duties for up to nine weeks, after which their young leave the nest.

Backyard & Beyond

Head toward the ocean or gulf to find brown pelicans. They are seen all along the southeastern coast, passing over surf at even the most crowded beach locations. Look for them in small flocks, slowly flapping over the water, wheeling and diving after prey.

Double-crested Cormorant

Phalacrocorax auritus

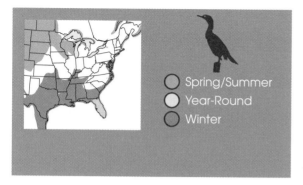

○ Spring/Summer
○ Year-Round
○ Winter

Often, the somewhat snakelike black neck and head is all that betrays the presence of a swimming double-crested cormorant. In general, this water bird is most numerous in the Southeast during late fall, winter, and early spring. Double-crested cormorants declined earlier in the mid-twentieth century due to disturbance and hunting at nesting grounds, followed by DDT and other pesticide contamination. Protection, wetland conservation, and the DDT ban have helped these birds recover.

All About
With practice, birders can easily distinguish a distant, flying double-crested cormorant from a pelican, goose, heron, or other large bird by its all-dark form, thick and somewhat wavy neck, longish tail, and slow wingbeats. The cormorant's bright orange throat, bill, and lores stand out on its otherwise black body. Even its heavy webbed feet are blackish. Immatures are dull brown with whitish necks and chests. In this species, it's usually not visible. On the Gulf Coast, from Texas to western Louisiana, watch for the smaller, thinner, longer-tailed neotropic cormorant. During spring, this smaller species has an angled, white fringe behind its smaller, orange throat.

Habitat & Range
Most double-crested cormorant populations are migratory, and these birds turn up at rivers, marshes, swamps, large lakes, bays, and along the coast. Because they travel widely during the day, don't be surprised to see cormorants flying over inland habitats in loose formation. Double-crested cormorants breed in western Alaska, central Canada, and down both coasts of the United States; they winter along the coast and well inland throughout the Southeast.

Feeding
Double-crested cormorants are very adaptable, seeking a wide variety of fish, and also crustaceans, amphibians, and other aquatic animals. Their webbed feet propel them under water after their aquatic prey, and much of their feeding is done not far beneath the surface.

Nesting
Double-crested cormorants nest in colonies in trees, on cliffs, and on islands. Females build much of the platform nest, while males provide the many sticks and other materials. Females usually lay three or four eggs, which both parents incubate for about a month. Young leave the nest 21 to 30 days after hatching, but are not fully on their own until after two months.

Backyard & Beyond
Watch for the "periscope" heads of partially submerged cormorants and try not to confuse them with those of the more dagger-billed anhinga or loons, which have slimmer, straighter bills and at least some light coloration on the head. After long swims, cormorants often sun themselves on dead trees and shoreline, holding out their wings to dry.

Great Blue Heron

Ardea herodias

○ Spring/Summer
○ Year-Round
○ Winter

North America's largest and most widespread heron is found, at one time or another, virtually wherever water and small aquatic creatures are found. Although the best known of our dozen heron species, the great blue heron is not always called by its correct name. Many non-birders call it a crane or a stork, but the heron can be instantly distinguished from these other large, long-legged birds by its folded-back neck in flight and the S-shaped curvature of its neck at rest.

All About

Adult great blue herons have a black stripe running from the eye to the back of the neck; immature birds have a blackish cap. Southern Florida is home to the great white heron, an all-white race of the great blue that can be distinguished from egrets by its large size and long, thick, orange bill and orange legs. The great blue heron's croaking *ccrraaaaaaaank* call is often heard as it takes flight.

Habitat & Range

Found across the United States, southern Canada, and up the Pacific coast to Alaska, the great blue heron ventures where few other herons dare. Many eastern birds migrate to the South or to the tropics—as far south as north-western South America—in winter. Outside of the Appalachians, great blue herons occur throughout the South all year.

Feeding

Great blue herons seek a variety of prey in a range of wet habitats. Fish are a mainstay, but amphibians, reptiles, birds, small mammals, and invertebrates feature on the menu, as well. Feeding strategy varies as well. They may hunt alongside each other, wading slowly up to their bellies, or may stand alone for long periods, waiting to thrust their bills at unsuspecting prey. Great blue herons sometimes stalk rodents in dry fields or haunt beaches and docks in search of live or discarded sea life.

Nesting

Great blue herons nest in large colonies, often in tall trees away from human disturbance. They will nest in the company of other water birds, often in areas with water beneath nesting trees, probably to thwart predators. Each year, great blue heron pairs form bonds through a series of posing displays, including stretching, preening, crest raising, circling in flight, and twig shaking. Males provide sticks, which females place in the large platform nest. Females usually lay three to five eggs, which incubate for almost a month. Both parents feed the young, which take flight 2 to 2½ months after hatching.

Backyard & Beyond

Despite their large size, great blue herons sometimes turn up at small backyard ponds seeking fish and frogs. They are far more frequent in marshes, swamps, rivers, lakes, and reservoirs.

Great Egret

Ardea alba

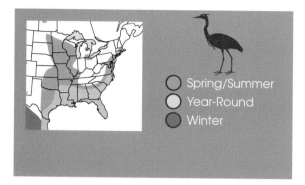

○ Spring/Summer
○ Year-Round
○ Winter

Once a favored target of plume-hunters, the great egret has rebounded over the last century following conservation measures and protection. Found on all continents except Antarctica, in few places is the great egret more common than in the Southeast, where these elegant white birds adorn many a lush, green wetland. Over the years, the great egret has had other names, including common and American egret and great white egret. The current name stresses the large size of the bird in relation to other egrets.

All About

The great egret is by far the largest of our four egret species, with the longest neck. Size and proportions, along with a combination of black legs and an all-yellow bill, help birders separate it from cattle and snowy egrets. At the height of breeding, bright lime-green decorates adult great egret's *lores*, the areas between eyes and bill. Also, during breeding season, the spray of famous white plumes, or *aigrettes*, spills over the bird's back. Like most other herons, the great egret's neck is S-shaped and folded back when the bird is flying. When disturbed or taking flight, the great egret may issue its croaking call, which is somewhat similar to—but lower than—the great blue heron's call.

Habitat & Range

Great egrets frequent a variety of watery habitats, including marshes, swamps, rivers, lakes, and large ponds, where you may find them alone or in small or large groups. They often feed in the company of other egrets, herons, cormorants, or ibis, especially where food is concentrated, as in fish-filled pools left during dry spells. Many northern nesters withdraw from their breeding range in winter, heading to the Southeast like "snowbirds," to add to the resident population.

Feeding

The great egret forages by standing very still, waiting for unsuspecting fish, frogs, crayfish, or other prey, but this long-legged bird may also slowly wade and strike at quarry, sometimes grasping prey with its bill and sometimes spearing it.

Nesting

Male great egrets stake out and hold the nesting area, which is often in a mixed colony of water birds. Both sexes build the platform nest out of sticks they gather nearby. They incubate their three to five eggs for just over three weeks, and feed their young by regurgitating food for them. Young egrets can fly by age six or seven weeks.

Backyard & Beyond

This large, white bird is frequently seen flying from one watery area to another. If you live fairly close to a lake or marsh, at least one or two may fly over your neighborhood. Watch for the long, all-yellow bill; deep-folded neck; and all-black legs and feet.

Snowy Egret

Egretta thula

○ Spring/Summer
○ Year-Round
○ Winter

To identify an adult snowy egret, think two-tone: the snowy egret has a yellow lore—the area between eye and bill—but an all-black bill; also, it has yellow feet but otherwise black legs, at least in adults. If you see this combination, you're watching a snowy egret. Like the great egret, this bird suffered severe declines after extensive plume-hunting in the late 1800s. Numbers have rebounded over the last century.

All About

The snowy egret's "golden slippers"—when not submerged in water or covered in mud—make identification of this white heron easy. However, the immature snowy egret has yellowish legs; identify it by its yellow lores and yellow feet. Snowy egrets often hunt alone, but they also frequently associate with white ibis, other egrets, and other water birds. Biologists have found that, in at least some circumstances, snowy egrets are more successful finding food when other birds are there to help stir up prey.

Habitat & Range

Snowy egrets can be found in freshwater, saltwater, and brackish wetlands. Away from the coast, they are more likely to be found in larger marshes and swamps. After summer, they withdraw from much of their inland range, favoring coastal sites for winter, including those in the Southeast. Other wintering snowy egrets travel as far south as South America.

Feeding

Hunting snowy egrets snap up small fish and a wide variety of invertebrates, including crabs, crayfish, worms, and snails. Reptiles, amphibians, and rodents also find their way into this wader's stilettolike, black bill. Snowy egrets are generally more active hunters than great egrets. As they stride in the shallows, their yellow feet may serve to catch the eye of fish and other creatures, drawing them closer or stalling them so the egret can strike.

Nesting

During breeding season, the adult snowy egret has a special courtship lacy plume, or *aigrette*, splaying from its crown, back, and breast. At the peak of nesting time, the area between its eyes and bill (the *lore*) flushes red. Snowy egrets nest in colonies, often in the company of other water birds. Both parents build the platform nest of sticks and place it fairly low in a tree or shrub. They incubate their three to five blue-green eggs for about three weeks; both feed the young, which can fly when about a month old.

Backyard & Beyond

Snowy egrets wander widely after breeding season. You may see them fly over your neighborhood even if there's no wet spot to draw them. When watching a flying bird, look first at the legs. Within a reasonable distance, the yellow feet and black legs can clinch your identification.

Little Blue Heron

Egretta caerulea

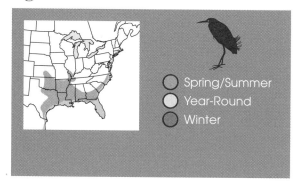

- Spring/Summer
- Year-Round
- Winter

"**D**ark blue egret" is a rough interpretation of this bird's Latin scientific name. Take a look at a whitish, immature little blue heron, and it's easy to believe that this bird is more closely related to a snowy egret than a great blue heron. The little blue heron is a familiar sight not only in inland freshwater marshes and swamps, but also in brackish or salty coastal marshes.*

All About

Far smaller and darker than a great blue heron, the adult little blue heron is easily confused with the tricolored heron, another mostly dark member of the genus *Egretta*. However, even from far away, you can see that the tricolored heron has a white belly. A closer look reveals the tricolored's yellowish bill (purple in breeding season) and a thin, white line running up the front of its long neck. In south Florida and along the Gulf Coast, the larger reddish egret may provide some identification challenges, but its rust-orange neck and pink-and-black bill differ from the little blue's purplish neck and blue-and-black bill. The white, immature little blue heron is separated from other egrets by its gray lores (even snowy immatures have yellow lores), blackish-tipped but otherwise pale gray bill, and dark-tipped wings in flight.

Habitat & Range

The little blue sometimes turns up in flooded fields, seeking grasshoppers and other prey. Immature birds and adults wander widely in late summer, and inland birds head to the coast or south for the winter. Others head farther south to Central America. In addition to their U.S. breeding range, little blue herons also nest in Mexico, central South America, and throughout the West Indies.

Feeding

Immature little blue herons may loiter and feed near each other after leaving the nest. Adults usually feed alone, though they are often near other waders, seeking food in the same places. Their diet varies by season and location and includes crayfish, fiddler crabs, a variety of small fish, and insects. Amphibians, small reptiles, and other small animals are also taken.

Nesting

Little blue herons nest in colonies in trees and bushes, often with other water birds. The female lays between two and five pale blue eggs in a stick nest constructed by both parents. Male and female both incubate the eggs for about three weeks. Hatched young stay in the nest up to three weeks, then perch near it until they fly at about one month old.

Backyard & Beyond

Watch for all-dark herons in flight. In the case of flying immatures, the combination of dull pale legs and bill and dark-tipped wings should help clinch the identification of a little blue heron.

Cattle Egret

Bubulcus ibis

- ○ Spring/Summer
- ○ Year-Round
- ○ Winter

The "great colonizer" would be an apt name for this bird. Once an Old World fixture, the cattle egret expanded its horizons—especially from the late 1800s to now, crossing over to South America from Africa and then to North America by the 1950s. It also spread from Asia to Australia and New Zealand. Antarctica is the only continent where they do not nest. While they usually nest in wetlands, they are less dependent upon these areas for food, preferring to find food down on the farm.

All About

Compared to other egrets, the cattle egret is thick-necked and short-legged. Also, its yellow bill is stubby in comparison with other egrets. During breeding season, it takes on a plumage far different from the others: Buff-orange feathers adorn its back, crown, and breast, and at the peak of breeding, the bird's bill and legs turn pink.

Habitat & Range

Now among the most numerous herons in the Southeast, cattle egrets are found in freshwater and brackish wetlands, but they most often appear in agricultural settings, particularly where cattle range or tractors plow up soil. The cattle egret's distribution reflects its traveling ways. This bird is a widespread and common breeder in the Southeast coastal plain and into the Mississippi drainage, but breeding colonies are widely scattered across much of the rest of the United States. After nesting, many cattle egrets disperse, popping up all over the continent, into southern Canada and interior Mexico.

Feeding

Characteristic feeding behavior is to follow cattle or other large animals that stir up small prey hiding in the grass. Cattle egrets are also regular tractor followers. Much of their diet consists of insects, such as grasshoppers and crickets, but frogs and other small animals are caught as well. Cattle egrets also frequent garbage dumps, where they find insects and a wide variety of other edible tidbits.

Nesting

Cattle egrets nest in colonies in trees or bushes, usually in wetlands or on islands, and in the company of other water birds. The female usually lays three to four eggs in a stick nest that she crafts from branches provided by her mate. Both parents incubate the clutch for three weeks or a bit longer; they then feed their young for more than a month after they hatch and before they fly off on their own.

Backyard & Beyond

As their name hints, cattle egrets often appear in pastures, following cattle, horses, or other large animals. Great and snowy egrets sometimes forage in fields, but if you see a flock of egrets in a dry frield with cattle, they mostly likely are cattle egrets.

Green Heron

Butorides virescens

- Spring/Summer
- Year-Round
- Winter

The green heron isn't exactly green, but it's the most greenish of the North American herons. Perhaps a better name would have been "squat heron" or "little heron" or "common pond heron." The bird was known until recently as the "green-backed heron," and this is an apt moniker since the adults have blackish green backs.

All About

The least bittern is our smallest heron, but the green heron is the smallest *easily seen* heron. While a green heron will sometimes stretch its neck out to peer at approaching birders or predators, its head is usually held close to the body, giving the bird a squat look. Identification of adults is straightforward: The back and crown are blackish with a green tinge, the neck and face are dark chestnut, and the belly is gray. Yellow legs flush to bright orange during breeding season. Young birds are brown streaked, and care should be taken not to mistake them for bitterns. Subadults are a mixture of brown and streaky and rusty necked. The piercing *KEEE-OWK* call will draw attention to flushed birds that might otherwise be missed.

Habitat & Range

In spring and summer, look for green herons along wooded streams and ponds, around lakes, at drainage ditches, and in marshes, often near woody cover. In winter, green herons move south from northern nesting areas, spending the winter in Florida and the Gulf States and south-ward into the tropics. Green herons also nest throughout the West Indies and in Central America south to Panama.

Feeding

Like stock-still balls of rust and greenish feathers, green herons wait patiently by the water's edge for fish, frogs, crayfish, various insects, and other small prey. They also slowly walk through the water and wait for prey to show. They have even been known to drop small baits, such as fish food pellets, bits of bread (from people feeding park ducks), or flower petals into the water to attract curious fish and other potential prey.

Nesting

Green herons nest in pairs or small clusters, but avoid large colonies. They nest in trees or shrubs that may either be near or fairly far from water and feeding areas. Three to seven eggs are laid in a stick platform nest primarily built by the female. Both parents incubate the eggs for about three weeks; both then feed their young, which can fly by three weeks of age.

Backyard & Beyond

Green herons may visit backyard ponds to investigate the goldfish or frogs. They also frequently fly over neighborhoods en route to golf course ponds, streams, lakes, or drainage ditches. Green herons are frequently overlooked until startled into flight.

White Ibis

Eudocimus albus

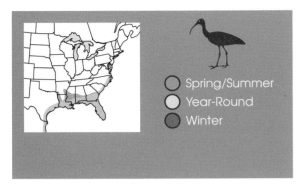

○ Spring/Summer
○ Year-Round
○ Winter

One of the most easily identified and familiar southeastern wetland birds, the white ibis wanders widely in search of crustaceans and other prey. In good light, these birds gleam when set against a marshy backdrop, and you can tell them from herons by their outstretched necks and flap-and-glide flight. Stragglers may be found alone, but most often white ibis are seen in small or large flocks.

All About

An adult white ibis is easy to identify—whether at rest, feeding, or flying—thanks to its red legs and red, down-curved bill, which stand out on an otherwise white bird. In flight, the wing tips flash black, as if they have been dipped in ink. Immature birds can be quickly differentiated from all-dark glossy ibis by their whitish underparts and orange bills, and by white back patches that are often visible when birds are molting into adult plumage.

Habitat & Range

A fixture in wetlands from Virginia (a recent expansion) and southward along the coast through Mexico to Central and northern South America, the white ibis can be found in a variety of shallow habitats—from swamps and marshes to rice plantations and coastal lagoons. They nest and most frequently occur in freshwater habitats, although adults also feed in brackish and saltwater wetlands. Most nesting occurs near the coast, with birds dispersing inland and up and down the coast after breeding season.

Feeding

The white ibis's diet is heavy on crustaceans where available, including fiddler crabs, crayfish, grass shrimp, and others. Insects and some small fish and snakes, frogs, snails, and other animals are also caught and eaten. Young birds cannot tolerate salt and must feed on freshwater prey, such as crayfish.

Nesting

The white ibis nests in colonies in trees and shrubs, often on islands where it finds protection from raccoons and other predators. It rarely nests on the ground. The nest, a platform of twigs and leaves, is most often placed between 6 and 10 feet above the ground. The female lays two or three eggs, which are incubated by both parents for about three weeks. After the chicks hatch, they stay close to the nest and usually don't leave the colony for at least six weeks.

Backyard & Beyond

You will find white ibis feeding in shallow water, where many other long-legged waders gather. Many national wildlife refuges, state wildlife management areas, and private wildlife sanctuaries along the Southeast coast protect white ibis nesting colonies or important feeding areas. The largest population once nested in the Everglades, but over the last century, numbers there declined after the area's water flow was altered by canal networks.

Canada Goose

Branta canadensis

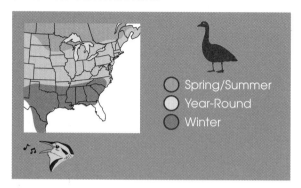

○ Spring/Summer
● Year-Round
○ Winter

The Canada goose enjoys an almost iconic status with human observers (though large, nonmigratory flocks can wear out their welcome). Their huge, V-shaped flights mark the passing of seasons, their honking is reminiscent of wilderness itself, and their strong family bonds (they mate for life) endear them to us. Many non-bird watchers mistakenly call this bird the Canadian goose.

All About

The Canada goose's black neck and white cheek strap are unmistakable. In flight, Canadas beat their wings deeply and slowly and show a black-and-white tail. Their familiar call is a deep, two-syllable *ha-ronk* and is given by mated pairs as well as flocking birds. Canadas also give a variety of softer cackling calls to each other, especially when they are on the ground. More than a dozen different subspecies exist in North America, and their sizes vary from 25 to 45 inches in length.

Habitat & Range

The Canada goose is a habitat generalist when it comes to water, settling in lakes, bays, rivers, and city parks and ponds. The species has enjoyed unprecedented success in living with or near humans, and today it nests all across the upper two-thirds of North America. Some re-established populations of Canada goose are year-round, nonmigratory residents, though many birds nesting in northern North America migrate to the southern United States in winter.

Spring migration begins early, and many females are incubating by mid-March.

Feeding

Aquatic plants, grasses, grains, and seeds are the Canada's primary foods. To reach submerged food, it will tip its tail in the air and extend its neck below the water's surface. Flocks leave roosting areas in the morning to forage in nearby fields, meadows, and marshes. Urban populations often live on handouts of cracked corn near city park lakes and golf course ponds.

Nesting

Located on a high spot near water, the nest is a small mound made of surrounding sticks and vegetation and lined with down plucked from the female. Half a dozen or more eggs are laid and incubated by the female for nearly a month while the male stands guard and brings her food. Within two days of hatching, young goslings are herded by their parents to the nearest water. Families stay together until the following breeding season, though young birds become self-sufficient in about two months.

Backyard & Beyond

Some housing developments and golf courses find them (and their droppings) a nuisance. To best see Canadas, visit a wildlife refuge where large flocks congregate during winter and during spring and fall migration. Watching hundreds of loudly honking Canadas is quite a spectacle.

Snow Goose

Chen caerulescens

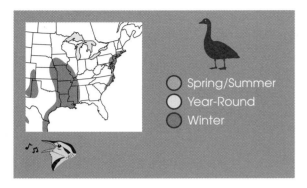

○ Spring/Summer
○ Year-Round
○ Winter

Like a distant line of dancing snowflakes, the bright white bodies of migrating snow geese flash in the sun as their nasal honking resonates in your ears. This species nests in the Far North, but winters in the southern United States and is one of our most successful waterfowl species. In fact, nesting colonies in the Arctic have been so successful that the snow goose's population has ballooned in recent years.

All About

The snow goose has a snow-white plumage overall, though the neck and head are often stained with reddish minerals from mud. The pink bill of the adult shows a black grin patch on the sides, a useful field mark to separate the large snow goose (26 to 33 inches in body length) from the smaller and less common Ross' goose (23 inches). Black primary wing feathers are obvious in flight, and the flashing black and white patterns of flying flocks have earned these birds the nickname "waveys."

Habitat & Range

Snow geese spend much of their time in transit. To take advantage of the short Arctic summer, they begin heading north as early as February, arriving on the breeding grounds by mid-May. By late August, fall migration begins and continues through December, when the last migrants reach the wintering grounds. At all times of year, snow geese prefer large, open bodies of water or large agricultural fields.

Feeding

Snow geese are mostly vegetarians, eating plant matter that includes grasses, leaves, seeds, and berries. Wintering flocks roost by night on water, leaving early in the morning to graze in fields and meadows.

Nesting

In their far northern breeding range, snow geese are almost always found within a few miles of the ocean. Nesting colonies can be huge, with more than a thousand pairs clustered together in some places, causing great damage to the surrounding habitat. Female snow geese select the nest site, scrape together surrounding vegetation and pluck their own down feathers to insulate the eggs as they are being laid. Two to six eggs are laid and incubated by the female for about 24 days before hatching. Within a day, goslings are mobile and the entire family roams about, foraging together. Snow goose families stay together for an entire year, breaking up upon returning to the breeding grounds the following spring.

Backyard & Beyond

Finding snow geese in winter means going to one of their preferred winter habitats: coastal marshes, large inland reservoirs, major river systems, and surrounding agricultural fields. They are gregarious birds by nature, so where you find one, you are likely to find anywhere from several dozen to several thousand birds. These wintering flocks are active, loud, and raucous.

Wood Duck

Aix sponsa

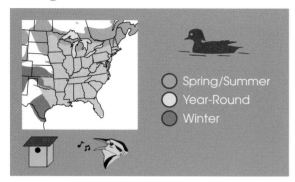

○ Spring/Summer
○ Year-Round
○ Winter

The up-slurred WHEEEP *of the wood duck is a familiar sound to anyone frequenting areas where woodland and fresh water mix. Patience and a bit of stealth will reward the birder seeking a good look at these cagey, dazzling ducks. Across much of the South, wood ducks abound, finding ample habitat and welcoming nest boxes.*

All About

The male wood duck takes its colorful plumage to an extreme. In breeding plumage, it has a green crown and black face offset by white slashes reaching up from its white throat. The bill looks painted, a bright red-orange with black and white touches. Breast and undertail are chestnut, while the sides are adorned with vertical white and blackish slashes followed by a panel of butterscotch yellow. The male's back is metallic green. These colors fade during summer, as the birds molt into *eclipse*, or nonbreeding, plumage, but the bright bill and eye and face pattern remain. Both male and female have backward-facing crests that give them a helmeted look. The female wood duck is easy to identify, not only because of her head shape, but also because of her white, tear-shaped eye rings. Otherwise, females are grayish brown and generously flecked with whitish spots on their sides.

Habitat & Range

The perfect setting for wood ducks combines tranquil fresh water with plenty of trees—bottomland swamps, riverside forests, and tree-lined ponds and lakes. Wood ducks are permanent residents in much of the South, except in the Appalachians, where populations withdraw during the cold months. Northern populations, from southern Canada through the Northeast, retreat to the South in winter.

Feeding

Wood ducks eat a variety of seeds and some fruits from aquatic and forest plants, including acorns. Sometimes, they eat grain. Insects and other small animals supplement their diet; though, for recently fledged birds, these are a mainstay.

Nesting

Wood ducks are cavity nesters, setting up house in holes high in mature or dead trees. They also nest down low in nest boxes. The nest is simply an accumulation of down placed on the cavity floor, where the female incubates her 8 to 15 pale eggs for between $3^1/_2$ and 5 weeks. Chicks usually tumble out of their nest the day after hatching. Females accompany them for about six weeks, and they can fly at about two months of age.

Backyard & Beyond

If you live near fresh water, you may see wood ducks fly over your property. If your property includes a pond or wetland, you may attract wood ducks with a nesting box, which ideally would be set in the water on a post fitted with a collar-like, predator baffle.

Mallard
Anas platyrhynchos

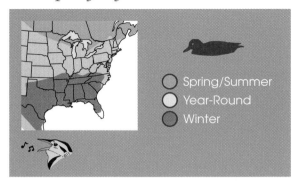

- ○ Spring/Summer
- ○ Year-Round
- ○ Winter

Of all the North American duck species, there's one that nearly everyone knows—the mallard. Abundant all across the continent, the mallard is known to interbreed commonly with black ducks and other wild duck species, as well as with domesticated ducks. Large numbers of semitame mallards exist on city park ponds, golf courses, and reservoirs, getting by on handouts from humans.

All About
The male mallard's green head and yellow bill are easily recognizable, but female mallards—with their overall dark brown coloration—can be confused with black ducks, mottled ducks, and other female ducks. Look for her orange and black bill and listen for the loud, raucous *quack*, *quack-quack*, *quack-quack* call, given only by female mallards. Mallards are fairly large ducks with a 23-inch body length.

Habitat & Range
Like other dabbling ducks, mallards prefer shallow bodies of fresh water at all times of year, including marshes, flooded woodlots, ponds, and swamps. They can be found year-round across most of the United States, but a large number of mallards breed in the Far North and spend the winter in the Southeast.

Feeding
Mallards feed by scooping up seeds and plant material from the water's surface, by tipping up—tails in the air—to reach submerged plants, and by grazing for waste grain in agricultural fields. They eat everything from seeds and vegetation to insects, small fish, crawfish, and frogs.

Nesting
Mallards pair up well before the spring breeding season. The hen mallard chooses the nest site, usually in or near thick vegetation on the ground. She then builds a small bowl out of nearby plant material and lines it with her own down. Between 7 and 12 eggs are laid and incubated by the hen for a month. Like other ducks, mallard ducklings leave the nest within hours after hatching and follow their mother to the nearest water. Though ducklings feed themselves right away, it's nearly two months before they are able to fly. Predators take a heavy toll on nests and young, especially in parks where natural predators are augmented by domestic pets.

Backyard & Beyond
If you want to feed the mallards in your local park, don't bother with stale bread, which holds little nutritional value for birds. Instead, offer some cracked corn. This inexpensive food is available at most stores selling birdseed and is relished by mallards. When you've got a hungry flock of panhandling mallards nearby, take time to look at the birds' fine plumage. Look, too, for wild ducks of other species that may be "hanging out" with the local flock of tame mallards, as well as for the many interesting hybrids that result from the mallard's promiscuous nature.

Blue-winged Teal

Anas discors

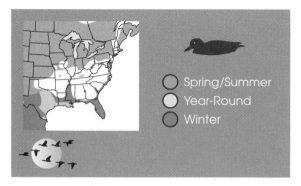

○ Spring/Summer
○ Year-Round
○ Winter

A fast-flying, small (14 inches long) duck, the blue-winged teal shows the blue shoulder patch for which it is named only when the wings are extended. Blue-wingeds fly in tight flocks and seem to be wary as they pass repeatedly over a body of water before landing. However, they are not as skittish as other ducks when approached by humans, perhaps because they know they can explode off the water and straight into the air in seconds.

All About

Males have a blue-gray head and a distinctive white face crescent and hip patch, making them easy to identify even from a distance. Females are a warm, gray-brown overall with a slight echo of the males' white face crescent. Identifying them is made somewhat easier by the fact that blue-winged teal pairs form in early winter and stay together through spring migration.

Habitat & Range

Blue-winged teal breed throughout the northeastern, central, and western United States, but bird watchers in the southeastern states are most likely to see them during spring and fall migration and in winter. Most blue-winged teal spend the winter south of the United States, as far as South America. They are considered fair-weather ducks by many bird watchers because they stay far to the south until spring is in full force. Perhaps it is their later spring arrival and their earlier fall departure that has earned them the nicknames "summer teal" and "August teal."

Their preferred habitats—at all seasons—are shallow, freshwater marshes and ponds.

Feeding

Teal feed on seeds and plant matter gleaned from the water's surface or by swimming with their heads submerged to find snails, aquatic insects, and crustaceans. Unlike other dabbling ducks, blue-wingeds do not "tip up" to feed on submerged vegetation.

Nesting

Like many other ducks, blue-winged teal nest on the ground in a spot concealed by thick vegetation. The female builds a shallow, basket-shaped nest out of dried grasses lined with her down. A clutch of nine or more eggs is laid and incubated by the hen for slightly more than three weeks. Teal ducklings leave the nest almost immediately and are able to feed themselves right away, but it will be six weeks before they are fully flighted.

Backyard & Beyond

The blue-winged's preference for shallow water means that it can show up almost anywhere—from farm or city ponds to coastal marshes, mudflats, and sewage settling pools. If you see a flock of small ducks flying pell-mell, twisting and turning as one, chances are they are blue-winged teal. You can clinch the identification by looking for the male teal's white face crescent, or for the flash of blue, white, and green in the wings.

Ring-necked Duck

Aythya collaris

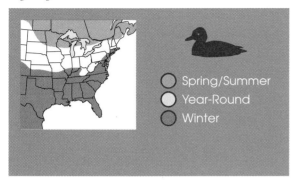

- ○ Spring/Summer
- ○ Year-Round
- ○ Winter

The ring-necked duck is a characteristic bird of the South—not because it nests there, but because of its widespread occurrence there in winter. Flocks of ringnecks frequent marshes, swamps, and sheltered and wooded corners of lakes. These birds are often found in areas where the only other regularly sighted ducks are wood ducks and mallards (in interior areas). Ringnecks are also found on open water and areas with a wider diversity of ducks.

All About

Closely related and superficially similar to the greater and lesser scaup, this diving bird has a few embellishments that easily set it apart from the scaup. Like the scaup, the male ringneck is blackish—in most light—on head, chest, and back. However, even at a distance, the adult male ring-necked duck has a vertical white comma that edges its gray sides. Its bill is three-toned: The tip is black, followed by a white band, then much gray, then a white border where bill meets head. Like the scaup, the female ringneck is more somber in coloration and markings, but she has a noticeably dark crown compared with the rest of the head. She sports a white eye ring, and usually has a clearly three-toned bill. As with the red-bellied woodpecker, the ring-necked duck's name was poorly chosen by "dead-bird-in-the-hand" early ornithologists: Only in rare circumstances will you see its namesake rusty collar.

Habitat & Range

Most ring-necked ducks winter in the United States, below the northern tier of states, and south into central Mexico. Others winter in the West Indies, and a few are found as far south as Panama. Unlike scaup, ring-necked ducks frequent small or smallish bodies of water, and they rarely enter salt water. Summer finds them nesting in Canada, Alaska, and a good number of northern U.S. states in freshwater wetlands, usually surrounded by forest.

Feeding

Ring-necked ducks dive for their supper, snipping roots and stems of plants, eating seeds, insects, and mollusks. Like other waterfowl, their recently hatched young eat mostly insects.

Nesting

The female ring-necked duck usually lays between 8 and 10 eggs in a nest of grasses or other plants clipped from nearby. She incubates the eggs for almost a month. After they hatch, she accompanies her chicks until they can fly, shortly before two months of age.

Backyard & Beyond

Early in the morning or in well-protected areas, you may catch close-up looks at ring-necked ducks on small ponds or lakes. Even at a distance, though, the gray, white, and black markings on the male's sides help identify these birds as they dive underwater and pop back up to the surface.

Hooded Merganser

Lophodytes cucullatus

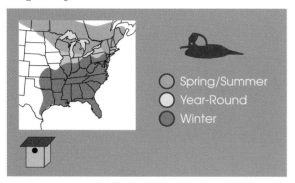

○ Spring/Summer
○ Year-Round
○ Winter

The hooded merganser is a hidden treasure of wooded wetlands, lakes, and bays, and is often spotted in small flocks skirting the back edge of fresh or brackish bodies of water. Of the three mergansers—ducks with narrow, serrated bills—the hooded is the smallest and has the shortest bill. Hooded mergansers occur in many areas also frequented by wood ducks.

All About

Both male and female hooded mergansers can be easily identified. The male is in gaudy plumage much of the year. Its head is an odd shape, either extremely round like a raised mushroom when its crest is raised, or bump-headed when its crest is relaxed. This shape influences the appearance of the dazzling white spot behind the bird's yellow eye. With raised crest, the white is like a fat inverted comma; with crest relaxed, it is like a horizontal blob. The male's bright coppery-orange sides contrast with a white chest pierced by two vertical black bars that bleed into the black back and head. The female lacks such bold coloration. A rich brown-rust on her head, she is an otherwise brown-gray. A dark bird, she lacks the white throat, bright orange bill, and gray to brown contrasts seen in female red-breasted and common mergansers.

Habitat & Range

Ponds, rivers, creeks, bays, and swamps are among the habitats used by this widespread species. Hooded mergansers breed from Canada to as far south as northern Florida and southern Louisiana. The situation changes during migration and winter, when many eastern hooded mergansers winter in the Southeast.

Feeding

While the other two mergansers are primarily fish-eaters, the hooded merganser has a more varied diet that not only includes small fish but also insects, crayfish, and other aquatic creatures. Like other mergansers, hoodeds dive for their food, apparently finding prey by sight.

Nesting

The female hooded merganser creates a shallow bowl at the bottom of a tree cavity or nest box, using whatever materials she finds there. She plucks down feathers from her undersides to line the nest. Up to a dozen white eggs are laid, which she incubates for up to 40 days. The young leave the nest at a day old and are attended by the female. Hooded mergansers often lay their eggs in the nests of other hooded mergansers and wood ducks, leaving their young to be raised by another mother.

Backyard & Beyond

The males of both hooded mergansers and wood ducks are equally gaudy in plumage, and both have odd head shapes. Look for "hoodies" in small flocks of males and females on freshwater lakes and ponds; they will often be hugging a wooded shoreline.

Turkey Vulture

Cathartes aura

Spring/Summer
Year-Round
Winter

Catharsis—a cleansing or purification—is the root of the turkey vulture's Latin name. It refers to this bird's invaluable service in ridding the landscape of animal carcasses—a necessity in the age of superhighways. The highway system, with its continual supply of shoulder fare, may have contributed to the turkey vulture's northward breeding range expansion.

All About

The tilting flight, with wings held in a shallow "V", immediately distinguishes a turkey vulture from most other large, dark birds in flight. At close range, the underwings appear two-toned, with the flight feathers having a reflective, pewter sheen. The small, naked head is red; the bill bone-white. On the ground, a turkey vulture appears to be all wing—a long blackish trapezoid, topped by a tiny red head. Hoarse hisses are their only sounds. Nestlings produce a continuous breathy roar when cornered in the nest.

Habitat & Range

Ranging widely as they search for food, turkey vultures prefer farmland pasture where carcasses might be found, and with nearby forests where they find nesting and roosting spots. Communal roosters, they may be seen warming themselves with wings spread open to the sun. Turkey vultures are migratory in the northern parts of their range, mingling with resident birds in the southern United States, some traveling as far south as Amazonia before returning in early spring.

Feeding

Powerful olfactory senses help the turkey vulture locate carcasses, and they may circle in groups, narrowing down the scent source, before spotting it. This allows them to find carrion in deep woods. One circling vulture brings sharp-eyed companions from miles around, and they share their plunder, rising with heavy flaps from roadsides when disturbed. Its bare head allows the vulture to reach into larger carcasses without fouling its feathers.

Nesting

Turkey vultures hide their nests on rock ledges, in hollow logs, under boulders, or in unused animal burrows. The female lays two eggs, which she and her mate incubate for around 28 days. The young are in the nest cavity and its vicinity for about 12 weeks, making first flights as early as 60 days of age. After a few weeks of exercising and being fed in the nest vicinity, they appear to be independent upon their first extended flight.

Backyard & Beyond

Turkey vultures have learned to exploit factory farms, especially chicken farms, for the inevitable carcasses they produce. They are closely attuned to spring calving and lambing times. Rather than being seen as harbingers of death, turkey vultures might be considered for their great beauty in flight and as a vital cleanup crew.

Black Vulture

Coragyps atratus

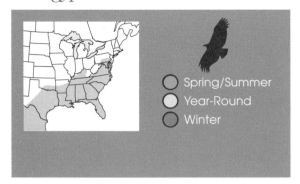

○ Spring/Summer
○ Year-Round
○ Winter

With its distinctive gray "light bulb head" and shorter, broader wings, the black vulture can easily be distinguished from the longer winged, more graceful turkey vulture. It makes smaller circles and flaps more, as if struggling to stay aloft. A long period of juvenile dependence and complex social structure also helps set it apart from the more aloof turkey vulture.

All About

Smaller and chunkier than the turkey vulture, the black vulture is also darker—a true soot-black. In flight, its extremely short tail and broad wings give it a distinctive headless and tailless silhouette. Labored, quick flapping is interspersed with gliding as the black vulture makes tight circles in the sky. A whitish spot at the base of the primary wing feathers is diagnostic. The voice is basic, with hisses, grunts, and low barks as a repertoire.

Habitat & Range

Black vultures are more common in flat, low-lying areas, especially agricultural areas with adjacent dense woodlands. They roost communally in isolated stands of trees, on utility towers, and on similar sites, where they are often persecuted by people who do not recognize their value as scavengers. Black vultures have expanded their range northward in recent years. They are migratory in the northern part of their range, resident in the southern.

Feeding

Lacking a well-developed sense of smell, this small cousin of the turkey vulture relies on its larger relative to find food. Black vultures fly higher than turkey vultures, presumably in an effort to keep them in view and hone in on their finds. Once there, black vultures will overpower turkey vultures and feed first. They primarily eat carrion, but they can kill small animals, including young pigs, calves, and lambs.

Nesting

Scattered, abandoned buildings provide nest sites for many black vultures, while others use caves, thickets, or hollow logs. The female lays two eggs, which she and her mate incubate for around 38 days. The young are in the nest cavity and its vicinity for about 90 days, when they are capable of following their parents. An extremely long juvenile dependency period follows. Young birds may be fed into the following spring, when it is time for the parents to nest once more. This long dependency period may contribute to the black vulture's complex social structure.

Backyard & Beyond

Black vultures use their communal roosts as an information-gathering tool. Birds that return from a successful day of feeding are followed the next morning by hungry birds. Black vultures associate primarily with "family," birds to whom they are related, and they frequently squabble with and oust unrelated individuals.

Sharp-shinned Hawk

Accipiter striatus

If the birds at your feeder seem skittish, they have a good reason—a sharp-shinned hawk could appear at any moment. Its primary prey, after all, is small songbirds. This songbird specialist is actually doing nature a favor by weeding out the slowest, weakest, or oldest birds, helping to keep bird populations healthy. Once thought to be an evil killer of innocent birds, thousands of sharpies and other hawks used to be shot, a practice that has since been outlawed.

All About

Built for speed and maneuverability with short rounded wings, a slender body, and long narrow tail, the sharp-shinned hawk can chase fleeing songbirds into and through thick cover. Adult sharpies have reddish breasts, and a dark gray head and back. Young birds have brown backs and white breasts coarsely streaked with brown. Sharpies appear small-headed and slighter when compared to the similar, but larger, Cooper's hawk. Flying sharpies almost always follow this rhythm: flap, flap, flap, glide.

Habitat & Range

Forest habitats of almost any type can support sharp-shinned hawks, but they are most likely to be found where songbird populations are thriving. Sharpies have a vast breeding range, but they prefer large tracts of woodland for nest sites, so they are rarely observed on the nest. In fall most migrate southward, their movement triggered by passing cold fronts. Some migrate as far as Central America, but many spend the winter in the continental United States.

Feeding

Hunting sharp-shinned hawks use surprise and speed—emerging suddenly from behind a line of trees or bursting forth from a quiet, concealed perch. As surprised birds scatter, the sharpie pursues one and grabs it with its long, taloned toes. If undisturbed, the hawk may finish its meal on the ground, or it may carry it away to a safer location. Sharpies will take prey as large as ruffed grouse and as small as hummingbirds.

Nesting

The sharp-shinned hawk's nest is made of sticks and is built by the female high in a tree. She lays four to five eggs and incubates them for about a month. After hatching, the female broods the young birds for about 20 days, all the while being fed by her mate. A month after hatching, young hawks are ready to leave the nest, though they spend several more weeks being fed by the parents.

Backyard & Beyond

Your first reaction to a sharp-shinned hawk in your backyard might be horror, but you have to respect the bird's ability as a predator. Watch the hawk's intense focus when it's perched, and listen for how the songbirds warn each other about the hawk. It's like a television nature show, live from your living room window!

Red-shouldered Hawk

Buteo lineatus

- Spring/Summer
- Year-Round
- Winter

The South is the heartland for this colorful raptor, which flourishes in swamps and along wooded riversides. Its strident KEEah, KEEah, KEEah call directs birders to soaring birds overhead or those coursing through the woods. Development strikes a blow to red-shouldered hawks, birds that normally shun the open habitats that are favored by the slightly larger red-tailed hawk.

All About

Robin-orange shoulder patches and breast barring are hallmarks of the adult red-shouldered hawk. Although chunky, the red-shouldered is slimmer than the red-tailed hawk, and its tail is comparatively longer and barred in black and white. In flight, especially while soaring or gliding, light or clear crescents can be seen at the base of the bird's flight feathers, areas called *windows* by birders. These windows are an important field mark to differentiate red-shouldered hawks from similar red-tailed and broad-winged hawks. The broad-winged hawk is also orange below, but its tail exhibits mainly one large, wide white band, while several bands are visible on the red-shouldered's tail. The red-shouldered hawk's underwings are darkish, contrasting with its light windows, while the broad-winged hawk's is almost all whitish underneath, bordered in blackish. Immature red-shouldered hawks are brown and white, with heavy teardrop streaks below and brown and whitish barred tails. Southern Florida adults are pale, with frosty heads and backs.

Habitat & Range

Red-shouldered hawks hunt in forests found near water. They nest throughout the eastern U.S. Many reside year-round, though some northern birds migrate south in winter. Red-shouldered hawks occupy the same habitats as barred owls— one hunting by day, the other by night.

Feeding

During warm months or in warm areas, red-shouldered hawks seek a variety of small animals, including various insects, frogs, snakes, and lizards. In colder weather, rodents and small birds play a larger role in their diet.

Nesting

The nest will most likely be located high in a mature tree in deciduous woods that do not have much undergrowth. The large stick nest is lined with softer materials, such as bark and grassy or leafy stems. The female lays two to four eggs, which she incubates for about a month. The male brings food. Young leave the nest after about six weeks, but parents feed them for two more months before they gain full independence.

Backyard & Beyond

Some suburbs sit within hearing or soaring range of red-shouldered hawks breeding in nearby woods; listen for their telltale scream. Migrating immatures often turn up in backyards, perching in large trees in wooded districts. Riverside walks will often yield sightings, as will trips to swamps.

Red-tailed Hawk

Buteo jamaicensis

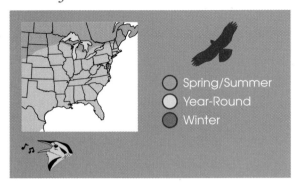

○ Spring/Summer
○ Year-Round
○ Winter

This bird is the large raptor people most often see doing "lazy circles in the sky." The red-tailed hawk inhabits open terrain across the continent and south to Central America. It thrives in habitats opened up by human activities, such as farming or forest clearing. They are also the large raptor most commonly seen perched along roadways and power lines.

All About

Red-tailed hawks occur across the continent in quite a variety of plumage colorations. In the East, however, count on a few easy field marks to help identify adult birds: the reddish-orange tail, a dark-streaked belly band, and a white chest. This hat trick of field marks can easily be seen in many soaring redtails, as well as in perched birds. Additionally, two chocolate-colored bars adorn the leading edge of the underwing. Overall, soaring red-tailed hawks are bulkier and more formidable in general appearance than slimmer red-shouldered hawks and broad-winged hawks, which have shorter tails. Red-tailed hawks younger than two years old lack the telltale reddish tail, but they still exhibit the belly band and white chest.

Habitat & Range

Look for red-tailed hawks along highway edges, over farm fields and forest clearings, and in almost any other open habitat with at least some telephone poles or trees on which they can perch and scan for prey. From tundra to tropical forests, the red-tailed hawk is a formidable pred-ator. They breed as far south as Panama and on various Caribbean islands, thus the species name *jamaicensis*. For nesting, they usually avoid areas with a lot of human activity, even though they nest in New York City's Central Park and pass through suburbs during migration.

Feeding

Many farmers appreciate seeing red-tailed hawks flap over their acreage, as they eat many voles, mice, rats, rabbits, squirrels, and other small mammals. Other prey can include a variety of birds and reptiles. Red-tailed hawks may glide down from a perch to grab prey, dive down, or hover and then drop on prey.

Nesting

Nests are usually found in tall trees, although these birds will nest on cliffs and sometimes even buildings. Both mates build the large stick nest, which they line with softer materials. The female usually lays two or three eggs, which both parents incubate for about a month. The male hunts for food, passing it to his mate, who feeds their young. Nestlings fly after about 10 weeks.

Backyard & Beyond

You may hear the red-tailed hawk's blood-curdling cry around its nesting grounds. Because they range widely and some populations migrate short or long distances, you may see red-tailed hawks soaring or gliding over your home.

Bald Eagle
Haliaeetus leucocephalus

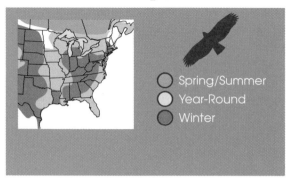

○ Spring/Summer
○ Year-Round
○ Winter

The bald eagle barely edged out the wild turkey when our founding fathers were voting on a national symbol. Skilled fishing bird, scavenger, and pirate, the bald eagle is an opportunistic raptor that's been given a second chance thanks to improved conservation and bans on DDT, which dramatically impaired the birds' breeding and sent their population into steep decline in the decades following World War II.

All About
There is no confusing the adult bald eagle, with its huge size and gleaming white head and tail. Adult plumage is not attained until after the third year. Until then, immature birds are dark brown with varying degrees of white mottling on their backs, wings, bellies, and, in older birds, heads. Depending upon age, the large bill is blackish or accented in the bright yellow seen in adults. Immatures and adults have strong, bright yellow talons.

Habitat & Range
Water plays a strong role in where bald eagles hunt and nest. In the process of rebounding in many areas, bald eagles now nest in most states, where they are often local nesters tied to specific sites. They are particularly common from Florida to coastal South Carolina, but the largest breeding populations are in Alaska and western Canada. During winter, bald eagles often congregate at wetland areas, rivers, and dams, where fishing or carrion feeding is particularly productive.

Feeding
Bald eagles hunt from perches or swoop down after sighting prey during soaring. While fish are preferred prey (frequently grappled from the water in the eagle's mighty talons), eagles also eat a wide variety of other foods, depending upon individual, time of year, and location. Carrion—particularly dead fish, birds, and mammals—plays an important dietary role. Many live animals are also caught: muskrats, reptiles, amphibians, crustaceans, and birds—as large as great blue herons—have been documented. Bald eagles also steal fish from ospreys and other birds.

Nesting
Bald eagles usually nest high in large trees in huge, bulky stick nests that are often used again over the years. Both mates collect sticks, and nest building may take several months. The female usually lays two eggs, which she and her mate incubate for just over a month. Once the first chick hatches, both parents incubate and *brood*, or cover, the eggs and hatchlings. Both parents feed their young, which leave the nest between 8 to 14 weeks after hatching.

Backyard & Beyond
Recently, bald eagles have started nesting in closer proximity to human development, thanks to protection from disturbance. If you see a large, dark raptor soaring slowly in the sky, with flat wings, look for the other clues of the bald eagle's identity.

Osprey
Pandion haliaetus

○ Spring/Summer
○ Year-Round
○ Winter

The bold chocolate and white "fish hawk," so familiar to boaters and fishermen, is happy to exploit artificial nesting platforms, from power poles to those built specifically for it. Though osprey populations declined by 90 percent from the 1950s to the 1970s (poisoned by persistent organochlorides), they have made a heartening rebound in recent decades.

All About
Chocolate-brown above and pure white below, the osprey is armed with long, pale green legs and grappling-hook talons for seizing fish. Fierce yellow eyes are ringed in black, making the bird look as though it is wearing aviator's goggles. A banded gray tail and ragged crest complete this gangly bird's unusual look. Females have streaked upper breasts and are larger than males. When disturbed, ospreys give a series of high, piercing, chicklike peeps and thin screams.

Habitat & Range
One of the most widespread species, the osprey inhabits rivers, lakes, and coastlines throughout much of the United States. It is still reclaiming territory in the interior United States, helped by osprey reintroduction programs. Lacking body down, ospreys must migrate to stay warm and to find sufficient food in unfrozen waters, traveling down both coasts of Mexico and Central America.

Feeding
The only North American raptor to feed exclusively on fish, the osprey soars and hovers over shallow, clear waters of estuaries, marshes, lakes, and rivers, searching for fish. Spotting prey, it folds its wings and plunges, feet first, often completely beneath the surface. Unique cylindrical, recurved talons and horny spikes on the soles of its feet hold the fish securely until the osprey reaches a "carving block," usually a dead snag, where it can eat. Fish are always carried with the head facing into the wind, and are sometimes eaten as a snack on migration, far from water.

Nesting
The huge stick nests ospreys build are a familiar site on channel markers, dead trees, and artificial nesting platforms along coasts. Nesting pairs add sticks yearly until the nests assume enormous proportions. In the soft, grass-lined center the female lays two to three eggs, which she and her mate incubate for around 37 days. The male provides all the female's food during this time. Chicks stay in the nest for about 55 days, taking short flights, and are fed on or near the nest for around two weeks after first attaining flight.

Backyard & Beyond
Though artificial nesting platforms have had a positive influence on osprey populations, they are by no means out of danger. Overfishing, pesticide contamination, and persecution on Latin American wintering grounds (where they are shot by the hundreds at fish farms) continue to limit populations.

American Kestrel

Falco sparverius

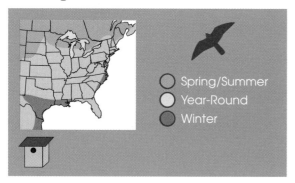

- ○ Spring/Summer
- ○ Year-Round
- ○ Winter

North America's smallest falcon is also the most familiar to many, hovering over farm fields and air strips, perching on telephone poles and wires, and nesting in boxes put out by concerned landowners, who welcome these insect and rodent eaters. In some regions, kestrel numbers have fallen in recent decades, probably due to large-scale landscape changes, as farm areas have reverted to forest and as cities and suburbs have stretched out to once-rural areas.

All About

In flight, the kestrel has sharp-looking, pointed wings and a slender, long tail. In comparison to the merlin and peregrine falcon, it is slim. Sharp-shinned and Cooper's hawks also have long tails, but their wings are broad, not pointed. While soaring, the kestrel's wings look more rounded and the tail fans. Adult males are brightly colored, with blue-gray wings and crown, rufous tail, and a rusty back embellished with black barring. Black spots speckle the underparts. Both sexes have two vertical stripes on the face and a black spot on the back of the neck. Adult females lack the male's blue-gray wings, have barred tails, and—instead of black spots—sport rusty lines of spots on their underparts.

Habitat & Range

The American kestrel is not strictly a farm bird, although many farms provide the ideal habitat for them. They also nest and hunt in open urban areas, open forest, clearings, and even deserts. They are truly American in the New World sense, nesting from Alaska to southern Argentina. In the South, numbers swell in the winter, when northern birds move south en masse to winter in warmer areas.

Feeding

Grasshoppers and other large insects are important prey to kestrels, but voles, mice, and other rodents also play a part in their diet, as do small birds, reptiles, and other small animals.

Nesting

American kestrels are cavity nesters. Females usually lay their four to six eggs in a tree hole or other cavity, sometimes in a crevice in a building or cliff or in a nest box. Both parents share the month-long incubation duties. Young fly about a month after hatching, and parents feed them until about two weeks after they leave the nest.

Backyard & Beyond

Provision of nest boxes in rural areas has helped American kestrel populations, and this is one potential way to attract kestrels to your property if you live in an open area. Kestrels also pass through suburban areas during migration. In the South, they may frequent open suburbs rich in grasshoppers and such prey as small birds and lizards. They will use snags placed in the middle of grassy meadows as hunting and eating perches.

Northern Bobwhite

Colinus virginianus

○ Spring/Summer
○ Year-Round
○ Winter

Conservationists are struggling to find out why the distinctive bob-WHITE call of the northern bobwhite no longer rings out in parts of its wide breeding range. Many suppose that large-scale landscape changes—such as the prevention of naturally occurring fires, which rejuvenate brushy fields—and the widespread use of herbicides have caused bobwhite populations to dive throughout much of the Southeast over the last three decades. In the northern parts of their range, hard winters often knock down populations.

All About

The bobwhite is the East's only quail. This plump, football-shaped bird more often runs than flies and, when not disturbed, picks at the ground for seeds like a chicken. Males have a striking head pattern, with white throat and supercilium (line above eye to back of head) cutting through an otherwise dark chocolate-brown head. Females are similarly marked, but have buff (rather than white) and rust (rather than dark brown) head coloration. Bobwhites have cinnamon-rust bodies embellished with long white streaks below, and they have very short tails.

Habitat & Range

Far more often heard than seen, the northern bobwhite occurs from Massachusetts west to Wyoming and south to the Mexico-Guatemala border. Some introduced populations inhabit western mountain states as well. Bobwhites feed and breed in a variety of open habitats. They favor farm fields and those just reverting to rank, weedy meadows; pastures; pine forests; and mixed pine and deciduous forests with undergrowth kept open by managed fire or regular cutting.

Feeding

Adult bobwhites are opportunistic seedeaters. Depending upon season and locality, they consume a wide variety of weed seeds, as well as agricultural seeds and those from various forest plants. They also eat some insects and berries, buds, and other plant foods. Until two months of age, young bobwhites mostly eat insects and other small invertebrates.

Nesting

During one breeding season, a bobwhite pair could ideally produce 25 or more young in several broods; however, they suffer high mortality rates and are rarely this productive. Bobwhite pairs build their grass or other vegetation-covered scrape nest in a well-camouflaged spot within their tangled habitat. There they incubate a dozen or more eggs for just over three weeks. Young hatch able to run and feed themselves. Parents usually loiter nearby.

Backyard & Beyond

Where prime habitat is carefully maintained, there are plenty of these quail left for hunters and birders alike. If you live on a large piece of land, you can create a bobwhite habitat by cutting (or, with local fire department supervision, burning) fields every one to five years.

Wild Turkey
Meleagris gallopavo

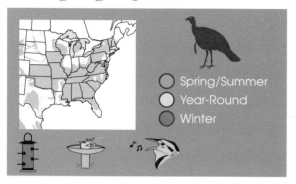

○ Spring/Summer
○ Year-Round
○ Winter

When restocking programs abandoned using farm-raised birds and turned to releasing wild-caught birds in the 1940s, the repopulation of wild turkeys into their former haunts took off. Today, the large dark forms of wild turkeys are a familiar sight along many highways, and the birds even come to backyard feeders.

All About
A tall, strong-legged bird, the wild turkey's feathers are iridescent with dark bronze, shot with hints of copper and acid green. Displaying in spring, the male erects its plumage in the strut posture, its enormous tail fanned, wings drooping, and wattles ablaze. A "beard" of wiry, barbless feathers sprouts from the center of his breast. Hens are visibly smaller and paler than gobblers, with a brown cast to their plumage and without distensible wattles. Along with the male's explosive gobble, turkeys employ a great variety of calls, including yelps and hollow *putt* sounds, in their intraflock communication.

Habitat & Range
Dense deciduous forests—either uplands or bottomlands—with some clearings are ideal turkey habitats. The nuts from oaks and other nut trees make up an important component of their diet. Some exploit agricultural fields for spilled grain. Wild turkeys are nonmigratory and may fast for more than a week in severe weather.

Feeding
The wild turkey's strong legs and feet help it scratch its way across the forest floor, raking away debris to uncover acorns, tree seeds, and invertebrates. Turkeys pluck buds and fruits as they walk or clamber through branches, and they strip grasses of their seeds by running stems through their bills. Young poults take a number of insects and invertebrates.

Nesting
Gobblers display—gobbling and strutting—in early spring to attract visiting hens. After mating, the hen lays about a dozen eggs in a feather-lined bowl in the ground at the foot of a tree or under brush. She incubates them alone for about 26 days. When all chicks have hatched and imprinted on the hen (from one to three days later), they leave the nest, following her every move. She feeds them for the first few days; after that they pick up their own food. She broods them on the ground until they are able to join her in a roost tree at night; she still shelters them with spread wings on the roost.

Backyard & Beyond
Wild turkeys may, in some rural and suburban situations, be attracted into yards with cracked corn spread on the ground. A small flock can consume as much as 50 pounds per week. Fascinating social behavior and courtship behavior is a rich reward. Rotate feeding areas to prevent the spread of disease.

American Coot

Fulica americana

- Spring/Summer
- Year-Round
- Winter

What looks like a duck and acts like a duck, but is not a duck? It's the American coot, of course. Coots are duck-like in many ways, but they are actually members of the rail family and are the most common (and most commonly seen) of all the rails. Like ducks, coots are excellent swimmers and use this ability to find and eat aquatic vegetation. However, coots are reluctant and awkward fliers—they must run, pattering across the water's surface and flapping madly to lift their heavy bodies into the air.

All About
Chunky and almost all black with a contrasting white bill and red eyes and forehead patch, the coot is hard to mistake for anything else. The common moorhen and purple gallinule are similar in shape, but both are more colorful (the gallinule much more so) and less common than coots. Coots swim using the lobed toes on their powerful feet, and when swimming they bob their heads back and forth with a "funky chicken" motion. Coots are raucous, loud birds that utter a variety of grunts, cackles, and croaks.

Habitat & Range
American coots are widespread across North America, especially in winter when they can be found in huge flocks on large bodies of water. They breed throughout the central and western portions of the continent, and they are year-round residents in spots in the South. During the breeding season, coots prefer ponds, lakes, and marshes of almost any size, provided that they have large stands of tall reeds, such as cattails.

Feeding
Finding most of their food on or below the surface of the water, coots dabble, swim, and dive when foraging. They are equally at home on land, grazing on the grass of city parks and golf courses. Their diet is largely vegetarian with the main menu items being duckweed, algae, and various pondweeds and sedges.

Nesting
The female coot builds a floating, basket-shaped platform of vegetation with a lined cup to hold the eggs. She lays up to a dozen eggs and incubates them for about 23 days. Young coots have shiny, bald, red heads and golden down, an adaptation that is thought to trigger feeding by the parents. Babies leave the nest after a day or so and are able to find food on their own shortly thereafter.

Backyard & Beyond
Though they may not be a backyard bird, coots should be easy to find in nearby parks and on golf course water hazards. In winter, look for flocks of coots on almost any body of water, from reservoirs to sewage ponds.

Killdeer
Charadrius vociferus

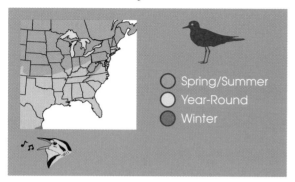

- Spring/Summer
- Year-Round
- Winter

The killdeer is a large, double-banded plover that screams its name across farm fields and other grass- and dirt-covered habitats. If you see an orange-tailed, stripe-winged bird calling KILL-DEEE, KILL-DEEE, you can rest assured that it's this plover. Despite their lousy-tasting flesh, many killdeer were shot during the late 1800s, along with a wide range of other shorebirds. These species are now protected from harm by federal and state laws.

All About

On its white breast, two black bands stand out. Other plovers—such as the smaller but similar semipalmated plover—have only one band or none at all. Otherwise, killdeer are wet-sand brown above and clear white below, with white around the front of the face and eye. The killdeer is one of our largest and longest-tailed plovers, so even mixed with a few other species on a mudflat, they stand out, especially when you spot those two breast bands. Much of the tail is orange, except the tip, which is black punctuated with white dabs.

Habitat & Range

Unlike most other plovers, killdeer often forage or nest far from water. You may find them on ball fields and airport runways, on turf, in pastures, and in farm fields, as well as on mudflats. They are found throughout North America, but northern birds head south for the winter. In the South, only the Appalachians lose their killdeer during cold months.

Feeding

A farmer's friend, the killdeer spends its foraging time searching for beetles, grasshoppers, caterpillars, and other insects. Crayfish, centipedes, spiders, and other invertebrates are also eaten, as well as some seeds.

Nesting

A simple scrape in the dirt or gravel (including gravel-covered roofs) will do for a killdeer pair, although they sometimes add embellishments, such as a lining of pebbles, grass, or other small materials. Females lay three to five blotched eggs, which both parents incubate for just less than a month. Nesting in exposed habitats, killdeer rely on camouflage and deception to keep their eggs and chicks safe. If an intruder approaches the nest, an adult killdeer may feign injury—dragging a wing as if it is broken and exposing its bright tail—then lure the person or predator away from the nest. Adults watch over their hatchlings, little puffballs that can run around and find food by themselves shortly after hatching. They can fly before they reach one month old.

Backyard & Beyond

Killdeer are attracted to large areas of grass as well as to short-cropped fields, so you may see them on your property if it's relatively treeless and large. Their cries carry long distances, so you may also hear killdeer passing by or calling from nearby nesting grounds.

Lesser Yellowlegs

Tringa flavipes

○ Spring/Summer
○ Year-Round
○ Winter

Lesser yellowlegs is a tall shorebird commonly seen in a variety of saltwater and freshwater situations. It winters in the Gulf States and along southern seacoasts, both east and west, so wherever you live in North America you stand a chance of seeing this species at some time during the year. Lessers often travel in large flocks and may be found together with greater yellowlegs.

All About

True to its name, this bird has bright yellow legs, which really stand out against its dark back and speckled underparts. The sexes are alike. When alarmed, it will take flight with a loud *tu* or *tu-tu* call, trailing its long yellow legs behind. The only species the lesser yellowlegs is likely to be confused with is the equally common greater yellowlegs, a nearly identical, but larger, close relative. In flight, both show white on the rump. The smaller lesser yellowlegs has a shorter, straighter bill than the greater, and overall it has a much more delicate appearance.

Habitat & Range

During migrations, the lesser yellowlegs is more likely than the greater yellowlegs to visit fresh water. It occurs widely and may stop at small ponds or wetlands, temporary rainwater puddles, coastal marshes and mudflats, and flooded fields.

Feeding

Lesser yellowlegs feed in shallow water where they find their prey—aquatic insects, snails, small fish, and crustaceans—on or just beneath the water's surface. They sometimes swing their heads back and forth underwater in an effort to stir up food. On land, the lesser yellowlegs may snatch up terrestrial insects and worms from the ground, or pick flying insects out of the air.

Nesting

Breeding at the edge of the northern tundra, lesser yellowlegs nest in natural clearings with small clusters of vegetation. The nest is merely a scrape in the ground, softened with a few fallen leaves and placed next to a fallen log or under a low shrub, usually within 200 yards of a water source. Nesting starts as early as May, with the male calling loudly from the top of a tree or other elevated perch. The female lays three to four eggs, and both parents share the 18- to 20-day incubation. Within hours of hatching, the young are able to leave the nest. As soon as the chicks are self-sufficient—as early as July—the adults leave for the south. The youngsters start south a few weeks later.

Backyard & Beyond

Any marsh or wetland in your neighborhood might host lesser yellowlegs during migration. If you live in the winter range of this species, you should be able to find it easily at mudflats and marshes, mingling with other shorebirds.

Willet

Catoptrophorus semipalmatus

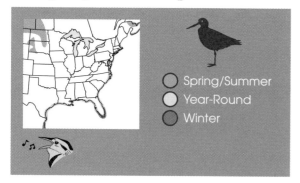

○ Spring/Summer
○ Year-Round
○ Winter

Anyone coming upon a willet standing on a winter beach may be excused for thinking it a dull bird. It seems to be without distinguishing characteristics, a brown-and-white wallflower among better-dressed kin. But then it opens its wings, and you see that there is more to this bird than meets the eye.

All About

Large (14 to 16 inches long) and long-legged, the willet is a muted gray-brown above and white below, with a long dark bill and bluish legs. Even in breeding season, there is no gaudy transformation to its basic look. But the willet's glory lies in its boldly striped, black-white-black wings that, when opened, identify this species at a glance. Willets seem to sense this, too, flexing their wings often and stretching them to their fullest upon landing, as if to say, "Look at me!" These common shorebirds also call attention to themselves with cries of *pill-will-willet* from which they get their common name.

Habitat & Range

There are two distinct breeding populations of willets in North America—one in the salt marshes of the Atlantic and Gulf coasts, and the other in the prairie grasslands of the central United States and Canada. During migrations, willets may be found widely and in a variety of habitats, from marshes, wet meadows, and mudflats to grassy dunes and beach margins.

Feeding

Willets use their bills to probe for food in soft mud or sand, or to pick small items directly from the ground. What's on the menu depends on location and season. In saltwater habitats, willets eat fiddler crabs, mollusks, and small fish; in freshwater situations, aquatic insects are a staple. Occasional vegetable matter—grasses, seeds, and even rice—rounds out their diet.

Nesting

Willets are semicolonial nesters, especially the coastal populations. Large groups may settle on a secluded, grassy island or along the edges of dunes. The nest is made of grasses in a scrape in the ground. Four or five eggs are laid, and both parents share incubation duty, with the male taking the night shift. After 22 days the downy chicks emerge, and within hours they are ready to run after their parents in a daily search for food. Young willets achieve flight capability at about four weeks. Female willets leave home when the young are three weeks old, at which point the male takes over the child-rearing chores.

Backyard & Beyond

Visit beaches and tidal creeks, marshes and shallow wetlands in the proper season for your area, and scan the flocks of small shorebirds for this species, which will appear larger, plainer, and chunkier than most others. Watch for those telltale black-and-white wings, a sure giveaway if you see them.

Sanderling

Calidris alba

○ Spring/Summer
○ Year-Round
○ Winter

The name sanderling *basically means "little one of the sand," and that's often where you'll find this bird. This is the sandpiper that thrills many beachgoers who enjoy watching the waves chase the little white-and-gray birds. To reach the beaches, mudflats, and other habitats, sanderlings must fly thousands of miles, though they are often only pausing en route to somewhere else—either north to the tundra for nesting, or south as far as Central and South America to spend the winter.*

All About

The sanderling is the sandpiper most often encountered near where the waves crash. To make a safe identification of an adult sanderling *outside of spring*, note what the sanderling does *not* have: streaks, spots, or brown markings. Adults are smooth and silvery above and clear white below. Often, a blackish shoulder patch is visible. The dunlin, another common migrating and wintering bird, has browner tones and a far longer, slightly drooped bill. The sanderling has a stout, straight, mid-length bill. In spring and summer, migrating sanderlings can be seen in their breeding plumage, sporting rusty-orangish tones on head, breast, and back. Immatures have blackish backs stippled with white. Next to a smaller species, such as the semipalmated sandpiper, a sanderling appears larger, more robust, and also more gray and white (except in spring).

Habitat & Range

Ocean beachcombers much of the year, sanderlings also turn up on jetties and mudflats, but they nest on stony barrens on the high Arctic tundra.

Feeding

The sanderling's typical feeding behavior is to scurry onto wet sand as waves recede to probe for small mollusks and crustaceans, fleeing as the waves crash down and the surf rolls toward it. It will also scuttle up the beach onto dry sand, where it snatches up insects. On far northern nesting grounds, this bird eats insects and some plant material.

Nesting

Sanderlings nest during the short summer of far northern Canada and Greenland (and also northern Europe and Asia). There they may nest as a single pair or next to each other in small groups. The female, most likely, scrapes a depression in gravel that she lines with leaves or lichens. There she usually lays four eggs. Both sexes incubate the eggs for up to a month. Young leave the nest not long after hatching and can feed themselves, though they cannot take flight for about two more weeks.

Backyard & Beyond

Relax, grab a novel, a towel, and some sun block, and head to the beach to see sanderlings—but don't be surprised if you also find them on rocky jetties or mudflats.

Laughing Gull

Larus atricilla

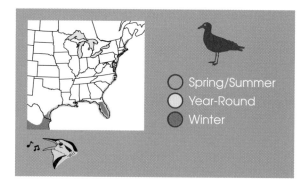

Spring/Summer
Year-Round
Winter

The laughing gull is the most common black-headed gull of eastern beaches, and its ringing calls are one of the familiar sounds of summer all along the Atlantic and Gulf coasts. Social and gregarious, the laughing gull has adapted well to humans and is quick to take advantage of the amenities of civilization—from nesting on artificial spoil banks to feeding on refuse from fishing boats.

All About

The laughing gull is an extremely handsome bird. A summer adult wears dark gray on the wings and back, contrasting with a snow-white body and inky black head. White crescents outline the eyes, and a red bill and legs complete the image. The wing tips are solid black. Male and female laughing gulls look alike. Winter adults are less striking, having only a smudge of black on the head and a black bill and legs at that season. Immatures are sooty gray and dirty white, with a white rump and a wide black band across the end of the tail, but they are often seen together with the more recognizable adults.

Habitat & Range

A bird of beaches, bays, and salt marshes, the laughing gull is seldom seen more than a few miles inland at any season, though occasionally an individual may be blown far astray by a hurricane or other major storm.

Feeding

The diet of the laughing gull is varied and includes everything from small fish to insects, crustaceans, snails, and garbage. Laughing gulls may invade a tern colony to take eggs or even small chicks, but they do not do this as commonly as some larger gulls do. Laughing gulls may also visit flooded fields to skim off earthworms and other invertebrate prey.

Nesting

Laughing gulls are colonial ground nesters, often choosing small, low, island locations with no predatory mammals. Many birds arrive at the colony site a full month before breeding begins to secure the best nest locations. The nest is a loose cup of grass and sticks placed in a shallow scrape and is made by both sexes. After the three to four eggs are laid, the male shares the 20-day incubation duties. Both parents feed their newly hatched young as the chicks wander near the nest until they can fly at five weeks.

Backyard & Beyond

Laughing gulls often perch on docks or visit marinas where humans gather, so a visitor to an Atlantic or Gulf coast beach in the right season should find this species easily. Flocks of these birds follow ferries and other boats in hopes of handouts; they are quite adept at catching tidbits thrown into the air by amused passengers, calling loudly all the while.

Ring-billed Gull

Larus delawarensis

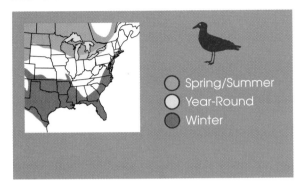

○ Spring/Summer
○ Year-Round
○ Winter

T his gull might almost be called the inland gull. Though found in coastal areas like most gulls, it is also the most numerous and widespread gull away from the seacoasts, sometimes found in huge flocks. At first glance it looks like a slightly smaller version of the herring gull, but it has a personality all its own.

All About

The ring-billed gull is a medium-sized (19 inches long) gull, and in adult plumage it has a light gray back and wings on a pure white body. Its wing tips are black with white spots, and it has a black ring near the end of its yellow bill. Males and females look alike. Young ring-billed gulls take three years to mature, during which time their bodies and wings are varying shades of mottled brown and gray, with a white tail that has a prominent, black terminal band. These gulls are smaller, lighter, and more graceful-looking than similarly patterned herring gulls, and they have a more buoyant appearance in flight.

Habitat and Range

In addition to the beaches and bays of the sea-coasts, ring-billed gulls may be found at large lakes and rivers, in newly plowed fields and pastures, and at sod farms, garbage dumps, and parking lots throughout their range.

Feeding

Ring-billed gulls are omnivorous, thriving on whatever food is on hand. Fish are a favorite item, but insects and earthworms are high on the list, along with grains, refuse, and even small rodents. They will eat the eggs of other species, and they are not averse to taking handouts from humans at parking lots and picnic grounds. (French fries, caught in midair, are popular. Ketchup is optional.)

Nesting

After a courtship routine by the male (which includes bowing, throat-puffing, and a ceremonial walk around the female, enlivened by many odd gesticulations), the mated pair will build its nest on the ground in a fairly open area near water. The ring-billed is colonial, so there are usually lots of similar nests nearby. Both sexes build the flimsy nest of grasses, sticks, and moss; and both take turns incubating the two to four eggs for up to four weeks until hatching. The downy young are tended by their parents in the general vicinity of the nest until they attain flight at about five weeks of age.

Backyard & Beyond

Look for ring-billed gulls in large, open fields after spring or autumn rainstorms, or watch for them anywhere there is an infestation of large insects, such as grasshoppers or locusts. If there is a landfill nearby, it may attract gulls from a wide surrounding area and can make for productive gull watching.

Herring Gull

Larus argentatus

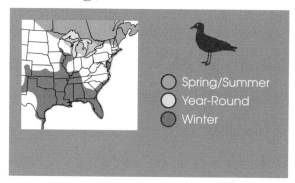

Spring/Summer
Year-Round
Winter

This is the bird that most people think of when they hear the term seagull. Large, abundant, and widespread, the herring gull is an imposing bird—and, in its adult plumage, it is certainly beautiful. Picture a dozen or more sitting on a pier with ocean waves lapping below, and you have a perfect coastal postcard scene.

All About

Measuring up to 26 inches in length, the adult herring gull has silver-gray wings tipped in black and white, a dazzling white body, bold yellow bill, and pink legs. Males and females are alike, and they are considerably larger than similar-looking ring-billed gulls. Immature herring gulls wear varying shades of brown or gray-brown and are not fully mature until their fourth year. All ages join in making the yelping or trumpeting calls, which are a constant fact of life throughout the herring gull's entire range and which define the seacoast in the minds of anyone who's ever walked a beach.

Habitat & Range

Herring gulls are birds of shorelines, major lakes and rivers, garbage dumps, and, occasionally, farmlands—especially recently tilled fields. Their population, once confined to the northern states, has been spreading southward for decades and breeding birds may now be found as far south as Cape Hatteras, North Carolina.

Feeding

Herring gulls eat almost anything, which is one reason for their success. Fish, along with all manner of other seafood, are a staple of the herring gull diet, but they also eat the eggs and chicks of other bird species (they can decimate a tern colony if given the opportunity), all kinds of garbage, large insects and grubs, and even carrion. They are smart and have learned to drop clams onto rocks or pavement to open them. They are quite willing to steal food from other seabirds. In the gull world, there is no such thing as a guilty conscience.

Nesting

Herring gulls nest on the ground, preferably in the lee of a rock or some other natural feature. Both sexes help scrape out a site and line it with grass, weeds, and feathers. Many nests contain a ball of some kind—whiffle ball, tennis ball—which may be a courtship gift from the male. The usual clutch is three eggs, and both parents share the month-long incubation. The young, downy and active from the start, depend on their parents at least until they fly at about 50 days of age.

Backyard & Beyond

Check the range map above to see when herring gulls might be expected in your area, and then visit the nearest beach! These birds also hang out at sewage outlets, dams, or anywhere that human activity may generate a reliable food supply.

Great Black-backed Gull

Larus marinus

○ Spring/Summer
○ Year-Round
○ Winter

Known as the *"king of gulls,"* the great black-backed gull is the largest and heaviest gull in North America. It is bold and seemingly fearless and, in contests of will with smaller gulls or other seabirds, it will usually win. For such a large bird, the great black-backed gull is amazingly graceful on the wing, especially when soaring.

All About

In its adult plumage (achieved in its fourth year), the great black-backed gull is strikingly dressed, with ebony back and wings and a snow-white head, body, and tail. The yellow bill is large and heavy, with a red spot near its tip, while the legs and feet are pink. It measures up to 31 inches in length, and the sexes are outwardly the same. Immature birds have brown wings, dirty-white bodies, and black-tipped tails; they gradually assume the adult appearance. Though it can be confused with herring or lesser black-backed gulls, the dark black back and huge size are usually the decisive field marks.

Habitat & Range

Originally a bird of the North Atlantic seacoast, the great black-backed gull has expanded its breeding range southward along the eastern seaboard for decades and now nests as far south as North Carolina. It seldom ventures inland, except along the St. Lawrence River and into the Great Lakes where there is an established population.

Feeding

Voracious and opportunistic, the great black-backed gull will eat almost anything, especially fish, other marine life, and the eggs and chicks of other gulls and terns. It readily takes carrion and is a frequent scavenger at garbage dumps and refuse piles. It sometimes follows fishing vessels and takes discarded, undersized fish that have been thrown overboard. It is also known to prey on small migrating songbirds, and even on larger water birds when the opportunity arises. It frequently steals fish from other marine birds.

Nesting

Ground-nesting great black-backed gulls are colonial and frequently mix with herring gulls. The two species nest in close proximity, on islands just offshore, protected from terrestrial predators. The nest may be a mound of loose grass, seaweed, and moss, hollowed out and lined with finer grass. Two or three eggs are laid, and both parents incubate them for about four weeks. Upon hatching, the downy young begin exploring in the vicinity of the nest within a few days. They fly when they are seven or eight weeks old.

Backyard & Beyond

Generally speaking, you must visit the Great Lakes or the eastern seaboard to see a great black-backed gull. They occur along the entire Atlantic coast—except for southern Florida—at some time during the year, and in adult plumage they are unmistakable.

Royal Tern

Sterna maxima

- ○ Spring/Summer
- ○ Year-Round
- ○ Winter

*R*oyal terns are a common sight for much of the year along warm-water coastlines in the United States. They are noisy while feeding and foraging, issuing their loud keet-keet or kir-reet calls constantly, a habit that makes them very difficult to overlook. If there's a royal tern in the vicinity, it usually gets noticed. And because of its size and appearance, it gets remembered, as well.

All About

The large (18 to 21 inches long) and striking royal tern is easily recognized by its size, white body, pale gray wings, crested black cap, and orange bill. The only bird it may be confused with is the even larger Caspian tern, but that bird has a blood-red bill and no visible crest. Royal terns are graceful fliers for their size. Slim, with long, pointed wings and a wingspan that reaches nearly 4 feet, they have delicate, deeply forked tails and are well designed for life on the wing.

Habitat & Range

Royal terns are almost always associated with salt water, so inland records are rare. After breeding, royal terns may wander up the Atlantic coast and are sometimes found as far north as Cape Cod, Massachusetts.

Feeding

Royal terns subsist primarily on small fish, 4 inches or less in length, which they seize by hovering in the air and then diving into the water below. Crabs are another favorite food, as are oysters. Sometimes royal terns will fly close to the sea's surface, scouting for schools of small fish and then dipping their bills repeatedly into the water to secure their meal.

Nesting

Royal terns are colonial nesters and usually opt for a sandy site on an offshore island, where hundreds or even thousands of pairs congregate in such close proximity that the nests are nearly touching. Each nest is merely a depression in the sand. Both parents incubate the single egg (there are occasionally two), which hatches at four to five weeks. When the young can move about on their own, two or three days after hatching, they join as many as 10,000 other tern youngsters in a sort of avian day-care center that ornithologists call a *crèche*. Families recognize each other by sound, and each chick is fed only by its own parents. The young royal terns do not achieve full independence until they are nearly eight months old.

Backyard & Beyond

Royal terns are found only in warm, saltwater situations, so you must visit the seacoast at the proper time to find one. One hint: This species, unlike some other terns, is more likely to forage near the shore, usually over breaking waves and pounding surf, and in quiet inlets and bays.

Forster's Tern

Sterna forsteri

- ○ Spring/Summer
- ○ Year-Round
- ○ Winter

Named after the nineteenth-century German naturalist Johann R. Forster, Forster's tern is often confused with the similar common tern; and even John James Audubon did not recognize all the differences. Today's bird guides make the differences very clear, and most birders can tell them apart. Forster's tern seems more at home on the wing than on land and can fly effortlessly for hours. It is graceful as it rides on the winds or skims the waters below.

All About

Forster's tern—pearl-gray and white with a black cap and orange-red bill—is a slim and agile flier with a deeply forked tail and long, narrow wings. Males and females look alike. Measuring about 15 inches in length, the Forster's tern has a wingspan of 30 inches. Immatures and adults in winter plumage (as shown in the photo) have white (not black) caps and a dark black mask through the eye and ear. This mark is very obvious and identifies this species even at a distance.

Habitat & Range

Forster's tern may be found from coastal beaches, bays, and salt marshes, to freshwater marshes and lakes well inland. Seasonally this species prefers marshes in spring for breeding purposes, while in winter they are more common along the coastlines. During migration, small flocks or individual birds often show up on small lakes or ponds.

Feeding

Forster's terns hunt from the air and take a great variety of prey. In the ocean, they will dive for small fishes. They seize flying insects, such as dragonflies or caddis flies, or swoop low to the ground to snatch up grasshoppers, beetles, or locusts. Forster's terns have also been known to take dead frogs from the surface of a pond, and they regularly catch aquatic insects, often without getting a single feather wet.

Nesting

This species nests almost exclusively in marshes, both saltwater and freshwater, often in loose colonies. The nest may be placed on the ground, on top of a muskrat den, or on a floating mat of vegetation. It usually consists of a mound of marsh reeds and grasses, hollowed out at its center. Both sexes help to build it, and the usual clutch is three eggs. After a shared incubation period of over three weeks, the young terns emerge, covered in down but still dependent on their parents. They continue to be tended and fed for several weeks.

Backyard & Beyond

Forster's terns are easiest to distinguish in their immature or winter plumage, which is worn from August until the following spring. With the black mark across the cheek and through the eye, they are instantly recognizable. In spring, visit marshes in their breeding range for the best chance to see one.

Black Skimmer

Rynchops niger

○ Spring/Summer
○ Year-Round
○ Winter

The black skimmer is a crow-sized bird of the seacoasts. In general body shape, it is a lot like a large tern—except for its huge, scissorlike bill. Not only is this bill very long and vertically flattened, which makes it seem massive, but it is actually uneven—the lower half is one-third longer than the upper half. It almost looks as if it's been broken off. The skimmer's bill evolved to suit a very specialized way of feeding.

All About

The black skimmer has white underparts, black wings and back, and a short notched tail. The unusual, dual-length bill is red at the base and black at the tips. The sexes are alike in plumage, though males are larger than females. Skimmers have an unusual vocalization that has been compared to the bark of a dog.

Habitat & Range

Black skimmers are birds of beaches, bays, and inlets, seldom seen far from the coast. They avoid heavy surf areas and prefer more sheltered locations, such as lagoons and estuaries, which are more conducive to their feeding style.

Feeding

Black skimmers fly low over water—*skimming* it—with their bills open, the lower half cutting through the waves, the upper half in the air. When they encounter a fish, shrimp or other morsel, the bill snaps closed and with a quick movement of the head, the food is swallowed. This is usually accomplished in less time than it takes to describe, and the skimmer never misses a wingbeat during the entire process. Immature black skimmers do not have the uneven bill shape at first. While in the nesting area, they need ordinary bills so they can pick up morsels regurgitated onto dry land by their parents, a task that would be almost impossible if the upper and lower mandibles were not the same length. They do not develop the longer, lower mandible until they can fly—and fish—on their own.

Nesting

Black skimmers are very social, forming close flocks in all seasons. Mated pairs scrape out their nests in the sand, quite close to each other, sometimes hundreds of nests together in one crowded, noisy colony. Taking turns, the parents incubate their three to five eggs for about three weeks until hatching. The chicks are then fed by regurgitation for about a month until they can fly.

Backyard & Beyond

Dusk is the best time to search for skimmers, as they frequently fish during the darkness. Their basic hunting method is entirely by feel, not dependent on sight. Many of them thus become active at twilight, after having rested on a handy sandbar (all facing the same direction, into the wind) all afternoon.

Mourning Dove

Zenaida macroura

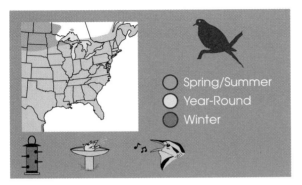

Spring/Summer
Year-Round
Winter

Whether you regard them as songbirds or living skeet targets, if you feed birds, you probably have mourning doves as constant companions. These tapered, graceful brown and pinkish birds wholeheartedly embrace human alterations of the natural landscape, finding their greatest abundance in agricultural and suburban areas. Doves love water, but may foul birdbaths by sitting around the rim, tails in.

All About

The mournful *oooahh, oooh, ooh, ooh* song of the mourning dove is a song of the South, echoing from power lines and treetops in early spring. Mourning doves travel in flocks, breaking rank only to nest and raise young. Males defend their mates as a kind of mobile territory, defending her and the immediate nest site—but not much else—from other birds.

Habitat & Range

The only habitat shunned by mourning doves is deep, contiguous forest. They are most common in agricultural areas with hedgerows and shelterbelts. They are also abundant in suburban areas as well, where visits to feeding stations are an integral part of their daily routines. Mourning doves migrate, especially far northern populations, but some individuals are resident year-round.

Feeding

Streamlined, fast, and powerful flyers, mourning doves travel in flocks, descending to feed on a great variety of grains and weed seeds that they peck from the ground. They are often seen in ranks on power lines over farm fields. A capacious crop allows mourning doves to gorge—sometimes to the point of being misshapen—and then digest their stored food later when resting.

Nesting

Mourning doves may mate and nest in any month of the year, but males begin to tune up their songs in late winter. They have a production-line breeding mode, following one brood with another as often as six times in a season. The twig nest platform, placed in a wide variety of tree species, but frequently in a pine, is often flimsy enough so that eggs show through from beneath. Two eggs are incubated by both members of the pair, and they hatch in 14 days. Young doves are fed first on crop milk, a secretion unique to the pigeon family, and later on regurgitated seeds. Young remain in the nest for another 15 days but may fledge much earlier. The male feeds them until about day 30, while the female re-nests. Immature birds are visibly smaller and have fine, buff feather edges overall.

Backyard & Beyond

Mourning doves take any seeds that might be offered at feeders, preferring sunflower seeds, cracked corn, millet, milo, and other grains found in seed mixes. They become adept at emptying hopper feeders into their ample crops, and then sitting for long periods afterward to digest their food.

Rock Pigeon
Columba livia

- ○ Spring/Summer
- ○ Year-Round
- ○ Winter

Originating in northern Europe, Africa, and India, rock pigeons—largely gone from their former wild haunts—have spread to cities and towns worldwide thanks to their domestication some five thousand years ago. Evidence of this domestication lies in their highly variable coloration; a flock may contain birds in every color from pure white to reddish to solid black.

All About

A substantial bird with a small head, deep chest, powerful wings, and a square tail, the rock pigeon is built for flight. Wild-type birds are slate-blue with a white rump, black terminal tail band, and two black bars on the secondary wing feathers. Pinkish green iridescence adorns the neck. Pigeons have short, reddish legs and a short, straight bill. Their song is a series of soft, resonant coos—*ooh-ga-rooogh*—and a harsh *Woogh!* serves as an alarm call. Pigeons can be found in flocks except when tending young.

Habitat & Range

It is rare to find rock pigeons in natural habitats, though there are still some cliff-nesting populations in North America. Most consider tall buildings, with their myriad ledges, to be ideal nesting grounds and are happy to take foods, such as bread and popcorn, from city sidewalks. Pigeons are nonmigratory, though their celebrated homing skills are exploited by pigeon racing clubs across the world.

Feeding

Walking and pecking with rapidly bobbing heads, pigeons find their preferred food—grains, seeds, and some fruits—on the ground. Urban birds have highly developed scavenging skills, raiding trashcans and fast food litter for high carbohydrate fare, such as bread.

Nesting

It's easy to watch pigeons display and even mate; the male's spinning, bowing, and cooing may be conducted underfoot on city sidewalks. Pigeons mate for life, guarding females zealously. They may lay eggs and raise young anytime. Building ledges, highway overpasses, barns, bridges, and other structures may be selected as the site on which to build a stick-and-grass nest and lay two eggs. Both male and female incubate for about 18 days. The rubbery, black-skinned squabs stay in the nest for a variable period of 25 to 45 days. Fat at fledging, they may be forced to shift entirely for themselves upon leaving the nest.

Backyard & Beyond

Thanks to the flocking habit of pigeons, most feeder operators are less than delighted when they descend. The most effective deterrents seem to be sturdy feeders enclosed by wire caging that excludes pigeons while admitting smaller birds. Some people opt to spread food at a distance to keep pigeons from overwhelming seed feeders. Pigeons will eat anything that might be offered, but millet and cracked corn are special favorites.

Yellow-billed Cuckoo

Coccyzus americanus

- ○ Spring/Summer
- ○ Year-Round
- ○ Winter

The yellow-billed cuckoo is a furtive, skulking bird of thickets and brushy woodland edges and, though it is fairly large, its retiring habits make it far more easily heard than seen. It often hides deep within the foliage and, when perching in the open, it tends to remain very still. The yellow-billed cuckoo makes a unique repetitive clucking sound that is a sure clue to identification.

All About

Slender and long-tailed, the yellow-billed cuckoo has a plain brown back and creamy white breast. The underside of the tail shows a pattern of bold white spots against a black background, and bright rufous wing patches are visible in flight. The lower part of the bill is yellow. Male and female yellow-billed cuckoos look alike. The only other species they are likely to be confused with is the related black-billed cuckoo, which lacks the rufous wing color and has a black bill, among other differences.

Habitat & Range

Yellow-billed cuckoos inhabit deciduous woodland edges, thickets and tangles along watercourses or roadsides, willow groves, and overgrown orchards. Yellow-billed cuckoos are not generally found in deep interior woodlands, as they prefer some kind of "edge" to their habitat.

Feeding

Yellow-billed cuckoos eat great numbers of hairy caterpillars and many large insects such as dragonflies, cicadas, grasshoppers, crickets, and beetles. Small fruits are a minor but regular part of their diet in summer. Most yellow-billed cuckoos forage by slowly and methodically exploring branches, twigs, and leaves for hidden insects, but they occasionally may act like flycatchers, darting into the air for a meal on the wing, or hovering to seize a caterpillar at the edge of a leaf.

Nesting

Once paired, cuckoos survey the surrounding area for a leafy and secluded nest site, five to ten feet off the ground. Both help build a loose shell of twigs and stems, lining it with fine grasses. Three to five eggs are laid, and both parents share the incubation and feeding of the young. The entire process, from egg laying to fledging, takes only 17 days, one of the shortest such periods for any bird species.

Backyard & Beyond

If you have mature trees rimming your backyard, you may have an occasional yellow-billed cuckoo stopping by on migration—listen for its patented clucking calls. An old folk name for the yellow-billed cuckoo is "raincrow," because these *kowp-kowp-kowp* calls are so often uttered on hot summer afternoons, when thunderstorms are likely to follow. Knowing the cuckoo's call will be helpful in finding this secretive bird; otherwise, check the thickets and edges of your local woodland or park for a chance to find this species.

Great Horned Owl

Bubo virginianus

- ○ Spring/Summer
- ○ Year-Round
- ○ Winter

Huge, powerful, and widespread across North America, the great horned is the king of all of our owls. Armed with incredible vision, the great horned sees and pounces on prey, using its powerful talons and bill to dispatch its victim. The deep, hooting call of the great horned—whoo-who-o-o-o-who-who—a staple of movie and television soundtracks, is most often heard in nature just after sunset.

All About

The great horned owl is named for its large size (up to 24 inches tall, with a wingspan of 44 inches) and its long feathered head tufts (horns). A deep rusty brown and buff overall, this owl has large, golden-yellow eyes. Its thick, soft feathers provide excellent insulation from either heat or cold, permitting the great horned to nest as soon as early to midwinter even in regions with harsh winter weather.

Habitat & Range

A nonmigratory bird throughout the Americas, great horned owls can be found as far north as the tree line, and as far south as South America—and in nearly every conceivable habitat and setting. Great horned owls are equally at home in urban and suburban settings, as well as in deep woodlands, grasslands, and deserts.

Feeding

Mammals (rabbits, hares, and large rodents) are the primary prey item of great horned owls. They also eat earthworms, fish, snakes, and even birds as large as great blue herons. They are one of the few predators that will readily kill and consume skunks. Within a great horned owl's territory, it's unusual to find other, smaller owls—they may have been eaten by the resident great horneds. Their primary hunting mode is to perch, watch, and pounce on prey.

Nesting

Great horned owls most often take over an old stick nest built by a hawk, heron, or squirrel, but they will also nest on cliff ledges, in tree cavities, and even on the ground. Two to four eggs are laid and incubation by the female lasts slightly more than a month. The male brings food to his mate on the nest each night. Six weeks or so after hatching, the young owlets venture from the nest to nearby branches. They remain dependent on the adults for many months, but leave the nest area before the next breeding season.

Backyard & Beyond

If you live in or near older woodlands, chances are good that great horned owls are your neighbors. Though there is little you can do to attract great horned owls to your property, listen just after dusk and before dawn for their deep hoots, which carry for great distances. Watch for the great horned's silhouette at dusk along woodland edges, especially in treetops and on power poles.

Barred Owl

Strix varia

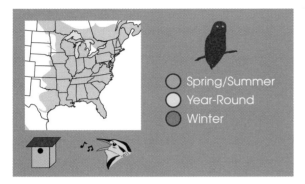

Spring/Summer
Year-Round
Winter

Who cooks for you? Who cooks for you all? *The wild hoots of the barred owl echo through swampy, deciduous woodlands throughout the South. Its dark, liquid eyes give it a deceptively gentle look, but this owl is a top-of-the-line predator, taking everything from fish to rabbits. Though it does some daylight hunting, most of the barred owl's foraging takes place at night.*

All About

A rounded, earless outline, smoky gray-brown plumage that is heavily mottled and barred with white, broad brown streaks on a white belly, and dark eyes distinguish the barred owl. Its bill and feet are yellow. Its familiar eight-hoot call gives way to raucous and sometimes frightening caterwauling in breeding season. This species is more apt to call in daylight than any other; it may call all day during overcast conditions.

Habitat & Range

Like its famous endangered cousin the spotted owl, the barred owl prefers old forest, probably in part because the large nesting cavities it requires occur in trees of ample girth. It is commonly associated with lowlands, but occupies upland sites as well. The barred owl does not migrate, but may wander in harsh winters.

Feeding

Anything it can kill is fair game for this medium-large owl. Small mammals, as small as mice and up to the size of rabbits, make up at least half the barred owl's diet. It makes acrobatic strikes after squirrels, sometimes turning completely over in flight. Birds, amphibians, reptiles, insects, and other invertebrates compose the rest of its diet.

Nesting

Most barred owls select large nest cavities, such as those formed when a large branch breaks off a hollow tree. They will also use a hollow in a broken tree trunk, as well as the nests of other raptors or squirrels. Two to three eggs are incubated by the female alone. They hatch from 28 to 33 days later. The male feeds the family for the first two weeks of the chicks' life, after which the female leaves them and helps bring in food. Young owls, clothed in buff-colored down, begin venturing onto branches when they are around five weeks old, before they can fly. They give a hideous, rasping screech as a location call and may be found and observed discreetly from a safe distance. Fledglings are fed by their parents until early autumn, when they strike out to find new territory.

Backyard & Beyond

Surprisingly enough, the barred owl will accept nest boxes, because tree cavities large enough to contain them are hard to find. Plans for a wood duck nest box with a seven-inch entrance hole should accommodate them. This should be mounted as high as possible in a large tree.

Eastern Screech Owl

Megascops asio

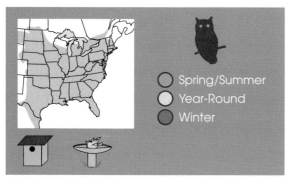

- ○ Spring/Summer
- ○ Year-Round
- ○ Winter

Eastern screech owls are very acclimated to humans, but their nocturnal habits and cryptic coloration keep us from seeing them regularly. Even when perched in full view in daylight, screech owls have a remarkable ability to conceal themselves. Found commonly in cities and towns, the screech owl's success may be due not only to its secretive nature, but also to its ability to take a wide variety of small prey.

All About

A small bird (8½ inches long), the eastern screech owl occurs in two color variations: reddish and gray, with gray being more common. The screech owl's plumage appears very bark-like. When a "screech" sits with its body elongated and ear tufts extended, it looks like a broken branch stub. This bird's name is misleading; a screech is rarely voiced. The call most bird watchers hear is a series of descending, whinnying whistles and tremolos on a single note.

Habitat & Range

A nonmigratory, resident bird throughout the eastern United States, the screech owl is found wherever woodlands are mature enough to have cavities. Unlike many other owl species, the screech owl is commonly found in urban parks and suburban backyards.

Feeding

Eastern screech owls will eat almost anything— from mice and voles to moths, earthworms, crawfish, frogs, and fish. In spring and summer, they prey upon small and medium-sized songbirds, but during winter small mammals are more common prey. Screech owls perch in a tree, waiting and watching for potential prey, most of which is captured with the owl's feet in flight or by pouncing on the ground.

Nesting

Screech owls nest in natural cavities and will readily use nest boxes. They begin nesting early, from mid-December in the South to late March in the North. From two to six eggs are laid and a month-long incubation period ensues. The female incubates the eggs and broods the young owlets, while the male delivers all the food. Owlets remain in the nest for a month before venturing into nearby trees. They remain dependent on their parents for two months.

Backyard & Beyond

You may very well already have eastern screech owls in or near your backyard. Spend some time outside at night—especially when the moon is full—listening for the screech owl's wavering calls. Check natural tree cavities during the day for roosting or nesting owls—they may be peering out of the hole. You can attract screech owls with an owl nest box. Boxes should be about 12 to 14 inches deep with an internal floor size of 7×7 inches and a 2³/₄-inch diameter entry. Place the box above 10 feet high in a shady spot on a tree trunk wider than the box's width.

Chuck-will's-widow

Caprimulgus carolinensis

○ Spring/Summer
○ Year-Round
○ Winter

The chuck-will's-widow is more often heard than seen, and—like its close relative the whip-poor-will—it says its name, chuck-will's-widow, *over and over again at night, primarily at dusk and dawn. The "chuck" is more common throughout the Deep South than the whip-poor-will. Both species are most active at night and therefore are less well known than many of our common birds.*

All About

Chuck-will's-widow is a buffy-brown, black, and gray overall. Like other members of the goatsucker family (such as the common nighthawk and whip-poor-will), it is most active at dawn and dusk, foraging and calling. Mostly inactive during the day, chucks usually perch lengthwise along a large tree branch, and their cryptic coloration camouflages them well, making them difficult to see. About 12 inches in length, with a wingspan of 26 inches, the chuck is larger than either the nighthawk or whip-poor-will.

Habitat & Range

A common breeding bird throughout the southeastern United States, the chuck-will's-widow is a spring and summer resident in dry, open, mixed woodlands and coastal dunes. Fall migration begins in August, and the chucks head southward to spend the winter in the Caribbean islands, Mexico, and Central America, returning to the southern United States by early April. Some birds remain year-round in southern Florida. They prefer a more open habitat than whip-poor-wills.

Feeding

Chuck-will's-widow is a nocturnal, insect-catching machine. As it flies along woodland edges, its wide-opening mouth closes around a variety of beetles, moths, and other insect prey. Stiff feathers called *rictal bristles* surround the bill and serve to funnel insects into the bird's mouth. Chucks will also eat small songbirds during migration or when insect prey is unavailable.

Nesting

As a ground nester, chuck-will's-widow builds no nest. In a concealed spot on the ground, two eggs are laid and incubated by the female for about 20 days. After hatching, the young chucks remain in the nest for two weeks; they are able to fly at about 18 days old. John James Audubon reported that when the nest was threatened, chuck-will's-widow adults moved the eggs in their mouths to a new location.

Backyard & Beyond

The chuck-will's-widow, unlike its close relative the common nighthawk, is not a bird of cities or towns. Instead, this species prefers partially wooded rural areas where large insects are present. People living near prime chuck habitats are treated nightly to the bird's insistent and incessant calling, a familiar sound of southern summer nights. Drive slowly along rural gravel roads at dusk and watch for the orange-red gleam of the chuck's eyes—the birds often rest and call from roadsides.

Common Nighthawk

Chordeiles minor

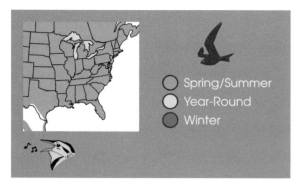

- Spring/Summer
- Year-Round
- Winter

Peent! *is the nasal flight call of the common nighthawk, a familiar sound in cities and towns, though it is usually mistaken for an insect call. This call accompanies the batlike flight of the nighthawk as it courses through the sky, hawking insects. Despite its name, the nighthawk is not a hawk and is active both day and night.*

All About

The common nighthawk is a long-winged, dark bird with characteristic white wing slashes. Its distinctive bounding flight can be used to identify it from a distance as it forages over fields, towns, and woods. Nighthawks belong to the goatsucker family, a name based on the old myth that they drank milk from livestock at night.

Habitat & Range

A common breeding bird throughout North America, nighthawks can be seen in flight over almost any habitat. In cities and towns, nighthawks are attracted to the insects around streetlamps. Beginning in late July, nighthawks can be seen at dusk in large migratory flocks, sometimes numbering dozens of birds. Nighthawks winter in South America, returning to the southern United States by early April.

Feeding

A specialist in catching flying insects, the common nighthawk's mouth opens wide to capture its prey. The nighthawk sees its prey—most often flying ants, beetles, moths, and mayflies—and pursues and catches it. When a nighthawk needs water, it swoops low over a lake or river and skims a drink from the surface.

Nesting

Historically, nighthawk nests were found on the ground in grasslands and in open patches of soil, gravel, or sand. The nest is a shallow depression near a log or stone that helps to shade and conceal it. Now, nighthawk nests are more commonly found on gravel roads or on flat, gravel-covered rooftops in urban areas. The female selects the nest site, lays two eggs, and handles the 18-day incubation. Young nighthawks are brooded by the female for 15 days, protecting them from sun and weather. The male feeds both his mate and the young in the nest. After 20 days, the young birds are able to fly, and the male then takes over their care while the female starts a second nest.

Backyard & Beyond

Nighthawks have good success nesting on gravel roofs, but not so on roofs lined with rubber or foam, materials that pool water and retain heat. Watch and listen for nighthawks in the sky at dawn and dusk. You may hear their *peent!* before you see them. During courtship, male nighthawks perform a diving display near females, swooping swiftly toward the ground. As the male comes out of the dive, he flares his flight feathers, creating a booming sound much like a large truck shifting gears.

Chimney Swift

Chaetura pelagica

○ Spring/Summer
○ Year-Round
○ Winter

Known by bird watchers as "the flying cigar," the chimney swift is a familiar sight in the sky over cities and towns during the spring, summer, and fall. Its nickname aptly describes the swift's elongated flight silhouette. The twittering calls of chimney swifts are one of the most common bird sounds of summer. The chimney swift is named for its preferred nesting and roosting site—the inside of chimneys. This species spends much of its life on the wing, stopping only to sleep and nest.

All About

Chimney swifts are a dark charcoal-gray overall with a small black bill, eyes, and tiny feet. Indeed their feet are almost useless for walking, but are perfect for clinging to the inside of a chimney. The chimney swift is nearly all wing—with a 5-inch long body and a 14-inch wingspan. Four hundred years ago, all chimney swifts nested in hollow trees and caves, but the arrival of European settlers and their stone chimneys soon provided abundant nesting sites. Today most chimney swifts nest in chimneys and other human structures, such as unused smokestacks and abandoned buildings.

Habitat & Range

Widespread and common across the eastern half of the United States and southern Canada, the chimney swift is found wherever there are suitable nest sites. Fall migratory flocks of swifts are a magnificent spectacle as they form a swirling, chattering cloud descending to roost in a large chimney at dusk. In winter, this tiny bird migrates to South America, returning again in March to the southern United States.

Feeding

An all-insect diet is captured and consumed on the wing. Swifts often are seen flying high in the sky when foraging.

Nesting

A pair of swifts chooses a nest site—usually a chimney. The nest is a half-saucer shape made of sticks held together and made to adhere to the wall of cavity by the birds' saliva. Swifts break small twigs off trees, grabbing them with their feet as they fly past a tree. Two to five eggs are laid, and both parents share incubation (15 days) and brooding duties until the young swifts fledge at about 19 days after hatching.

Backyard & Beyond

Allowing chimney swifts to nest in your older, unused chimney is really easy—just let the swifts find it. They pose no danger and, if not for the sounds of hungry nestlings during a two-week period, you might not know they are there. If hosting swifts is not your cup of tea, check around your town or region for chimneys being used by swifts. Watch for them entering or leaving the large brick chimneys on schools and old factories. Modern chimneys with metal caps and flues are impossible for swifts to use.

Ruby-throated Hummingbird

Archilochus colubris

○ Spring/Summer
○ Year-Round
○ Winter

The only breeding hummingbird east of the Great Plains, the rubythroat enlivens many gardens and yards with its presence. Males are fiercely combative and will defend a single nectar source against all comers. Spectacular pendulum flights, constant chittering, the low hum of beating wings, and the occasional smack of tiny bodies colliding are familiar to anyone lucky enough to have rubythroats at their nectar feeders.

All About

Seen in direct sunlight, the male's ruby throat patch dazzles. Both male and female are iridescent green above. The female's underparts are white, and she sports white spots on her rounded tail. Males appear smaller and darker overall, with grayish-olive underparts and a slightly forked, all dark tail. A squeaky *chip* is uttered constantly while feeding. Males sing a seldom heard, monotonous song from exposed perches at daybreak.

Habitat & Range

Rubythroats prefer mixed deciduous woodlands with clearings, where wildflowers and abundant small insects can be found. They're fairly common in forested areas across the entire eastern United States, falling off abruptly at the Great Plains. Virtually all rubythroats leave for the winter, many making the arduous nonstop flight across the Gulf of Mexico on fat reserves alone. Rubythroats winter in Central America.

Feeding

Though they are usually regarded as wholly nectivorous, rubythroats take a great number of small insects, which they catch by gleaning or in aerial pursuit. They may even rob spider webs of their catch. They are strongly attracted to red or orange flowers, but rubythroats will take nectar from flowers of any color. They hover and probe rapidly, often perching to feed.

Nesting

Once a male rubythroat has mated, his investment in the offspring is over. The female constructs a walnut-sized, thick-walled cup of plant down and spider silk, bound tightly with elastic spider web and encrusted with lichens. This well-insulated nest protects the two lentil-sized eggs when she must leave to forage. The young hatch after about 13 days and remain in the nest for about 21 days. The female regurgitates small insects and nectar into their crops. They are fed for at least a week or longer after fledging.

Backyard & Beyond

Attract rubythroats with a 1:4 solution of table sugar (sucrose) and water. Wash feeders with hot soapy water every few days and replace the solution. Boiling the solution briefly helps it keep longer. Artificial coloring in the solution is unnecessary (feeders have ample red parts). To thwart a bullying male, hang several feeders within a few feet of each other. He'll be unable to defend them all.

Belted Kingfisher

Ceryle alcyon

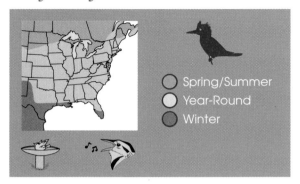

The belted kingfisher is a bird many recognize but few know well. Kingfishers take wariness to new extremes, uttering a loud rattle of alarm and swooping off at the slightest disturbance. The belted kingfisher's piercing rattle call, usually given as it takes flight, is more often heard than this wary bird is seen. They are a thrilling presence on streams, rivers, lakes, and marshes—wherever clear water and small fish abound.

All About

Almost comical in proportion, the belted kingfisher has an oversized crested head and a heavy spearlike bill, but diminutive feet. It cannot walk, but only shuffle, and it relies entirely on flight for most of its locomotion. Slate-blue upperparts, a stark-white collar and underparts, and a bluish breast band complete the ensemble. The female wears a "bra"—another rufous breast band below the blue one.

Habitat & Range

Because it is a sight hunter, the belted kingfisher seeks out clear water. Most often found along clear running streams, lakes, and ponds, it will also hunt salt estuaries and marshes. Nesting requires an exposed earthen bank. Kingfishers are migratory in northern latitudes. Though they can survive winter temperatures, they require open water year-round; thus, southern birds may migrate only as far as they must to find open water.

Feeding

Most of its hunting is done from a perch, but the belted kingfisher also hunts on the wing. Suspended in midair like an angel, it hovers, seemingly weightless, over a riffle. Spotting a minnow, it closes its wings and plunges bill-first into the water. It carries the fish in its bill to a sturdy perch (usually a dead snag or partially submerged branch), where it subdues its prey by whacking its head against the perch with sideways flips of its bill. The fish is then swallowed head first. Belted kingfishers also take crayfish and (to a much lesser extent) amphibians, reptiles, small mammals, and young birds.

Nesting

Kingfishers occasionally are forced to commute, if they are unable to find a dry earthen bank near their chosen feeding territory. They may use sand and gravel pits, landfills, or road cuts. This species excavates, digging rapidly with tiny feet straight into the bank, creating a round entrance hole and an upward-sloping tunnel that may extend as much as six feet into the bank. A chamber at the end holds five to eight eggs, which both male and female incubate for about 22 days. Young stay in the burrow for up to 29 days and are fed by their parents for three more weeks.

Backyard & Beyond

Any clear body of water, including backyard ponds with plump goldfish, can host a hunting kingfisher.

Red-bellied Woodpecker

Melanerpes carolinus

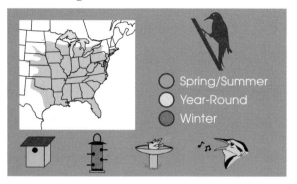

- Spring/Summer
- Year-Round
- Winter

The red-bellied woodpecker is so common, vocal, and eye-catching that it might be elected "most familiar woodpecker" in a vote of bird watchers in the eastern United States. Although occasionally misidentified as a red-headed woodpecker because of the male redbelly's bill-to-nape stripe of bright red, the red-bellied woodpecker actually is quite different in appearance—and much more common—than the real red-headed woodpecker, which sports an all-red head.

All About

A medium-sized (9¼ inches long) woodpecker with a stout, chisel-shaped bill and a zebra pattern of black-and-white horizontal strips on the back, the red-bellied woodpecker is named for a feature we rarely see—a light wash of pink or red on its belly. Hitching up tree trunks with the aid of its strong feet and stiff tail, the bird's red belly is almost always obscured. Adult males have a solid strip of red from the top of the bill and head and down the back of the neck (the nape). Females have a red nape, but are brownish on the top of the head. The redbelly's loud, rich call sounds like *qurrrr*, and its longer version is more rattling and harsher—*chrr, chrr, chrchrchrchr*.

Habitat & Range

A year-round resident across the eastern United States, the redbelly is an adaptable bird, found wherever there are mature trees. They do not migrate, though some northern birds may move southward in winter.

Feeding

The redbelly is an expert at excavating insects from trees using its bill as a chisel and its long, barbed tongue to extract food items. It will also eat berries, fruits, nuts, tree sap, salamanders, mice, and even small nestling birds. At bird-feeding stations, redbellies relish peanuts, suet, sunflower seeds, and cracked corn.

Nesting

The male redbelly begins courtship by drumming (a rapid pounding with the bill) on a tree trunk or branch to attract the female's attention. Both male and female excavate the nest cavity, which is usually located in a dead tree below an overhanging branch. The 8- to 12-inch deep cavity will accommodate four eggs. Incubation duties are shared and last about 12 days. Nestlings are fed in the nest cavity by both parents for almost a month before they fledge; afterward, they remain near the nest and are fed by the parents for several more weeks. Nest hole competition from European starlings can be fierce and usually results in the redbellies being evicted and forced to excavate a new nest elsewhere.

Backyard & Beyond

Peanuts and suet are the redbelly's favored foods, but you can also offer apple halves stuck on a tree stub, sunflower bits, and grape jelly (in a small dish). Listen for the redbelly's loud, ringing calls and watch for its swooping flight.

Downy Woodpecker

Picoides pubescens

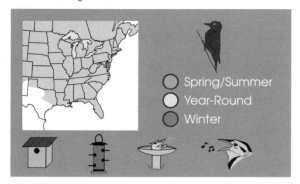

○ Spring/Summer
○ Year-Round
○ Winter

Downy woodpeckers are a favorite of backyard bird watchers because they are often the first woodpeckers to visit bird feeders. Common in any habitat with trees, downies are as equally at home in backyards as they are in remote woods. In all seasons, downy woodpeckers give a rattling whinny that descends in tone. They also utter a sharp pik! call regularly while foraging.

All About

The downy is the smallest ($6^3/4$ inches long), most common, and most widespread woodpecker. Its black-and-white plumage is similar to that of the larger ($9^1/4$ inches long) hairy woodpecker. In both species, the males have a red patch at the back of the head. Downy woodpeckers have an all-white breast and belly and a white stripe down the middle of the back. The wings and tail are black with spots of white.

Habitat & Range

A common resident of woodlands throughout North America, the downy is a habitat generalist—found anywhere there are trees or woody plants on which to find food. Though their population appears stable, downies suffer from nest site competition and from the removal of dead trees, which they need for nesting and feeding.

Feeding

Downy woodpeckers use their stiff tails and strong, clawed feet to propel themselves along tree branches or trunks. As they move along, downies probe and chisel at the tree's bark, searching for insects, insect eggs, ants, and spiders. They also eat fruits, such as sumac and poison ivy. At bird feeders, sunflower seeds and bits, suet, peanuts, and peanut butter are favorite foods.

Nesting

Like all woodpeckers, downies are cavity nesters. Each spring they excavate a new nest hole in the dead stub or trunk of a tree—usually one that is already rotting. The nest hole is placed underneath an overhanging branch higher than 12 feet above the ground. Excavation can take as long as two weeks—even with the male and female participating. Clutch size is usually four to five white eggs, with both sexes incubating. Hatching occurs at 12 days, and both parents feed the young for about three weeks until they fledge.

Backyard & Beyond

Telling the downy and hairy woodpecker apart can be difficult. A way to remember which is which is: *Downy is dinky; hairy is huge.* Downies have a small body, small head, and a small, thin bill. Hairies have a big body, a big head, and a large, chisellike bill. Though downies rarely nest in nest boxes, they readily use them for nighttime roosting, especially in harsh weather. Leave a dead tree or large dead branch on a tree in your yard (in a safe location), and you will be much more likely to attract woodpeckers.

Northern Flicker

Colaptes auratus

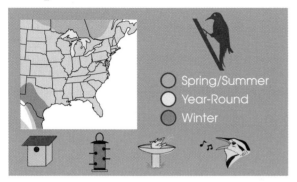

○ Spring/Summer
○ Year-Round
○ Winter

A *familiar and fairly large (13 inches long) wood-pecker, the northern flicker is a distinctively marked bird that—unlike other woodpeckers—is often seen foraging on the ground. The eastern form of the flicker is known as the yellow-shafted flicker for its bright lemon-yellow underwing and tail color. A red-shafted form of the northern flicker occurs in the West. There are more than 130 different names by which the flicker is known, including high-hole, yellowhammer, and yawkerbird.*

All About

The northern flicker is all field marks with its bright yellow wing flashes, white rump, spotted breast, and barred back. It is not easily confused with any other bird. In the East, both sexes have a red crescent on the back of the head, but only males show a black "moustache" mark on the cheek. The flicker has several calls including a single note *kleer*, a short *wickawicka* series, and a monotonous *wickwickwickwick* song. It also communicates by drumming on the resonating surface of a tree, pole, or even metal downspouts and chimney flues.

Habitat & Range

Widespread across North America, the northern flicker is found almost everywhere wooded habitats exist, though open woods and woodland edges are preferred. Flickers in the northern portion of the range migrate southward in winter, while southern birds are nonmigratory.

Feeding

Flickers feed on the ground where they specialize in eating ants. A flicker pokes its long bill into an anthill and uses its long, sticky tongue to extract the ants. They also eat other insects, as well as fruits and seeds. At bird feeders, they will eat suet, peanuts, fruits, and sunflower bits.

Nesting

Excavating a new nest cavity almost every year, flickers perform a much-needed service for many other hole-nesting birds—from chickadees to ducks—that use old flicker nests. Both sexes excavate the nest cavity in a dead tree or branch. The female lays between 5 and 10 eggs; both sexes share the 11-day incubation period. Young flickers leave the nest after about 25 days. Flickers will use nest boxes with an interior floor of 7×7 inches, an interior height of 16 to 24 inches, and a 2¹/₂-inch entry hole. Because excavation is a vital part of courtship, boxes packed full of woodchips are more attractive. Competition for cavities from European starlings is fierce and may be causing a decline in flickers.

Backyard & Beyond

Offering suet, corn, or peanuts and nest boxes in your wooded backyard is one way to attract flickers. Equally important is the presence of ground-dwelling insects (leave those non-threatening anthills alone!) and dead trees or dead branches. A large, dead tree branch placed vertically in your yard may entice a flicker to stop.

Pileated Woodpecker

Dryocopus pileatus

- ○ Spring/Summer
- ○ Year-Round
- ○ Winter

People who have never had a good close look at a pileated woodpecker invariably utter an exclamation when they finally see one. This is a magnificent, flashy, loud, but shy bird—the largest living woodpecker in North America. Its name is Latin for "capped," a reference to its crest. The pileated and its crazy laugh was the inspiration for Woody Woodpecker, but there the similarity ends.

All About

Both male and female pileated woodpeckers sport a red crest; the female's forehead is brownish and the male's is scarlet. A dull, dark charcoal-gray overall, pileateds reveal a large amount of white in the underwing when they take flight. Seen crossing high over a road, their wingbeats are slow and steady, the wings seeming to close between each beat. The call is a high, wild *yik-yik-yik-yik-yik*, suggesting a flicker, but not as monotonous. The pileated's hollow, sonorous drum roll fades away as it finishes.

Habitat & Range

Such a large bird needs large diameter trees because it roosts and nests in cavities that it excavates with its chisellike bill. Older-growth forests with standing dead trees, usually in bottomland or near watercourses, are preferred. In autumn, wandering pileateds may show up unexpectedly along roadsides and in yards, feasting on sumac, firethorn, dogwood, viburnum, or other fruits. Pileateds are resident throughout their range.

Feeding

Loud, chopping blows herald the presence of a feeding pileated woodpecker. They sometimes sound not so much like a woodpecker as a strong person wielding an axe. Palm-sized pieces of bark and punky (soft and rotted) wood fly as the bird strips bark or excavates to reach the ant galleries and beetle larvae it needs. It is a surprisingly agile fruit plucker, clinging like an overgrown chickadee as it eats small fruits. Pileateds also glean bark and branches for insect prey.

Nesting

Pileated pairs stay together year-round and presumably mate for life. Male pileated woodpeckers do most of the nest cavity excavation. The female lays four eggs, and both she and her mate incubate them; they hatch after about 16 days. Young remain in the cavity for up to 30 days, after which they have a long apprenticeship of learning to procure food with their parents.

Backyard & Beyond

People with heavily wooded yards are sometimes successful in attracting pileateds to raw suet or peanut butter suet mixtures offered in sturdy cages affixed to the trunk of a large tree. Having such an impressive bird in one's yard is an event; successfully feeding one is well worth the extra effort. These birds occupy the same territories throughout their lives, so it could be the start of a long relationship.

Eastern Phoebe

Sayornis phoebe

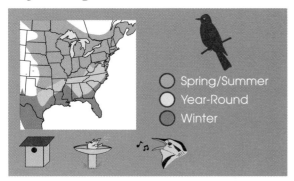

○ Spring/Summer
○ Year-Round
○ Winter

A very adaptable flycatcher, the eastern phoebe often nests on human structures, such as on building ledges, inside barns, under bridges, and in culverts. Nesting in such proximity to humans, phoebes are used to our activity and this apparent tameness allows us to think of them as "our phoebes." Many bird watchers consider the early spring return of the phoebe (and not the American robin) to be the most reliable sign of spring's arrival.

All About

The eastern phoebe, unlike most other flycatchers, is relatively easy to identify. A medium-sized bird that constantly wags its tail, the phoebe also gives a vocal clue to its identity by softly uttering its name—*fee-bee*. Phoebes are a dark, drab gray-brown on the back, with faint wing bars and a light breast and belly, often washed with yellow.

Habitat & Range

Wherever there is a suitable nesting ledge (with abundant flying insects nearby), phoebes may be found. Natural habitats include woodland edges and small streams. Common throughout most of eastern North America during the spring and summer (eastern phoebes breed far into northern Canada), in winter many phoebes migrate to the southern Atlantic Coast and along the Gulf Coast into Mexico.

Feeding

The eastern phoebe is a perch-and-wait hunter, watching for flying insects from an exposed perch and making short flying forays to nab its prey. Phoebes consume vast quantities of flying insects, but will also pluck food items from the ground or vegetation. Wasps, bees, flying ants, moths, and butterflies constitute much of their prey. In fall and winter, when insects are scarce, phoebes will eat small fruits and berries.

Nesting

Phoebes are early nesters throughout the breeding range, and nest building often begins almost immediately after a male attracts a mate to a likely site. Favored natural nest sites include rock ledges and caves, but they also nest in barns or outbuildings, and on handy ledges or sills on house porches. The female builds the cup-shaped nest out of mud, moss, and grass. Four to six eggs are laid and incubated by the female alone, for just over two weeks. Young phoebes, unless disturbed earlier, fledge after about 16 days.

Backyard & Beyond

Bird watchers love phoebes not only because they are common, but also because they are so full of energy and seem willing to make their nests in close proximity to humans. To attract phoebes to your property, place nesting shelves (about 6×8 inches in size) about a foot below the eaves of your house, garage, or outbuilding. Choose a site that is away from human activity and is as safe as possible from predators, such as snakes, raccoons, and cats.

Great Crested Flycatcher

Myiarchus crinitus

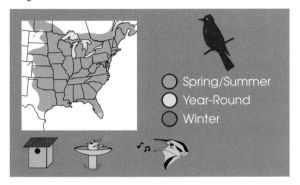

○ Spring/Summer
○ Year-Round
○ Winter

Although one of the largest and most common eastern flycatchers, the great crested is raucous enough that it is usually heard before it is seen. A loud, enthusiastic wheeep! or whit-whit-whit-whit call is most often heard in woodland clearings during the summer months. The great crested is unusual among eastern flycatchers in that it is a cavity nester, relying on old woodpecker holes, hollow trees, and even birdhouses for nest sites. Adding to this bird's preference for the unusual is its habit of using shed snakeskin in its nest construction.

All About

One of our larger flycatchers at 8½ inches tall, the great crested is a pleasing blend of colors with a lemon belly and underwings and a rufous tail, set off by a gray head and olive back. Males and females are alike in appearance, and both will aggressively defend their nesting territory against trespassing birds of almost any species.

Habitat & Range

Great crested flycatchers can be found in open woodlands, forest clearings, and even in wooded city parks throughout eastern North America during the summer months. Winter finds most of them in southern Mexico and southward to South America, though some spend the winter in south Florida. Fall migration starts in late August, with spring migrants returning to the Gulf Coast by late March.

Feeding

Capturing flying insects is the great crested's main foraging mode, but it will also glean insects from vegetation and supplement its diet with small berries and fruits. Butterflies, moths, beetles, and grasshoppers are its most common foods. Great cresteds usually forage high in the treetops or from a high, exposed perch.

Nesting

A cavity nester that cannot excavate its own nest hole, it must rely on finding old woodpecker holes, naturally occurring hollows in trees, or human-supplied nest boxes. After inspecting possible nest sites with her mate, the female begins nest building using an incredible array of material, including animal hair, feathers, pine needles, string, cellophane, and shed snakeskin. Why great cresteds use such a variety of materials is a mystery. Five or more eggs are laid and incubated by the female for about two weeks. Two weeks after hatching, young flycatchers leave the nest.

Backyard & Beyond

Any backyard with large shade trees and adjacent woodland in the eastern United States has the potential to attract nesting great crested flycatchers. To encourage them, leave standing any dead or hollow trees, especially ones with knotholes or existing woodpecker holes. Nest box dimensions should be: interior floor of 6×6 inches, inside height of 12 inches, entry hole of 1¾ to 2 inches. Mount at a height of 10 to 20 inches.

Eastern Kingbird

Tyrannus tyrannus

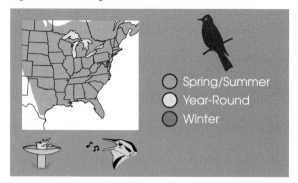

- ○ Spring/Summer
- ○ Year-Round
- ○ Winter

High in the treetops a medium-sized, black-and-white bird flutters out to catch flying insects and aggressively attacks other birds in flight, all the while emitting a sputtery series of sharp notes that sound like the zapping of an electric current. This is the eastern kingbird, whose Latin name translates into "tyrant of tyrants," the most common kingbird found in the East.

All About

The eastern kingbird is an excellent flier, able to catch flying insects and aggressively defend its breeding territory with its aerial mastery. Both sexes are blackish above and white below. The female's chest is grayish. Male kingbirds have a small, red-orange patch of feathers on the crown, though this is rarely seen. A thin, white band on the tail margin clinches the identification.

Habitat & Range

Spending the breeding season in open areas with scattered trees, eastern kingbirds prefer locations near water, probably for the bounty of insects. Fairly common in agricultural areas, pastures, city parks, and suburban neighborhoods with large trees and open understory during summer, most eastern kingbirds migrate to Central and South America in winter. In migration, the kingbird travels in loose flocks, and it is not uncommon to see a dozen or more birds in one tree in spring or fall.

Feeding

The eastern kingbird, or beebird, is an insect eater, specializing in bees, wasps, moths, butterflies, and other large, flying insects. Sit-and-watch hunters, kingbirds find an exposed perch and wait for something edible to fly past. They then sally forth and grab the prey in their bill, returning to the perch to stun and eat the insect. Kingbirds also eat fruits at all seasons, including mulberries, cherries, and elderberries. Fruits make up the bulk of their winter diet in the tropics.

Nesting

The kingbird's nest is placed high in a tree and is a large, loosely woven cup of bark, twigs, and weed stems. Females do all of the nest building and incubation. A typical clutch is two to five eggs with a 15-day incubation period. Hatchling kingbirds spend about 16 days in the nest before fledging, after which they are attended to by both parents for several more weeks.

Backyard & Beyond

Kingbirds can often be seen perching high in a tree or along fences or power lines, hunting for insects. They are very active in their territories in summer, so watch for their fluttery flycatching flights and listen for their loud zapping calls. The old myth that eastern kingbirds prey primarily on honeybees resulted in many of these birds being shot. Studies have now shown that kingbirds eat relatively few honeybees, mostly drones.

Loggerhead Shrike

Lanius ludovicianus

○ Spring/Summer
○ Year-Round
○ Winter

"Loggerhead" refers to this bird's large-headed appearance, but what really sets the loggerhead shrike apart is its hawklike feeding behavior. Its Latin name Lanius means "butcher," a reference to its habit of impaling prey on thorns or barbed wire to aid in carving them up. Look for signs of their presence by checking barbed-wire fencing for impaled insects, toads, or other prey items.*

All About

With just a quick glance at a loggerhead shrike, you might mistake it for a mockingbird, as both birds are a blend of gray, black, and white. A closer look reveals the shrike's flesh-tearing bill (shaped like a falcon's bill), black mask, and its overall big-headed appearance and compact shape—quite different from the lanky mockingbird. In flight, loggerhead shrikes flash white wing and tail spots. Its song is a rich, burry warble, underscoring its standing as our only truly predatory songbird.

Habitat & Range

The loggerhead shrike is much more common in the southern portions of its range, where it is a year-round resident. In the Northeast, this bird has vanished as a breeder due to reforestation, competition from other birds, and the effects of pesticides. Loggerhead shrikes prefer open country, such as pastures and grasslands with short grass and scattered, thorny trees or fencerows with barbed wire. They perch—body horizontal—in the open on wires and fences.

Feeding

Grasshoppers are the loggerhead's primary prey, but small amphibians, reptiles, mammals, and birds are also taken. Lacking the strong talons of a hawk, the shrike carries prey items to a convenient thorny perch, where it impales its victim. This holds the food item in place, allowing the shrike to tear it apart with its sharp, toothed bill—hence the common name "butcherbird." When prey is abundant, the shrike will impale prey for later consumption. One such "larder" in North Carolina held 15 small snakes on a single, thorny bush.

Nesting

The female shrike builds the nest in a tree or thorny shrub from materials collected by the mated pair. The cup-shaped nest is woven from bark strips, twigs, and plant stems and is lined with soft animal fur, feathers, or grass. About five eggs are laid, and the female alone handles the 16-day incubation period, though her mate brings her food. Young loggerhead shrikes remain in the nest for up to 20 days, and then remain in the nest area for about a week after fledging.

Backyard & Beyond

In the Deep South, loggerhead shrikes can be found in almost any open habitat, including city parks, golf courses, and along mowed roadsides. But across most of their range, they are most commonly seen in open pasturelands.

Red-eyed Vireo

Vireo olivaceus

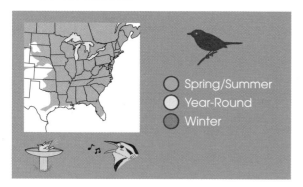

○ Spring/Summer
○ Year-Round
○ Winter

Easy to hear and hard to see, the red-eyed vireo is one of the most numerous summer birds of the eastern American woodlands. It arrives in April or early May from its South American wintering grounds, and its song rings out from every wooded tract. Foraging high in the emerging leaves, the vireo sings almost endlessly—one patient listener counted 22,197 songs from the same bird in one summer day!

All About

The red-eyed vireo is about 6 inches long—an olive-backed, white-bellied bird with a gray cap and bold white stripe over its bright red eyes. Males and females are similar. They have sharp, slightly hooked bills designed to catch insect prey. Despite their small size, they are strong fliers; their twice-yearly migration carries them to the Amazon and back. Red-eyeds, like all vireos, are more deliberate in their movements than warblers.

Habitat & Range

Red-eyes are usually found in open deciduous or mixed woodlands with a strong understory of sapling trees. They sometimes occur in large city parks, orchards, or even wooded suburban backyards.

Feeding

Like many small neotropical migrants, the red-eyed vireo feeds mostly on insects. It gleans its food from the upper story of tall deciduous trees, singing as it moves slowly along the branches, peering under and around the leaves. Occasionally, it hovers to snatch a bug from an otherwise unreachable surface. In late summer, the red-eyed vireo will supplement its diet with berries of many kinds.

Nesting

The female selects a suitable site, usually 5 to 10 feet off the ground on a horizontal forked twig. She builds a tightly woven nest of fine grasses and strips of grapevine, suspending it below the fork and decorating it with bits of lichen on its outer surfaces. Here she incubates her four eggs for 11 to 14 days. Both parents feed the nestlings for 10 to 12 days until they are ready to fledge. Red-eyed vireos are frequent victims of cowbirds and only rarely do they fight back by building a floor over the cowbird egg and laying another clutch. Most of the time they simply accept the cowbird chick, to the detriment of their own.

Backyard & Beyond

The best way to find a red-eyed vireo is to learn its song, then listen for it in the spring and summer woods. It is sometimes written as *Here I am, look at me, over here, here I am* sung over and over in a clear sweet voice, usually from high in a tree. Finding the singer will take some persistence and a good pair of binoculars. In fall, silent red-eyed vireos may be spotted in hedgerows and tangles, looking for berries.

Blue Jay
Cyanocitta cristata

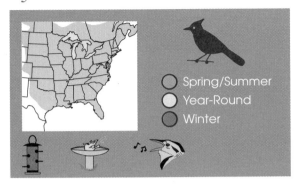

Spring/Summer
Year-Round
Winter

Blue jays are smart, adaptable, and noisy birds. They will often mimic the call of a red-tailed or red-shouldered hawk as they approach a bird feeder, in an apparent attempt to scare other birds away from the food. Sometimes persecuted by humans as nest robbers or bullies at the feeding station, blue jays are one of our most ornate and lovely birds. Bird watchers visiting the United States from abroad are astounded that such a beautiful bird is common in our suburban backyards.

All About

No other eastern bird is blue and crested, making the blue jay almost unmistakable. Males and females are similar. Besides the standard *jay jay* or *jeer jeer* call often used as a scold, blue jays also emit a variety of squeaks, rattles, and croaks, in addition to mimicking other birds' calls. If you hear a sound in the woods that is loud and unmusical, chances are good that it's coming from a blue jay.

Habitat & Range

Blue jays are common in wooded habitats, especially those with oaks. Indeed the blue jay has a special relationship with oaks, burying as many as five thousand acorns in fall caches for future consumption. Many of these acorns are never retrieved, so jays are credited with helping with forest generation. Resident throughout their range, especially in the Deep South, blue jays in northern latitudes migrate southward in early fall, traveling by daylight

in flocks of 10 or more birds, many carrying acorns in their bills.

Feeding

Blue jays will eat almost anything. Grasshoppers and other insects, and acorns and other nuts are their primary foods. Bird eggs or nestlings, mice, frogs, and a variety of human-supplied foods are also eaten. When storing acorns, blue jays will carry as many as five acorns in the throat and bill to the cache site, drop them in a pile, and bury them one at a time. They will return to recover only some of these acorns.

Nesting

Males help gather nesting materials, but females do most of the building in a tree. The twig nest is woven into a cup and lined with wet leaves and rootlets. Suburban blue jays often incorporate string, plastics, and paper (human trash) into nests. The female lays four to six eggs and incubates them for 18 days, followed by about 20 days of nestling care before the young jays fledge.

Backyard & Beyond

A common feeder visitor, blue jays are attracted to suet, peanuts, sunflower seeds, and even dog food. A source of water is highly attractive to blue jays, too. Look for blue jays along woodland edges and listen for their raucous cries, almost always the first clue to their presence.

American Crow

Corvus brachyrhynchos

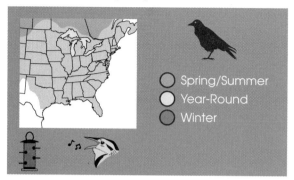

- Spring/Summer
- Year-Round
- Winter

Noisy, sly, opportunistic, and ubiquitous, the American crow lives among us; yet, comparatively little is known about it. Like other bold, brash corvids (the blue jay being a prime example), the crow is downright sneaky where its personal life is concerned. Few people know that crows may breed cooperatively in groups of up to a dozen birds, helping tend the dominant pair's nest.

All About

An unrelieved glossy black from bill to toenail, crows are armed with a stout, strong bill that acts as a chisel, axe, shovel, or forceps, among other uses. Its distinctive wingbeats appear to row the bird through the sky. Crows are well known for their raucous *caw*. Evidence suggests that crows have different "words" for different situations (assembly, dispersal, mobbing); their language is complex, as is their social behavior. Few people are privileged to hear the crow's song, given by both sexes, which is a long recitation of rattles, coos, growls, and imitations of sounds.

Habitat & Range

Though they are strongly associated with agricultural areas, crows find perfect conditions in cities and suburbs, where they raid pet dishes, bird feeders, and garbage cans. In the northern part of their range, crows are migratory, but all spend the winter within the continental United States. Throughout their range, crows use communal roosts when not breeding, and these can swell to massive proportions by late winter.

Feeding

There's almost nothing edible an American crow will not eat. At roadkills, landfills, and compost piles, crows will load their distensible throat with food and fly heavily off, often caching it under leaves or sod for later enjoyment. Crows forage by walking slowly on the ground—hunting invertebrates and vertebrates alike—and are constantly scanning roadsides and fields as they fly, descending to investigate anything that might be edible.

Nesting

Crows stay in family units composed of a pair and their young from the previous year. These yearlings may help build the nest, incubate, or feed the incubating female or her young. Four or five eggs are laid in the bulky twig nest, which is usually hidden high in a pine. The female incubates for around 17 days, and young fledge at around 36 days of age. Their strangled, nasal calls sometimes betray the nest location.

Backyard & Beyond

Crows are always up to something, and feeding them gives us an opportunity to observe their always-intriguing behavior. To find something a crow might like, open the refrigerator. Freezer-burned meat is a favorite. Cracked or whole corn is irresistible as well. Neighbors may wonder, but crows are well worth watching.

Purple Martin

Progne subis

Spring/Summer
Year-Round
Winter

No other North American bird has a closer association with humans than the purple martin. For more than four hundred years, martins in eastern North America have nested in human-supplied housing, at first in hollow gourds offered by Native Americans and today in a variety of specialized housing. Generations of people and martins have grown up together. Even non-bird watchers can appreciate this friendly and familiar bird.

All About

Our largest swallow (at 8 inches), the purple martin is a graceful flyer with a bubbly, liquid song. The adult male has a deep blue body and black wings and tail. Females and youngsters are gray and black with some blue on the back. In flight, martins can be confused with European starlings, but martins have a notched tail and call out almost constantly.

Habitat & Range

Purple martins breed across eastern North America, except for the extreme north. They spend winters in South America but return to the southern United States in mid-January, their arrival eagerly anticipated by their human landlords. Because of their reliance on human-supplied housing, most martins are found around cities, towns, and settlements.

Feeding

Martins eat flying insects almost exclusively, but—contrary to popular opinion and marketing hype—martins do not eat many mosquitoes. Instead, their diet includes larger flying insects, such as beetles, flies, dragonflies, wasps, butterflies, and moths. In cold, rainy weather, martin landlords often resort to feeding them mealworms and bits of scrambled egg in an effort to keep their beloved birds alive. Some landlords even shoot mealworms into the air with a slingshot just so the martins can catch their food.

Nesting

Martins are rather selective in choosing colony nest sites, but one thing is certain: They like to be with other martins. Research has revealed that they prefer white housing with a large (8×8×8-inch) interior and an $1^{1}/_{2}$-inch entry hole. The housing should be mounted near a human dwelling in an open area. Martins build a loose cup nest inside the cavity out of pine needles and grass, lined with green leaves (which limit parasites). The female lays four to six eggs and does most of the incubation, lasting about 16 days. Both parents feed the nestlings for the month-long period before fledging.

Backyard & Beyond

The most successful martin landlords are those willing to put in the extra effort to care for their tenants with predator-proof housing, elimination of competing house sparrows and starlings, and regular monitoring. Your chances of attracting martins are greatly enhanced if there is an existing colony within a mile of you.

Northern Rough-winged Swallow

Stelgidopteryx serripennis

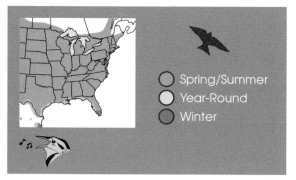

○ Spring/Summer
○ Year-Round
○ Winter

For such a common species, the northern rough-winged swallow is not well known. In farm country it is often overlooked among the barn swallows, while anyone encountering it at a nesting site may be tempted to call it a bank swallow. Its rather nondescript plumage only adds to the confusion. But this little bird has characteristics all its own, and a very distinct personality that makes it worth knowing.

All About

Only 5 to 5¹/₂ inches long, the northern rough-winged swallow is brown-backed with dirty-white underparts, a short notched tail, and narrow pointed wings. The rough-winged swallow lacks the distinct dark breast band of the bank swallow. Its legs are short, and its feet adapted more for perching than for walking. The rough-winged swallow is not very vocal at any time, but it does utter short, harsh *zeep* sounds in flight. The small serrations on its outer wing feathers, for which the species is named, produce fluttery noises during courtship displays.

Habitat & Range

Like all swallows, the rough-winged is a bird of open country. It may be found from sea level to 6,000 feet or more, and it is often (though not always) found near some kind of water. In all except the southernmost parts of the country, these are seasonal birds, arriving in early spring and departing by mid- to late fall.

Feeding

Its diet consists almost entirely of flying insects that are snatched in midair. Like other birds that catch their prey in flight, rough-winged swallows have wide gaping mouths to maximize their chances for success. Flies, wasps, winged ants, moths, and damselflies are favored items. They drink on the wing, barely breaking the surface of the water in a lake or pond to satisfy their thirst without wetting their wings.

Nesting

Rough-winged swallows breed in sandbanks or other vertical sites, such as road cuts or soft cliffs. Using their feet, they excavate a deep (up to six feet) burrow. Two or three pairs may nest in proximity, but this species does not breed in large colonies like the bank swallow. The pair constructs a twiggy nest at the end of the burrow. Five to seven eggs are laid, and incubation by the female takes 12 to 16 days. Both parents feed the nestlings, which leave the nest at about 20 days of age.

Backyard & Beyond

Look for rough-winged swallows in spring going into gravel banks or sandy road cuts, or near small bridges where they may nest in drainpipes. In late summer, they often perch with other swallows on roadside wires, and a careful observer can distinguish them clearly by their buffy, unbanded breast.

Tree Swallow

Tachycineta bicolor

Spring/Summer
Year-Round
Winter

The lovely tree swallow is making a breeding range expansion into the southern United States, first nesting in North Carolina in 1979 and then in Georgia in 1982. Limited by the availability of the nesting cavities they require, tree swallows are benefiting greatly from artificial nest boxes erected to attract bluebirds. Their liquid twitters, sharp blue-and-white coloration, and trusting ways make them a welcome addition to the Southern birdlife.

All About

Long triangular wings, snow-white underparts, and glossy teal-blue upperparts make the tree swallow a beautiful signal of spring. Soaring kitelike, then rising with rapid flaps, they course and dive over meadows and ponds in their search for flying insects. Their jingling calls have been likened to the sound of someone shaking paperclips in a tumbler. Females are somewhat browner above and a duller blue than males.

Habitat & Range

Tree swallows prefer open fields, preferably near water, for nesting, though they will inhabit upland sites. Marshes—fresh and salt—also provide the flying insects they require. The tree swallow's habitat for breeding range extends across Canada and the northern tier of the United States and is expanding into the Southeast at a good clip. Tree swallows winter in coastal areas from South Carolina to Florida, and along the Gulf Coast into Mexico and Central America.

Feeding

Eighty percent of the tree swallow's diet is insects; fruits make up the other portion, largely bayberries that sustain them in adverse winter weather. "Myrtle swallow" would be a more apt name for these birds, as myrtle is another name for bayberry. This ability to eat fruit helps tree swallows survive cold snaps as they make their way northward to breed. Insects are caught on the wing in spectacular zigzag flights and are stored in the throat to be fed to nestlings.

Nesting

A foundation of coarse grass leaves and stems is lined with large body feathers, usually white. Tree swallows are mad for feathers in nesting season and can often be induced to take soft white feathers from the hand. A New York study showed that eggs hatched and nestlings survived better in nests insulated with more feathers. The female incubates four to seven eggs for an average of 14 days. Young leave the nest 15 to 25 days later, flying strongly. Second broods are rare, but seem to be more frequent in the South.

Backyard & Beyond

Before the advent of artificial nest boxes, tree swallows were limited to old woodpecker holes—a hotly contested resource. A nest box with a 1 9/16-inch hole, mounted on a predator-proof pole in an open meadow near water, is the best bet for attracting tree swallows.

Barn Swallow

Hirundo rustica

Spring/Summer
Year-Round
Winter

One early naturalist estimated that a barn swallow that lived 10 years would fly more than two million miles, enough to travel 87 times around the earth. This species seems to define what it means to be at home in the air, and it has been compared to an albatross in its ability to stay effortlessly aloft. One of the most familiar and beloved birds in rural America, the barn swallow is welcomed everywhere as a sign of spring.

All About
Glossy blue-black above and orange below, the barn swallow is the only American swallow that has a true "swallow tail," with an elongated outer pair of tail feathers. Males and females are similar, but females are not quite as glossy or highly colored, and the fork in their tails is not quite as pronounced. Like all swallows, they have short legs and rather weak feet used for perching, not walking.

Habitat & Range
A bird of rural areas and farmlands, the barn swallow may be found over any open area, such as pastures, fields, and golf courses, as well as lakes, ponds, and rivers. It has adapted well to humans and is not shy of people, nesting close to settled areas as long as it has open space for feeding. Barn swallows travel in great flocks during migrations, often in company with other swallow species. They arrive in most of their U.S. range in April and leave in early to midfall.

Feeding
Foraging almost entirely on the wing, the barn swallow takes a variety of insect prey from flies and locusts to moths, grasshoppers, bees, and wasps. Occasionally small berries or seeds are added to the diet, but this is uncommon. Only in bad weather will barn swallows feed on the ground.

Nesting
Nothing says "country" more than a pair of barn swallows zipping in and out of the open doors of a working barn, darting after insects and chattering incessantly. Sometimes two or three pairs will share a favored site. The nest itself is a cup of mud and grass, lined with feathers and placed on a rafter or glued under an eave. Besides barns, barn swallows may use other open buildings, covered porches, or the undersides of bridges or docks. During second nestings, immatures from the first brood help feed and care for their younger siblings.

Backyard & Beyond
During breeding season, you may bring barn swallows into close range by throwing feathers into the air near a flock of soaring birds; the graceful fliers will swoop in to snatch them up for nest linings. Barn swallows also enjoy eating bits of baked eggshells (crumble them first) during breeding season.

Tufted Titmouse

Baeolophus bicolor

Spring/Summer
Year-Round
Winter

From deep mixed woods to old orchards, from city parks to leafy suburban backyards, this friendly and active little bird makes itself at home throughout the year. It is noisy and sociable, quite tame in human company, and fearless among other small birds with which it associates. Its cheerful calls of peter, peter, peter ring out even in midwinter, chasing away the January blahs.

All About
The tufted titmouse is 6½ inches long and dressed primly across its upperparts in gray, with a creamy breast and rusty flanks. A black-button eye stands out against its white cheek, and a crest adorns its head. Its small, sharp bill is black, as are its legs and feet. Titmice are very vocal and, besides their signature *peter* calls, they have a variety of whistled notes—similar to those of the cardinal and Carolina wren. Their harsh, raspy, scolding notes are similar to the chickadee's.

Habitat & Range
The tufted titmouse was originally considered a southern woodland bird, but for the past 50 years it has been expanding its range northward. The species' affinity for bird feeders and nesting boxes has played a part in this expansion. Titmice are nonmigratory and able to survive harsh weather if sufficient food is available.

Feeding
Tufted titmice eat mostly insects and seeds, depending on time of year. Caterpillars are a popular item in summer, but they also take wasps and bees, scale insects, beetles, the larvae of many species, and, in winter, insect eggs. Acorns are a mainstay in fall and winter. At feeders, titmice relish sunflower seeds, suet, suet dough, and peanuts.

Nesting
The natural nesting choice of the tufted titmouse is a tree cavity—an abandoned woodpecker hole, or crack caused by a lightning strike. Other sites include rotted fenceposts, drainage pipes, and nest boxes. The female builds the nest of grass, moss, bark, and leaves, filling up whatever size hole they have adopted. When the main structure is completed, the birds line it with hair—often plucked from a living animal—woodchuck, rabbit, dog, or even a handy human. Five or six eggs are laid, incubated by the female for 12 to 14 days. Both parents feed the young, which fledge at about 15 days. The family group stays together, sometimes into the next year, and year-old birds may help their parents care for the nestlings of the newest brood.

Backyard & Beyond
Tufted titmice sometimes breed in nest boxes, especially those with an entrance hole in the 1½-inch range. In winter they travel in mixed flocks with chickadees, sparrows, woodpeckers, and kinglets. Tufted titmice are easy to locate in woodlands by their noisy scolding calls.

Carolina Chickadee

Poecile carolinensis

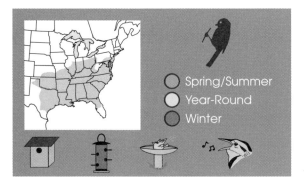

Spring/Summer
Year-Round
Winter

Gregarious and widespread, chickadees are just about everyone's favorite backyard birds. In the South, the resident chickadee is the Carolina, a slightly smaller but otherwise very similar cousin to the black-capped chickadee of the northern states. Chickadees travel in noisy little bands and draw attention to themselves with their frequent scolding chatter. Chickadees are often the first birds to discover a newly installed bird feeder.

All About

Only about 4^1/2 inches in length, the Carolina chickadee has a black cap and bib with a white cheek patch; gray back, wings, and tail; and pale underparts with buff-colored flanks. The bill is tiny and dark, the legs and feet black. Males and females are alike, and there are no seasonal differences in plumage. The *so-fee, so-fay* song of the Carolina chickadee is longer than the black-capped chickadee's—four notes as opposed to two or three—and its *chick-a-dee-dee-dee* call is higher-pitched and more rapid.

Habitat & Range

The Carolina chickadee is resident (nonmigratory) and, through most of its range, it is the only chickadee present. It is generally replaced by the black-capped chickadee at elevations above 5,000 feet in the southern Appalachians, though. Where the two species overlap they may occasionally interbreed, so identifying individual birds under such circumstances is tricky.

Feeding

Carolina chickadees have a varied diet. Nearly half of the food taken in the wild consists of insects, such as aphids, ants, moths, and leafhoppers. They also eat spiders, weed seeds, and the seeds and small fruits of many trees and vines. At feeders they are partial to sunflower seeds, suet, and peanuts.

Nesting

Cavity nesters, Carolina chickadees seek out natural holes in woodland trees, often adapting old woodpecker holes. They readily accept not only nesting boxes, but also crevices under eaves or porch roofs, hollowed out fenceposts, or drainpipes. The nest (made by the female) is a thick mass of mosses, bark, and grasses, enclosing a cup of soft hair. One side is built up higher than the other and can be pulled down like a flap to cover the young when both parents are away. As many as eight eggs are laid and incubated by the female for 11 to 13 days; both parents then share the feeding of the young until they fledge after two weeks.

Backyard & Beyond

It is easy to lure chickadees into your yard by providing black-oil sunflower seeds in hanging tubes or hopper feeders, and by offering suet or other fats, such as a peanut butter-cornmeal mix or "bird pudding." To induce a pair to stay and nest, install one or more nest boxes with entrance holes that are 1^1/4 to 1^1/2 inches in diameter.

White-breasted Nuthatch

Sitta carolinensis

Spring/Summer
Year-Round
Winter

Nuthatches are universally referred to as "upside-down birds," because they forage by probing the bark of tree trunks with their heads downward. During their journeys down the trunk of a tree, they often pause, and then raise their head so that it is parallel to the ground—an absolutely unique posture among birds. The most well-known member of the family is the white-breasted nuthatch, a bird of deciduous woods and well-treed backyards.

All About

At nearly 6 inches in length, the white-breasted nuthatch is the largest of its tribe. Males have gray backs with black caps, white underparts, and a beady black eye on a white face. Females are similar but wear gray, not black, on their heads. White-breasteds are thick-necked and short-tailed, with a stocky appearance. White-breasted nuthatch calls—uttered frequently in all seasons—are a nasal and repetitive *ank-ank*.

Habitat & Range

White-breasted nuthatches prefer deciduous woods, but are also found in large parks and leafy backyards. In northern coniferous woods, and at high elevations along the Appalachian chain, they are replaced by the smaller red-breasted nuthatch, while the brown-headed nuthatch displaces them in the dry pine woods of the South.

Feeding

The white-breasted nuthatch eats both insects and seeds, varying its fare with the seasons. Insects make up nearly 100 percent of their summer diet, with seeds being added in fall and winter. Autumn's extra seeds and nuts are sometimes stashed—or "hatched away"—in tree bark crevices, to be retrieved later—a habit that has given these birds their name. White-breasted nuthatches will come to feeders for sunflower and other seeds, or suet, but they tend to abandon backyard feeders almost entirely in spring and summer when insect prey is plentiful.

Nesting

Nuthatches maintain their pair bond and territory all year long. The nest is placed in a natural cavity, old woodpecker hole, or more rarely a nest box. Built by the female, it is a cup of grasses, bark strips, and twigs and is lined with hair. When the nest is finished, the nuthatches "sweep" the entrance with their bills, rubbing a crushed insect against the wood—the chemicals released may aid in repelling predators. The female incubates a clutch of eight eggs for two weeks. Both parents feed the young for at least two weeks until fledging.

Backyard & Beyond

Nuthatches are irregular feeder visitors, but they like black oil sunflower seeds and suet, peanuts, or peanut butter mix. In woodlands, listen for the nuthatch's nasal honking calls anytime. Male and female always forage near each other and, in winter, with other species in a mixed flock.

Carolina Wren

Thryothorus ludovicianus

○ Spring/Summer
○ Year-Round
○ Winter

Creeping and exploring around door stoops, garages, and tool sheds, Carolina wrens adopt a *mi casa, su casa* policy when it comes to nesting. If you find a nest cleverly hidden on a cluttered shelf or in a hanging flower basket, it's likely that of a Carolina wren. Their persistent songs, often given as a duet between pairs, brighten winter days and ring through the thick underbrush that they prefer.

All About
The Carolina wren is a rotund, warm-brown bird that often carries its tail cocked. Leading with its longish, curved bill, it resembles a little brown teapot. Reinforcing this impression is the phrase it often sings: *teakettle, teakettle!* The bright white line over its eye and its warm buffy underparts (paler in summer) help clinch the identification. Males and females are alike.

Habitat & Range
Wherever it occurs, the Carolina wren stays as a year-round resident. It's most common in swampy, mixed hardwood forests that are thick with vines, shrubs, and tangles, but it is happy in yards and gardens with plenty of shrubbery and outbuildings. Carolina wrens love poking about stacks of firewood, and they'll help themselves to the shelter of an open porch, garage, or shed, cleverly concealing their nests in our clutter.

Feeding
Insects and spiders make up virtually all the Carolina wren's natural food diet, which they capture while gleaning on or near the ground. At times, they will climb trees to glean insects hidden in bark or toss aside leaf litter while searching for prey. They'll bash large prey, such as katydids and moths, into manageable pieces and hunt cobwebby corners for spiders. In snowy winters, Carolina wrens resort to visiting feeders.

Nesting
Carolina wrens weave a surprisingly complex and bulky nest, hauling volumes of bark strips, fine twigs, leaves, grasses, green moss, and rubbish into a hidden nook, thick intertwining of vines, natural tree cavity, or cranny in an outbuilding. They often make a "porch" of such material leading to the nest. The entire affair is domed, and the finely-woven inner cup holds four eggs. The female incubates for 14 days, while the male feeds her. The young leave the nest from 12 to 19 days later.

Backyard & Beyond
Though they're unable to crack seeds with their fine, curved bills, Carolina wrens poke about for fragments of sunflower hearts and swallow white millet whole. They're most fond of peanut butter suet mixtures and mealworms, and they have been known to enter houses through open doors and windows to seek food. Highly intelligent, they easily find their way back out and make charming neighbors. Listen for their ringing whistles in any low-lying, tangled woods, and enjoy them in your yard.

House Wren

Troglodytes aedon

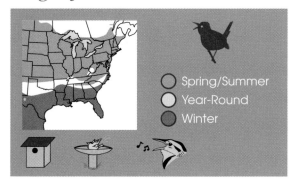

Spring/Summer
Year-Round
Winter

The rich and burbling song of the house wren is surprisingly loud for such a tiny (4³/4 inches long) bird. House wrens are named for their preference for living in close proximity to humans, often in tiny houses we provide for them. This mostly plain brown bird makes up for its small size and drab coloration by being a fierce competitor for nesting sites.

All About
House wrens are notable for their lack of field marks—the warm-brown upperparts and tail are matched by a grayish breast. Look closely at the house wren, and you'll see a variety of small white and black spots, the only variation in the bird's plumage. Males and females look alike and both have the wrenlike habit of cocking their tails up when perched. The thin, slightly curved bill is ideal for capturing and eating the house wren's insect prey.

Habitat & Range
Spending the summers in thickets and brushy edge habitat adjacent to woodlands, the house wren is a familiar bird in parks, backyards, and gardens, often—but not always—near human settlements. Some house wrens winter in the southernmost states in the United States, but many travel beyond our borders farther south.

Feeding
Insects make up the house wren's diet (grasshoppers, crickets, spiders, and moths are on the menu), but they will also eat snails and caterpillars. Most of their foraging is done in thick vegetation on or near the ground.

Nesting
House wrens nest in a variety of cavities from woodpecker holes to natural cavities and nest boxes. Like Carolina wrens, house wrens will also nest in flowerpots, drainpipes, and other such sites. They are very competitive about nesting sites, often filling all or most available cavities with sticks. The male builds these "dummy" nests, and the female selects one in which to nest. The twig structures are lined with soft materials, such as grass or hair, and the female lays six to eight eggs. She performs the incubation duties, which last from 12 to 14 days. Fledglings leave the nest two or more weeks after hatching. House wrens are known to pierce the eggs of other cavity nesting birds in their territories.

Backyard & Beyond
House wrens will readily accept nest boxes with interior dimensions of 4x4 inches and entry holes of 1¹/4 inches in diameter. Nest boxes placed adjacent to a brushy habitat or a wood's edge seem to be most attractive. The house wren's song and scolding calls are heard often wherever they are present. Nest boxes for bluebirds and tree swallows should be placed far from edge habitat, in the open, to avoid conflict and competition from territorial house wrens.

Blue-gray Gnatcatcher

Polioptila caerulea

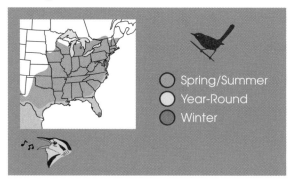

○ Spring/Summer
○ Year-Round
○ Winter

The blue-gray gnatcatcher is the birder's "mini-mockingbird," always in motion and usually talking about it. This graceful, delicate, miniscule bird seems to arrive too early in spring, sallying into swarms of midges from still-budding branches. Its slender, elongated form and flashy black-and-white paneled tail are hard to mistake, though the gnatcatcher often goes unnoticed. It's most likely to be spotted on its early spring migration, for it is a woodland denizen, often hidden by foliage after the trees leaf out.

All About

It's often the gnatcatcher's twangy, whining call—like a miniature banjo being tuned—that alerts us to its presence. Its song is a sputtering, wheezy, petulant-sounding jumble, punctuated by mews. The blue-gray gnatcatcher has been recorded mimicking other species, a talent not widely appreciated, perhaps because its high, whispery voice is beyond the hearing register of many bird watchers. A white eye ring and neat black eyeline, blue-gray upperparts, and a long, slender tail edged in white distinguish this elegant bird. Females are similar, but lack the black eyeline.

Habitat & Range

Blue-gray gnatcatchers are strongly associated with oaks in a wide range of habitats, sticking to woodlands dominated by broad-leaved species. They are more often seen along woodland edges than in yards and gardens, except during migration. Gnatcatchers winter in the western coastal scrub of Mexico and Central America.

Feeding

Perching on the outer twigs in the mid- to high canopy, gnatcatchers go out after flying insects or glean the outer foliage for insects and spiders. As they forage, they flick their white outer tail feathers, which is thought to create bursts of light that startles UV-sensitive insects into flight. The bill is a fine black forcep, good for grasping tiny prey.

Nesting

Gnatcatcher nests are often mistaken for those of hummingbirds, being neat, compact cups of silk (often gathered from tent caterpillar nests), plastered with lichens. They are usually saddled on a horizontal limb. It is often possible to witness construction because the male gnatcatcher escorts the nest-building female with much fanfare and conversation. Both male and female incubate four eggs for 13 days, and young birds leave the nest 13 days after hatching. They are still being fed by their parents three weeks after departing the nest but gain independence soon thereafter.

Backyard & Beyond

This species has expanded its range explosively over the past three decades, pioneering into the Northeast and southeastern Canada. However, its range expansion cannot be attributed to feeding stations, as has been postulated for the northward movement of tufted titmice, northern cardinals, and red-bellied woodpeckers. The gnatcatcher relies solely on insects for sustenance.

Eastern Bluebird

Sialia sialia

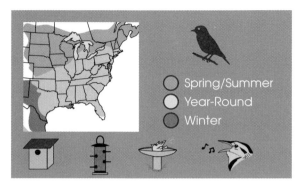

Spring/Summer
Year-Round
Winter

The eastern bluebird is our most famous thrush, even more popular than its cousin, the American robin. Its beauty, its song, and its willingness to live close to us has inspired many poets, songwriters, artists, and bird watchers. You can attract bluebirds to your property if you have a large open lawn, especially if you provide housing. Thanks to a concerted effort by bluebird lovers to provide nest boxes, the eastern bluebird has rebounded from its low population in the 1960s.

All About

The sky-blue back and rusty breast of the male bluebird are echoed in the female's more muted tones. There are three bluebird species in North America, but only the eastern is commonly found in the South. Bluebirds are often seen perched along fence lines, on wires, or high in trees. They may appear all dark in bright sunlight, so many observers miss seeing them. During spring courtship, paired bluebirds can be seen fluttering their wings near a prospective nesting site, uttering their rich *turalee turalay* song.

Habitat & Range

Bluebirds are resident (nonmigratory) throughout the eastern United States in open habitats, such as pastures, grasslands, parks, and large suburban lawns (especially where bluebird nest boxes are available). The two habitat requirements of bluebirds are large, open, grassy areas for foraging and cavities for roosting and nesting. In harsh winter weather, bluebirds may migrate short distances to find food or shelter.

Feeding

From an elevated perch, bluebirds watch for moving insects and then drop to the ground to pounce on them or to capture flying insects in midair. They eat insects year-round and will shift to fruits and berries when insects are scarce. Bluebirds visit feeders for mealworms, berries, and suet or suet dough.

Nesting

Bluebirds are cavity nesters and will use old woodpecker holes or natural cavities in trees where available. Human-supplied nest boxes are an important resource for the eastern bluebird. The female bluebird builds the nest inside the cavity using bark strips, grass, and hair. She lays four to six eggs and incubates them for 12 to 16 days. Both parents care for the nestlings until fledging occurs after 14 to 18 days.

Backyard & Beyond

If you offer housing, it's important to monitor and manage it to keep non-native house sparrows and starlings from usurping it and to keep predators from accessing the eggs or young. Place the houses (with $1^1/_2$-inch entrance holes) on metal poles with a pole-mounted baffle beneath the house. House location should be in the middle of a large, open, grassy lawn or field. Bluebirds catch insects on the ground in grassy areas, so they are particularly vulnerable to lawn chemicals.

American Robin

Turdus migratorius

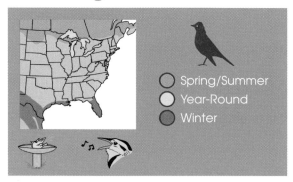

Spring/Summer
Year-Round
Winter

Almost all North Americans have grown up having a fairly intimate acquaintance with a thrush. The American robin, the largest and most widespread and most abundant North American thrush, has followed the watered lawn—with its plentiful earthworm prey base—westward across the continent. Only parts of Florida, Texas, and the Southwest, where the soil is too sandy to support the introduced common earthworm, lack robins.

All About

The robin's simple yet evocative *cheerily-cheerio* song meshes well with the thunk of basketballs and the drone of lawnmowers in suburban neighborhoods all across North America; yet, they also hide their nests in mountaintop spruce and fir forests, where they are as wary as any hermit thrush. Males sport brick-red breasts and black heads with broken white spectacles and a streaked white throat and lower belly. Females are paler.

Habitat & Range

The robin is primarily a bird of lawns with trees and shrubs, though it also breeds in high mountain forests near clear-cuts or openings. Few other species show its adaptability to diverse habitats, from landscaped parking lot islets to dense, secluded forests. Migration is marked in northern climes, but is less so in southern ones.

Feeding

Running, then standing erect and motionless on a lawn, the robin watches and listens for earth-worms and other invertebrates crawling in the grass. A quick stab captures them, sometimes resulting in a tug-of-war with a recalcitrant night crawler. Robins flock in fall to exploit fruiting trees and shrubs, fluttering and giggling as they reach for food.

Nesting

Most bird watchers are familiar with the robin's sturdy mud-and-grass cup, often nestled in an evergreen, a climbing vine, on a horizontal branch, or even on a windowsill. The female incubates three to four eggs for 12 to 14 days. Adults can be seen foraging with bills full of earthworms as soon as the young hatch. Young leave the nest, barely able to flutter, on about the thirteenth day. They are distinguished by their spotted, whitish breasts and reedy, begging calls. The male feeds them for another three weeks, while the female usually starts a second brood.

Backyard & Beyond

By mowing the lawn regularly and planting dense evergreens and fruit-bearing shrubs and trees, we unwittingly provide perfect conditions for robins. Robins seldom visit feeders, but will take bread, chopped raisins, and crumbled moistened dog chow in severe winter weather. Oddly enough, the American robin is the only member of its genus, *Turdus*, that breeds in any numbers in North America. The closely related clay-colored robin, which looks like a washed-out, American robin, breeds sparingly in south Texas.

Wood Thrush

Hylocichla mustelina

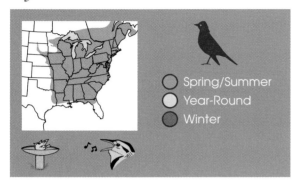

Spring/Summer
Year-Round
Winter

The lilting flutelike song of the wood thrush inspires bird watchers, naturalists, poets, musicians, and humankind in general. Few things are more beautiful than the evening song of the wood thrush as it echoes from deep within the forest. However, this species has suffered severe declines in population during the past thirty years due to loss of habitat, forest fragmentation, and nest parasitism from the brown-headed cowbird.

All About

This medium-sized (7³/4 inches in length) brown thrush has a bright rufous head and neck, olive-brown back and tail, and a white breast with large dark spots. Erect and robinlike in its posture, the wood thrush sings a multi-pitched and highly variable *eeeolay* song and utters a *whit-whit-whit* call when agitated. Wood thrush males do most of their singing at dawn and dusk, and usually from a midlevel perch in the forest.

Habitat & Range

Wood thrushes only spend their summers with us in eastern North America, arriving as early as April, but departing for the tropics by mid-August or later. Many make the flight across the Gulf of Mexico in both spring and fall. During the breeding season, they can be found in mixed deciduous forests with tall trees and a thick understory. Fragmented forest plots or those with cleared understory (due to deer browsing or human landscaping) are far less attractive to wood thrushes.

Feeding

Feeding much like a robin on the forest floor, the wood thrush sweeps aside leaf litter with its bill to uncover insects, larvae, millipedes, moths, ants, and even salamanders and snails. In fall, wood thrushes will feed in forest edge habitats to take advantage of fruits and berries.

Nesting

The female wood thrush builds a cup-shaped nest out of grasses, leaves, and rootlets, usually held together with mud, in the fork of a tree branch within 20 feet of the ground. She lays three to four eggs and incubates them for about 12 days before they hatch. Young wood thrushes are ready to fledge two weeks later. Wood thrush nests in fragmented forest habitats are more likely to be parasitized by the brown-headed cowbird, which does not build its own nest, but rather lays its eggs in the nests of other songbirds—often at the expense of the host species.

Backyard & Beyond

From spring through fall your best chance of locating a wood thrush is to listen for a male singing from patches of dense forest. Once you hear the song, patiently scan the upper, inner branches of the forest for this rusty-brown master singer. If you live in wooded habitat that is home to wood thrushes, be a good neighbor and keep pets restrained during breeding season.

Gray Catbird

Dumetella carolinensis

Spring/Summer
Year-Round
Winter

Named for its mewing catlike call, the catbird is actually a multitalented singer that is almost comparable to the mockingbird in its vocal versatility. Able to operate both sides of its syrinx, or vocal organ, independently, it can actually sing two different songs at once, and it's a mimic, too—not a bad resume for an otherwise plain gray bird.

All About

A slim, slate-gray bird about 9 inches long, the catbird is distinguished by a solid black cap and a bright chestnut patch under its tail. Because of its habit of cocking its tail, this patch is often visible. Catbirds are easy to recognize because—no matter what age, sex, or season—they all look the same. Very vocal, the male catbird makes an almost endless array of sounds, one after the other; some are his own and others are "stolen" from other birds or even from frogs, domestic animals, or mechanical devices heard in his travels. You can usually tell a catbird's song from that of other mimics, though, because each phrase is repeated only once, and the telltale *meouw* is thrown in from time to time.

Habitat & Range

In most of its U.S. range, the catbird is migratory, moving southward in winter, away from the coldest weather. Flying at night, migrant catbirds are often victims of collision, striking tall buildings or communication towers with distressing frequency. A few avoid the dangers of migration by remaining in their northern terri-

tories, a tactic that works if they are well fed and the season is not overly harsh.

Feeding

Foraging in thickets and brambles, the gray catbird eats mostly insects in spring and summer, adding small fruits as fall approaches. Favored insects include caterpillars, ants, aphids, termites, cicadas, and dragonflies. Among fruits it chooses grapes, cherries, and berries, followed by such late-lingering items as multiflora rosehips, catbrier, privet berries, bittersweet, and mountain ash.

Nesting

Singing from deep within a thicket, the male catbird courts his female in spring. After mating, she builds a bulky cup of twigs, weeds, and leaves, sometimes adding bits of paper or string and then lining it with fine grasses or hair. She incubates her three or four eggs for about two weeks; both parents then feed the nestlings for 10 to 12 days until they fledge. Two broods are common.

Backyard & Beyond

If a catbird remains in your neighborhood during winter it may be attracted by offerings of dried or fresh fruit, suet, doughnuts, peanut hearts, or table scraps. These birds are easily intimidated by other species, so they are more likely to respond to food scattered on the ground than concentrated in a small feeding dish.

Northern Mockingbird

Mimus polyglottos

Spring/Summer
Year-Round
Winter

This formerly southern species has been expanding its range for a century and now covers nearly every corner of the United States. Its rich, warbling voice and uncanny ability to imitate the calls of other birds—not to mention rusty hinges, frogs, dogs, and squeaky wheels—make it a superstar in any avian chorus. Five different states have chosen this popular songster as their state bird!

All About

The mockingbird is fairly large (9 to 11 inches long) with medium-gray upperparts and a pale breast and belly. Its long tail is edged in white, and there are prominent white patches on the wings that are especially visible in flight. The bill and legs are black. The sexes are alike. This bird's voice more than makes up for its plumage. It is loud, clear and—in spring and summer—nearly incessant. When the moon is bright, mockingbirds will sing at night. The mockingbird tends to repeat each phrase three times before moving on to the next. Both males and females sing.

Habitat & Range

Mockingbirds like to feed in short-grass areas with shrubby edges, so they are common in suburban towns, open city parks, small family farms, hedgerows, backyards, and similar situations. They are nonmigratory, present year-round in the areas they inhabit.

Feeding

The diet of the mockingbird is composed of insects (spring and summer) and fruits (summer, fall, and winter). Earthworms, spiders, snails, and other small meaty prey round out the menu. Multiflora rosehips are a mainstay in winter, and the range expansion of the mockingbird may have coincided with the spread of this alien plant.

Nesting

During spring courtship, a male mockingbird sings almost around the clock, often from a high perch, all the while jumping up in the air and waving his wings. When a female responds, both partners build the nest, a bulky mass of twigs around a cup of softer plant material, lined with moss and animal hair. Three to four eggs are laid and incubated by the female for about two weeks. The nestlings are fed by both parents for 12 days until fledging, and for about two weeks after as they learn to fend for themselves.

Backyard & Beyond

Though mockingbirds do not eat the usual feeder fare they may be attracted, especially in winter, with offerings of suet, peanut butter, doughnuts, or small fruits. This is not always a good idea, however, for mockers are very territorial, and individual birds may defend a winter-feeding area against all other species. If this happens, the easiest solution is to hang feeders on all sides of your house, so the aggressive mockingbird cannot see and defend all of them at once.

Brown Thrasher

Toxostoma rufum

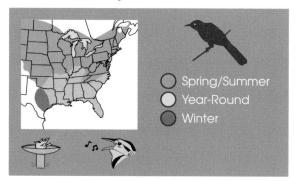

- Spring/Summer
- Year-Round
- Winter

The brown thrasher has a lush resounding voice, and sings a seemingly endless train of melodies—its own and others'—from one end of a spring day to the other, and it may stay hidden in a deep shrub all the while. The state bird of Georgia, the brown thrasher is common throughout its range, but not as well known as it ought to be. This mimic is a cheerful and friendly addition to any backyard.

All About

Nearly a foot long, the brown thrasher is a strong and handsome bird, equally at home in woodland edges or shrubby backyards. Its upperparts are bright cinnamon, broken only by two, thin, white wing bars; its white breast is heavily streaked in brown. It has a long tail, a long slightly curved bill, and strong sturdy legs well suited to "thrashing" about on the ground. Beginning birders may confuse a thrasher with one of the thrushes, or perhaps a fox sparrow, but the thrasher is much larger, with a longer bill and tail. The thrasher's song is almost as rich and varied as a mockingbird's, and it is very similar in quality, but where the mocker usually sings its phrases three times each, the thrasher utters his only twice.

Habitat & Range

Often seen on the ground, the brown thrasher is a bird of woodland edges, thickets, hedgerows, brushy riversides and parks, and shrubby backyards. It retreats from the northern reaches of its breeding range to spend the winter in less frigid areas, usually returning sometime in April. In most of the South, it is a year-round bird.

Feeding

More than half the brown thrasher's diet consists of insects—beetles, grasshoppers, cicadas, and caterpillars—most of which it finds on the ground as it rummages with feet and bill among the leaf litter. Brown thrashers also eat fruits, nuts, seeds, and acorns.

Nesting

The male brown thrasher sings vigorously upon first arriving at its breeding grounds, both to establish territory and to attract a mate. The mated pair builds a large, twiggy nest in deep cover, usually quite close to the ground. Both parents incubate four eggs for nearly two weeks. Chicks are fully feathered and ready to fly in just nine days, an adaptation to avoid predators, which are especially dangerous to low-nesting birds. Two and sometimes three broods are raised each year.

Backyard & Beyond

Brown thrashers will visit feeding stations for seeds and grains that are scattered on the ground. Nuts are popular, as are suet mixtures, cornbread, doughnuts, and raisins. Thrashers are not particularly shy of humans, but do require some shrubs or hedges nearby where they can retreat if they feel threatened.

European Starling

Sturnus vulgaris

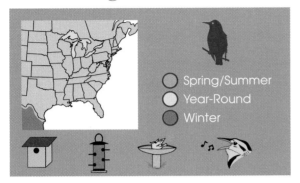

Spring/Summer
Year-Round
Winter

In 1889, there were no European starlings in North America, yet today—just over a century later—we have more than 200 million. Blame a fan of William Shakespeare. In 1890, a flock of a hundred starlings was released in New York's Central Park in an attempt to bring to America all the bird species mentioned in Shakespeare's plays. The adaptable starling soon spread westward in history's greatest avian population explosion.

All About

Glossy black overall, with a yellow bill during breeding season, the starling is one of the most familiar birds—not only because it is so common, but because it almost always lives close to human settlements. In winter, starlings are duller overall, covered with white spots (little stars, or "starlings") and with a blackish bill. In all seasons, starlings are very vocal, displaying an astonishing ability to mimic other bird songs, sirens, voices, barks, or mechanical sounds. In flight, starlings flap their triangular-shaped wings rapidly.

Habitat & Range

Starlings cover the entire North American continent year-round, except for the Far North in winter. In fall they form gigantic, noisy flocks roaming in search of food and roosting sites. Every habitat type can host starlings, but they prefer those altered by humans (farmland, urban, and suburban areas) and tend to avoid remote, pristine habitats except where humans are present.

Feeding

Insects, berries, fruits, and seeds are the starling's regular diet, but they are highly adaptable—as willing to eat French fries from a dumpster as they are to find bugs in our lawns or suet at our feeders. The starling's traditional foraging technique is to insert its long, sharp bill into the ground and then open it to expose beetle grubs and other prey.

Nesting

Starlings are cavity nesters that cannot excavate their own holes, so they use existing cavities, such as woodpecker holes, pipes, crevices in buildings, and birdhouses. Sites are often usurped from other, less aggressive cavity nesters, such as bluebirds or purple martins. Once a male has a site, a female will help finish the nest—a messy affair of grass, feathers, paper, and plastic. Between four and six eggs are laid and incubated by both parents for about 12 days. Young starlings leave the nest three weeks later.

Backyard & Beyond

Most Americans can see a starling simply by looking out their window. Many bird watchers consider them a pest at their feeders and birdhouses. To discourage starlings at your feeders, simply remove the foods they prefer: suet, peanuts, bread, and cracked corn. At nest boxes, an entry hole diameter of 1⁹/₁₆ inches or less will exclude starlings. Frequent removal of their nesting material will also discourage them.

Cedar Waxwing

Bombycilla cedrorum

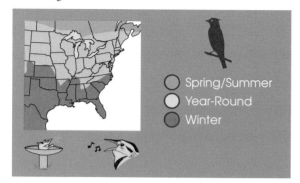

Spring/Summer
Year-Round
Winter

A beady, insectlike trill first alerts many bird watchers to the presence of cedar waxwings, so completely do they blend into canopy foliage. These wandering fruit-eaters appear and disappear seemingly without rhyme or reason, descending to strip a tree of its fruits, then whirling off to parts unknown. Fermented fruits may cause entire flocks to stagger about on the ground until the intoxication wears off.

All About

"Sleek" is the word most often used to describe the silky fawn plumage of the cedar waxwing. A velvety-black bandit mask hides the eyes, and a bright yellow band tips the gray tail. Older birds have red tips on the secondary wing feather shafts, which look like shiny drops of sealing wax. Cedar waxwings are most often seen in flocks in fall and winter.

Habitat & Range

The cedar waxwing's only real habitat requirement is the presence of fruit-bearing trees and shrubs; thus, it can be found everywhere except grasslands, deserts, and deep interior forests. Thought to be nomadic, the species does make a poorly understood migration that takes it as far south as southern Central America.

Feeding

Cedar waxwings travel in tight flocks to locate and feed on small fruits. They may be completely hidden in leaves as they flutter and pluck fruit, only to explode out with reedy calls and a rush of wings when startled. In late summer, they may be seen in twisting, dodging pursuits of winged insects over water.

Nesting

Though they defend no territory and in some places are semicolonial, cedar waxwings are monogamous. Both sexes help build a bulky, cup-shaped nest in the outer canopy of a tree. Leaves, straw, twigs, and string, often in a trailing mass, comprise the nest. The female lays four eggs and incubates them for 12 days, while the male feeds her. Young are fed on insects for the first two days, then solely on regurgitated fruits, leaving the nest around 15 days later. This fruit-based diet ensures that any parasitic brown-headed cowbirds hatching in their nests do not survive. Large flocks of immature birds (identifiable by their yellowish, streaked bellies) linger near breeding grounds for one or two months after the adults leave.

Backyard & Beyond

Attracting cedar waxwings is best accomplished by planting the trees and shrubs they prefer—serviceberry, hawthorn, firethorn, dogwood, chokecherry, viburnums, native honeysuckles, blueberries, cedars, and others with small fruits. They may also visit birdbaths, especially those with moving water. Worldwide, there are only two other species of waxwing: the Bohemian and Japanese waxwings. Waxwings are related to silky flycatchers, a largely tropical family.

Yellow-rumped Warbler

Dendroica coronata

Spring/Summer
Year-Round
Winter

One of the best-known warblers in the United States—and easily the most widespread and numerous in winter—the yellow-rumped warbler is a paradox: Its plumage and its habitats are very variable; yet, it is relatively easy to identify whenever you find it. Eastern birds of this species used to be called "myrtle" warblers, while their western counterparts were known as "Audubon's" warblers. They are now all yellow-rumped warblers, despite differences in plumage and habitat. Trendy birders stick to their own favorite name: "butterbutt."

All About

The yellow-rumped warbler is 5 to 6 inches long, with a sharp thin bill and slightly notched tail. In breeding plumage, the eastern male is blue-gray with a white throat and belly, black streaking on the back, a black face patch, two white wing bars, black bib, and yellow spots on the crown, shoulders, and rump. Spring females are browner and duller than their mates. Immatures and fall adults are brown above, with brown-streaked underparts and little or no yellow visible. The one constant in all plumages is the bright yellow rump. That, along with a frequent and distinctive *check!* note, will quickly identify these birds.

Habitat & Range

Breeding in the far north, the eastern race of the yellow-rumped warbler is known in most of the country only as a migrant or winter resident. Migrants can be found in woodlands, hedge-rows, thickets, and even along beaches as they stream through in large flocks. Winter birds congregate wherever they can find berries, their principal cold-weather food. In Florida, yellow-rumps are known to drink the juice of broken or fallen oranges, and throughout their winter range they will consume weed seeds large and small. Some yellow-rumps come to backyard feeders where they eat a variety of fare.

Nesting

For nesting, the yellow-rumped warbler selects conifer forests, generally spruce, pine, or cedar. The female builds the nest on a horizontal branch, anywhere from 5 to 50 feet high in the tree, using bark, twigs, weeds, and roots to create an open cup that is then lined with hair and feathers. The female incubates the four or five eggs for 12 to 13 days. When the chicks hatch, both parents feed them for 10 to 12 days until fledging, and then the male feeds them for a time afterward. There are usually two broods per year.

Backyard & Beyond

In winter, yellow-rumped warblers may visit feeders to eat suet, hummingbird nectar, orange halves, or grape jelly. It is possible to lure them with sprigs of bayberry or other wild fruits. Away from home, look for them where natural foods are plentiful, such as in bayberry thickets or stands of wax myrtle.

Palm Warbler

Dendroica palmarum

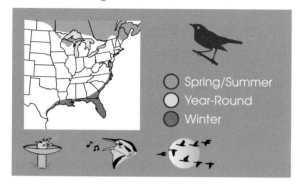

○ Spring/Summer
○ Year-Round
○ Winter

Many birds were misnamed by early ornithologists, and this is one. Except for the fact that it winters in warm climates, the palm warbler really has nothing at all to do with palm trees. It goes so far north to nest, in fact, and chooses such remote, inaccessible, and mosquito-ridden sites, that its breeding biology hasn't been fully studied to this day.

All About

Only 5 inches long, the adult palm warbler in spring has an olive back, yellow or yellow-white underparts with brown streaking, and a rusty cap edged with a yellow eyeline. The sexes are alike, but immatures (as well as fall or winter adults) are much duller—basically olive and cream with brown streaks, like little sharp-billed sparrows. Despite these variations in plumage, the palm warbler is easy to identify: All have a bright yellow patch under the base of the tail, and all have a habit of bobbing the tail constantly up and down. In fall or winter, when identification might seem difficult, no other bird combines these two characteristics.

Habitat & Range

In summer the palm warbler lives in muskeg regions of Canada and the extreme northern United States, but in migration and winter it is found widely. It spends a lot of time on the ground, in open areas such as large lawns, sod farms, and pastures, as well as along beaches, and in shrubby edge habitat of all kinds. Palm warblers often travel in flocks outside of the breeding season.

Feeding

Beetles, mosquitoes, gnats, aphids, and other small insects are the standard fare of the palm warbler, many of them picked up from the ground and others gleaned from leaves or even caught in mid-flight. This adaptable bird also consumes small berries when available and will take seeds on occasion.

Nesting

Palm warblers are early nesters, arriving in the North in April and getting started right away. Near the base of a stunted spruce at the edge of a bog, the female palm warbler will create an open cup nest, made of fine grasses and bark strips and concealed by taller grasses or a clump of moss. The four or five eggs are incubated for 12 days, possibly by both parents, and the chicks fledge at about 12 days of age.

Backyard & Beyond

Palms are not among the expected species at a bird feeder, but they may stop by on migration if you have an open lawn for them to forage on. Ball fields are another good place to look for them. The little birds may be found walking or hopping on the grass in these areas; the constantly wagging tails give them away.

Pine Warbler

Dendroica pinus

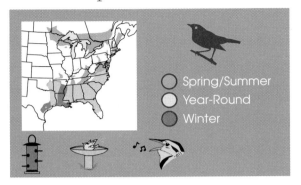

Spring/Summer
Year-Round
Winter

The pine warbler is unusual among North American warblers in that its winter range includes much of its breeding range, and almost the entire population remains in the United States year-round. A gregarious and cheerful little bird, it is often found in sizeable flocks in winter. Males sing their musical trill with abandon on all but the coldest days.

All About

A small (5 1/2 inches long) bird with a sharp warbler bill, unstreaked olive back, plain yellow breast, and two white wing bars, the pine warbler male in spring is not hard to identify. His duller mate, however, may cause confusion at times. Immatures in fall, lacking any yellow, are very like several other fall warblers, and frequently end up being called "UFOs", or Unidentified Feathered Objects. The pine warbler's song is a loose trill, similar to the notes of a chipping sparrow, but richer and more musical.

Habitat & Range

True to its name, the pine warbler is a bird of open pine woods and pine barrens, especially during the breeding season. In winter it expands its territory to include orchards, thickets, mixed woodland edges, and bottomland forests—and even suburban backyards, where it is not hesitant to seek food from a feeder.

Feeding

Like most warblers, the pine warbler prefers insect fare when available—beetles, ants, caterpillars, grasshoppers, and moths. But when this is scarce, it readily turns to alternate energy sources, such as pine seeds, grass seeds, fruits and berries, nutmeats, and animal fats. The pine warbler has mastered many different feeding techniques to fit any given situation, from foraging on the ground to climbing about on tree trunks like a creeper, clinging to a pinecone like a chickadee, or even flycatching. This adaptability is a principal reason for its population success and its ability to survive harsh weather.

Nesting

Pine warbler nests are placed high in a pine tree, well out on a limb and hidden from sight by pine needles. The female builds an open cup nest of weeds, twigs, and pine needles. The three to five eggs are incubated by both parents for about 10 days. Both parents also feed the nestlings, which leave the nest at about 10 days of age. There may be two or even three broods per year.

Backyard & Beyond

The pine warbler is one of the most willing of all North American warblers to come to backyard feeders, especially in winter. It readily takes suet, peanut butter mixes, crushed nuts, cracked corn, sunflower bits, and cornmeal from a variety of feeder types. To find pine warblers on their nesting grounds, visit appropriate pine woodlands and listen for their pleasant, trilling song.

Common Yellowthroat

Geothlypis trichas

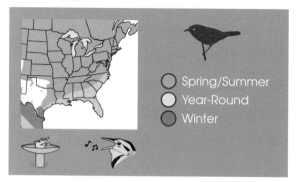

○ Spring/Summer
○ Year-Round
○ Winter

This charming bird may be the most popular warbler in North America. It is certainly one of the most widespread and well known. Its repetitive song, written as witchety-witchety-witch actually does sound like that, and beginners trying to learn bird songs find that the yellowthroat's is one of the easiest to master.

All About

Averaging about 5 inches in length, the common yellowthroat packs a lot of personality into a very small frame. Males are olive on top with a lemon-yellow throat and upper breast, white belly, yellow patch under the tail, and a bold black mask across the eyes, thinly bordered in white on top. The female is similar, but lacks the black mask. These are very active little birds and seem to be less timid than most warblers, possibly because they are nearly always low to the ground and therefore relatively easy to view. Their distinctive song continues well into the heat of summer.

Habitat & Range

Only in the dry southwestern states is the common yellowthroat hard to find during the breeding season. Everywhere else this little bird has no trouble locating the moist, shrubby, brushy conditions it needs for nesting. Even a relatively small patch of suitable habitat will do for a single pair, while large areas may host many nests. In winter and on migration, yellowthroats extend their interests to include shrubby backyards, dry woodland edges, and similar sites.

Feeding

Yellowthroats are almost exclusively insect-eaters, though they will add a few small seeds to their diet from time to time. Some favored insects are moths, aphids, leafhoppers, small caterpillars, mayflies, grasshoppers, and grubs. Foraging is done low to the ground, in dense cover.

Nesting

Female yellowthroats build a bulky cup nest quite low to the ground in thick weeds, using grasses, sedges, and other materials taken from the surrounding area. After lining it with fine grasses and hair, she lays three to five eggs and incubates them for 12 days. Her mate will bring her food during this time, and will then help her feed the nestlings for up to 10 days until fledging. The family stays together longer than most warblers, as the adults continue to feed the dependent young. Common yellowthroats are frequent victims of cowbird nest parasitism and do not seem to have an adequate defense against it.

Backyard & Beyond

In breeding season, thickets, hedgerows, marsh edges, and abandoned and overgrown farm fields are good places to look for common yellowthroats. Listen for their *witchety* song from spring through fall. In their southern winter homes, they may be harder to find, but their loud, scolding *chuck* notes will often give them away.

Summer Tanager

Piranga rubra

Spring/Summer
Year-Round
Winter

This trim and elegant neotropical migrant is sometimes called the "summer redbird" to distinguish it from the South's other "redbird," the familiar cardinal. It is shy and deliberate in its movements and, for such a colorful bird, can be surprisingly difficult to find. Luckily for the birder who seeks it, the summer tanager has several easily learned vocalizations, and it utters them often.

All About

Only the male summer tanager is red; the female is olive-backed with yellow-orange underparts. The male can be differentiated from the male cardinal by its more slender bill shape and lack of a crest on its head; it can be distinguished from a male scarlet tanager by its red (not black) wings and tail. Unlike the male scarlet tanager, the male summer tanager retains its red coloration throughout the year. The summer tanager is 7½ to 8 inches in length and sings a rich, warbling song that is similar in phrasing to a robin's. Its call is an explosive *perky-tuck-tuck!*

Habitat & Range

The summer tanager arrives on its U.S. breeding grounds sometime in April and departs, as a rule, by midfall. During migration the species covers a wide front; many birds fly nonstop across the Gulf of Mexico on their journeys north and south. Its preferred habitat is dry, open woods of oak, hickory, or pine, but many nest in wooded residential neighborhoods, as well.

Feeding

Summer tanagers are insect-eaters, and they are noted for their fearless predation on wasps, bees, and other stinging creatures. Beetles, caterpillars, cicadas, flies, and other insects are also taken, and in summer small fruits are eaten. Summer tanagers normally creep along tree branches scanning for insects, but they can also hover to glean insects from hanging leaves or capture flying insects with short flights from a perch.

Nesting

The nest of a summer tanager is a rather shallow, flimsy cup of weed stems, leaves, and fine grasses, built by the female on a horizontal branch well away from the tree trunk. The usual clutch of eggs is four, incubated by the female for 12 days. Both parents feed the nestlings until they leave the nest at about two weeks of age.

Backyard & Beyond

Look for summer tanagers near wasp nests in late summer—both adult wasps and larvae are favored food sources. Bee concentrations may also attract this species. You will improve your chances of finding a summer tanager if you learn to recognize both the warbling, robinlike song, and the *perky-tuck-tuck* call unique to this species. Summer tanagers are not generally attracted to bird feeders, but a few have been reported to eat orange halves or a peanut butter-cornmeal mix.

Scarlet Tanager

Piranga olivacea

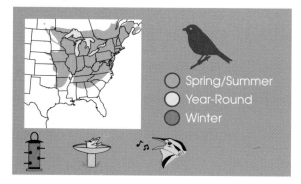

○ Spring/Summer
○ Year-Round
○ Winter

The male scarlet tanager in spring plumage ranks among the most stunningly beautiful birds in North America. One glance at his neon-bright plumage can turn even the most disinterested person into a confirmed bird watcher. Oddly, this dazzling bird's song has been compared to "a robin with a bad cold." A distinctive chick-burr call is often the first clue of a scarlet tanager's presence.

All About

The male scarlet tanager in spring plumage has a solid red body and jet-black wings and tail, with a black-button eye and bone-gray bill. The female is dull olive above with dark wings and pale yellow underparts. Immatures resemble females, and in late summer the adult males take on the muted olive-yellow plumage. In all plumages, the scarlet tanager's wings are darker than those of the summer tanager. At just 7 inches long, scarlet tanagers are the smallest of the four North American tanager species.

Habitat & Range

Preferring deciduous forests with oaks, maples, and beeches, scarlet tanagers generally inhabit areas farther north (or, in the South, at higher elevations) than summer tanagers. They arrive in April or May and depart by midautumn. Flocks of early migrants are sometimes decimated by sudden late-spring snowfalls or ice storms, which cause them to starve or freeze to death. Sometimes being the early bird is not such a good idea.

Feeding

Basically insectivorous, the scarlet tanager moves quietly about in the upper canopy of deciduous trees in search of prey. Small summer fruits—such as blueberries and mulberries—are also taken, as are fall staples, such as poison ivy berries and sumac fruits. Scarlet tanagers occasionally engage in flycatching, or hovering behavior, to obtain food. Early or late in the season, cold weather may force them to the ground to forage for bugs in sheltered microhabitats.

Nesting

Typically, the scarlet tanager nests in a large, unbroken, wooded tract and high in a deciduous tree—often, but not always—an oak. It will be situated well out from the trunk on a horizontal limb. Made by the female alone, it is shallow and loosely constructed of twigs, rootlets, weeds, and other plant material. Three to five eggs are laid, and the female incubates them for up to two weeks until hatching. Both parents feed the young during the 9- to 14-day nestling period and for two weeks more after fledging occurs.

Backyard & Beyond

Scarlet tanagers are not common at bird feeders, but they do—on occasion—respond to offerings of bread, doughnuts, orange halves, or a peanut butter-cornmeal mixture. They will also eat small fruits and, in fall migration, may be a regular sight along tangled hedgerows overrun by poison ivy or multiflora rose.

Northern Cardinal

Cardinalis cardinalis

Spring/Summer
Year-Round
Winter

Cardinals are the familiar and beloved "redbird" found all across the eastern United States. This bird's popularity is such that seven U.S. states and countless sports teams have chosen the cardinal as their official emblem. In spring and summer, cardinal pairs can be found together, often with the male perched high above, singing his what-cheer-cheer-cheer *song. In fall and winter, cardinals can be found in large loose flocks, especially during harsh weather.*

All About

A black face and a long red crest smartly set off the bright red plumage of the male cardinal. Females are a muted, brownish version of the male. Strongly territorial, mated cardinal pairs will vigorously defend their nesting turf from rivals, even going so far as to attack their own reflections in windows, mistaking the image for another cardinal. One of the cardinal's most notable behaviors is the "courtship kiss" in which a male feeds a bit of food to a female he is wooing.

Habitat & Range

Found in a variety of habitats—from deserts to wetlands to manicured backyards, cardinals prefer an *edge habitat*—a place where woodland and open space meet. They are resident (nonmigratory) and thriving throughout their range, which has expanded northward in recent decades—thanks in part to the availability of food at bird feeders.

Feeding

Cardinals forage on or near the ground. During warm weather, insects, berries, buds, and seeds are their primary diet. Gardeners appreciate cardinals for eating grubs, beetles, caterpillars, and other garden pests. In winter, cardinals shift to a greater reliance on seeds, nuts, and wild fruits. At bird feeders cardinals prefer sunflower seeds, but will also eat mixed seeds, suet, fruits, and peanuts.

Nesting

Female cardinals choose thick cover—vine or rose tangles or shrubs—in which to weave their shallow, cup-shaped nests out of grasses, rootlets, twigs, and bark strips. Into this nest, the female will lay three to five eggs and incubate them for nearly two weeks before they hatch. Both parents feed the youngsters for about 10 days before they fledge. In summer, young cardinals can often be seen following a parent around, begging to be fed. Males will take on this duty while the female starts a second brood.

Backyard & Beyond

You can enjoy cardinals all year long in your backyard by offering them the four things they need to survive: food, water, a place to roost, and a place to nest. A few bird feeders, a chemical-free lawn and garden, and some thick brushy cover will suit their requirements nicely. Watch for cardinals early and late—they are often the first birds active at dawn and the last ones to "turn in" at dusk.

Indigo Bunting

Passerina cyanea

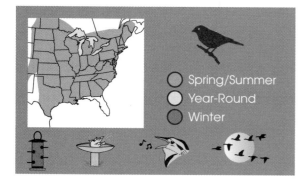

- ○ Spring/Summer
- ◐ Year-Round
- ○ Winter

Appearing all black against the light, a male indigo bunting properly lit is an unforgettable sight. A persistent late-season singer, he sings a jingly song comprised of paired notes that are often described as: Fire! Fire! Where? Where? Here! Here! Put it out! Put it out! *Much of what we know about celestial navigation in songbirds derives from work with captive indigo buntings at the Cornell Lab of Ornithology.*

All About

The breathtaking, all-blue male indigo bunting, with his silvery conical bill, is unmistakable. Females and immatures are a warm cocoa-brown overall. This bunting has a habit of twitching its tail to the side, and its *spit!* note is characteristic. Males change their blue feathers for brown in autumn, which makes for some interestingly mottled specimens. They molt again on the wintering grounds and return in spring, blue once more.

Habitat & Range

This species is common on roadsides and disturbed areas where "trashy" vegetation flourishes. Power line cuts, old fields, landfills, railroads, and hedgerows ring with the songs of indigo buntings, especially as summer reaches its fullest. Indigo buntings are strongly migratory, wintering in Central and northern South America.

Feeding

The indigo bunting takes insects when they are available, especially to feed its nestlings. Weed seeds are its mainstay, supplemented by berries and small fruits. It forages on or near the ground, as well as in low shrubs and trees. Watch for them in autumn, bending grass stems and flicking their tails side to side as they forage in weedy patches.

Nesting

Indigo buntings have a rather loose definition of monogamy, with extra-pair copulations being quite frequent. Males visit females in neighboring territories, and females visit males. Males vary in their tendency to feed young; some are attentive parents, whereas others leave most of the chick rearing to their mates. The nest is bulky but compact, cup-shaped, and constructed of bark strips, grass and weed stems, and skeletonized leaves, all bound with spider webs. It's often low in blackberry, sumac, or other brushy vegetation. These birds nest quite late in the season, reflecting their dependence on late-maturing weed seeds. Three to four eggs are incubated by the female for about 12 days, and the young leave the nest from 8 to 14 days later.

Backyard & Beyond

Lucky is the one who hosts indigo buntings! Spring arrivals are most often first seen feasting on dandelion seeds. Later, black-oil sunflower seeds and millet mixes prove attractive. The growing popularity of "meadows in a can" make for rich feeding grounds for indigo buntings, which flock to coneflower, Mexican hat, cosmos, coreopsis, and especially foxtail grasses.

Eastern Towhee

Pipilo erythrophthalmus

Spring/Summer
Year-Round
Winter

Drink your TEA! *sings the towhee throughout the brushy woodlands of the eastern United States. Formerly called the rufous-sided towhee (a much more descriptive name), this large (8½ inches long) sparrow is boldly patterned and spends nearly all its time on the ground scratching among the leaf litter, looking for food. The name towhee comes from the bird's call, which has also been transcribed as* chewink. *Many people know this bird as the chewink instead of towhee.*

All About

Clean, flashy colors have given the towhee the nickname "Hollywood robin." In flight, the bird's white wing and tail spots are noticeable. Female eastern towhees replace the male's black plumage areas with chocolate brown. Towhees' preference for thick cover and brushy habitat make them harder to see than other common species. The loud scratching of a foraging towhee sounds like a large animal walking through dry leaves; this is often your first clue to a towhee's presence.

Habitat & Range

Widespread across the eastern half of the United States and southern Canada, towhees in the northern part of the range are migratory, but those in the southern half are resident (nonmigratory). During mild winters, towhees may linger until harsh weather forces them to migrate or to seek the cover of wooded valleys and hollows. Brushy woodland thickets and edge habitats are preferred, but towhees are also found in older woodlands and suburban backyards.

Feeding

Towhees eat just about anything found on the woodland floor, including insects, seeds, fruits, and even snails, spiders, and millipedes. They prefer to scratch the ground under feeding stations for mixed seeds, cracked corn, and sunflower seeds (which they crack with their powerful bill).

Nesting

Towhees nest on or near the ground in a well-concealed spot. The female weaves a cup-shaped nest out of rootlets, bark strips, and grass. She also handles all the incubation duty, which typically lasts about 12 days. Normal clutch size is three to four eggs; young towhees fledge in about 10 days. Both towhee parents feed the youngsters, which allows the female to start a second—and sometimes a third—brood.

Backyard & Beyond

Spring is the best time to find an eastern towhee. Male towhees are especially vocal during the breeding season and will leave deep cover to sing from a high perch within their territory. Make your feeders much more attractive to towhees by adding a brush pile nearby to help these shy birds feel more at home. In summer, recently fledged towhees can be confusing and hard to identify with their streaky, gray-brown coloring. Their white tail spots and ground-scratching habits will give them away.

Chipping Sparrow

Spizella passerina

Spring/Summer
Year-Round
Winter

A *close look at this natty little bird reveals much to admire in its quiet and confiding ways. As common as it is around dooryards and gardens, we know surprisingly little about the chipping sparrow's mating systems. One Ontario study showed males not to be monogamous, as assumed, but to mate freely.*

All About

A rusty beret and bold, white eyeline are the best field marks of this slender little sparrow. Plain gray underparts, a streaked brown back, and a small, all-black bill set off its striking head markings. It is an under-appreciated bird, perhaps because it is so small and unobtrusive. Rather dry, monotonous trills, as well as its signature chipping notes, are the ambient sounds of a chipping sparrow's territory.

Habitat & Range

Before the massive expansion of suburbs, the chipping sparrow was limited to open, grassy coniferous forests and parklike woodlands with shrubby understories. Our suburban habitats have just the right mix of short grass, shrubbery, and conifers that chipping sparrows need, so we enjoy their company on doorsteps and sidewalks. Although northern populations are strongly migratory, southern birds flock up but tend to stay near their breeding grounds.

Feeding

Chipping sparrows forage primarily on or near the ground, feasting on weed and grass seeds and some smaller fruits. They feed insects to the young, however, sometimes flycatching on the wing. Winter flocks of up to 50 birds perch in trees, descending en masse to the ground to peck for seeds, then adjourning to treetops before the next feeding bout. At feeding stations, they'll peck on the ground or perch on hopper feeders.

Nesting

Female chipping sparrows weave lovely little nests of thin twigs and weed stems, with a center composed of animal hair. These are often concealed in low trees and shrubs, but are easily located by the shrilling of older nestlings. Females incubate the four eggs for around 12 days, and the young leave the nest about 9 to 12 days later. Streaky, brown, and nondescript, they're fed by their parents for three more weeks before forming juvenile flocks.

Backyard & Beyond

Chipping sparrows eagerly accept mixed seeds and suet dough mixtures offered on or near the ground. They're fond of rolled oats, and live mealworms will be taken straight to the young. They greatly appreciate baked and crushed eggshells strewn on a sidewalk. But it's most fun to offer them human or pet hair clippings. A trip to any salon can net a season's worth, and you may have the pleasure of finding a used nest lined with your own hair—the ultimate vanity piece for the discerning gardener.

White-throated Sparrow

Zonotrichia albicollis

Spring/Summer
Year-Round
Winter

Old Sam Peabody, Peabody, Peabody *is the sweet whistled song of the white-throated sparrow. In Canada, where this species spends the breeding season, the song is transcribed as* Oh sweet Canada, Canada, Canada—*but there's no arguing that the white-throated sparrow's song is easy to recognize. From September to March these northern breeders are with us, in loose flocks with other sparrows, brightening winter days with their cheery sounds.*

All About

The first field mark most bird watchers notice on the white-throated sparrow is not the white throat, but the black-and-white striped head pattern with a yellow spot between the eyes and bill. Even at a distance this striking pattern is obvious. Some white-throated sparrows have tan-striped heads and a tannish throat. These belong to the tan-striped variety of the species, though many ornithologists formerly thought these were young birds not yet in adult plumage. This medium-sized (6³/4 inches long) sparrow has a gray breast and a brown, lightly patterned back.

Habitat & Range

Spending most of the summer in the boreal coniferous forests of the far north and New England, the white-throated sparrow spends fall and winter far to the south, where it is a regular at bird feeders and in brushy edge habitat. It prefers a habitat with thick underbrush and is found near the edge of the woods, along hedgerows, and in brushy thickets in parks and backyards.

Feeding

White-throated sparrows prefer to feed on the ground. In spring and summer, the white-throated sparrow's diet is focused on insects—ants, grubs, and spiders—that it uncovers as it scratches through the leaf litter, much like a towhee does. In fall the diet shifts to include berries; in winter it includes mostly seeds from grasses. At bird feeders they are attracted to mixed seed, cracked corn, and sunflower or peanut bits offered on the ground or on a platform feeder.

Nesting

White-throated sparrows nest on or near the ground in a well-concealed spot. The cup-shaped nest is built by the female from grass, pine needles, and twigs and lined with soft material, such as rootlets or fur. The female incubates the four to five eggs for about two weeks; the male assists her in feeding the nestlings for the nine days prior to fledging. The young birds rely on the parents for food for about another two weeks.

Backyard & Beyond

Look for white-throated sparrows on the ground beneath your feeders from late fall through early spring. If your feeders are some distance from cover, consider moving them closer to the woods' edge, or add a brush pile nearby to make woodland birds (such as white-throated sparrows) feel more at home.

Song Sparrow

Melospiza melodia

○ Spring/Summer
○ Year-Round
○ Winter

Persistent singing, often year-round, makes this a well-named species. If there's a resident song sparrow in your yard, you'll probably hear its cheery notes at first light—as reliable as, but more pleasant than, a rooster's. One of the best-studied birds in North America, the song sparrow was the subject of Margaret Morse Nice's groundbreaking behavioral study in the 1930s. Much of what we understand about songbird territoriality began with this study.

All About

The classic "little brown job," the song sparrow has a heavily streaked white breast marked with a messy central spot. A grayish, striped face and crown and warm-brown upperparts complete the description. Flight is low and jerky, with the tail twisting distinctively. Three introductory notes leading to a variable jumble of trills and chips distinguish its song. Males and females look similar.

Habitat & Range

Though song sparrows occupy a wide range of habitats, they are most often found in shrubbery near water, from small streams to beach habitats. Song sparrows tend to be migratory in northern climes and year-round residents in the southern United States; this varies by population. The song sparrow is one of the most variable songbirds known. Populations in the Pacific Northwest, for example, are larger, darker, heavier-billed, and virtually unrecognizable compared to Southeastern coastal populations.

Feeding

The song sparrow's diet varies seasonally, with insects being its primary prey in spring and summer and with seeds and fruits dominating in fall and winter. Most of the song sparrow's foraging takes place on the ground, where it will scratch and kick about in leaf litter and grasses for weed seeds and insects.

Nesting

The persistent singing of song sparrows is linked to strong territorial behavior; where they are resident year-round, they tend to defend territories year-round. Territory boundaries are quite stable from year to year. Both sexes defend their territory, and they tend to stay with one mate. Females construct a bulky nest of bark strips and weed and grass stems, well hidden deep in a dense shrub. Small, ornamental evergreens are irresistible to song sparrows. The female incubates three to five eggs for about 13 days. Young leave the nest at only 10 days and may be fed by the parents for the next 20 days before they are fully independent.

Backyard & Beyond

Song sparrows readily visit feeders for sunflower seeds, cracked corn, and mixed seeds, preferring to feed on the ground. Peanut butter-based suet mixes are a favorite food, and song sparrows will appear to beg at windows for such fare. They are fond of water and will often nest near a water garden or backyard pond.

Dark-eyed Junco

Junco hyemalis

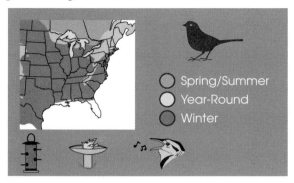

Spring/Summer
Year-Round
Winter

The dark-eyed junco is often called the "snowbird," because it seems to show up at our feeders and in our backyards at the same time as the first snows begin falling over much of the country. But even in the Deep South, this member of the sparrow family is a familiar winter visitor to backyards, gardens, parks, pastures, and feeding stations.

All About

Juncos are medium-sized (6¼ inches long) sparrows, but unlike most sparrows, their plumage lacks streaking. Dark-gray above and white below (or "gray skies above, snow below"), the junco has a conical, pinkish bill and flashes its white outer tail feathers in flight. Male juncos in the East are a darker gray than the brownish-overall females. Western junco forms show a variety of plumage colors, and many of these color forms were considered separate species until recently. Now they are all lumped into a single species: dark-eyed junco. Juncos make a variety of sounds, all of them high-pitched tinkling trills, especially when flushed from cover.

Habitat & Range

Few bird species' ranges cover North America more thoroughly than that of the dark-eyed junco. In winter it can be found in every state. Spring migration begins as early as March and continues through early June. During breeding season, juncos retreat to the far north woods and to coniferous and mixed woodlands at high elevations. Fall migration begins in mid-August through October. Their winter habitat preferences run to brushy edge habitat along woods, fields, and suburban backyards and parks.

Feeding

Juncos find their food on the ground. They are often seen scratching through the leaf litter, grass, or snow when foraging. In spring and summer the junco eats mostly insects, including spiders, caterpillars, ants, grasshoppers, and weevils, but it will also eat berries. In fall and winter the diet shifts to grass and weed seeds, along with birdseed gleaned from the ground beneath feeders.

Nesting

The junco's nest is a simple, open cup of grasses and leaves, loosely woven and lined with finer grasses, fur, or feathers. Nests are normally located on the ground in a concealed spot and built by the female. She incubates her three to five eggs for almost two weeks; the male helps with feeding chores once the young hatch. Within two weeks the young birds leave the nest, and the parents are free to start another brood if the season permits.

Backyard & Beyond

Where there is one junco, there is almost surely a flock. Seek them along the edges of woodlots, old pastures, and in areas with a thick growth of underbrush. Watch for the flashing white in the tail and listen for the juncos' trilling calls.

Eastern Meadowlark

Sturnella magna

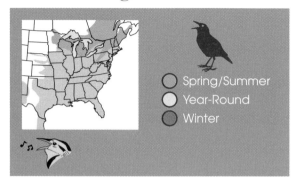

○ Spring/Summer
○ Year-Round
○ Winter

The eastern meadowlark's sweet whistled song—*spring of THE year!—is a sign of spring's arrival, as is its lemon-yellow color, adding a brightness to the most dreary of spring days. Ironically, this beloved "country" bird of open farmland is actually a member of the blackbird family, a clan that gets little affection from farmers. Echoes of the meadowlark's blackbird relatives can be heard in the bird's chattering scold calls given by territorial males in spring.*

All About

A familiar bird of rural farm fields, meadows, and grasslands, the eastern meadowlark is known by its distinctive field mark: a bright yellow breast with a "V" of black. Meadowlarks will sing from the ground and in flight, but they often use an elevated perch, such as a fencepost, tree, or power line. In flight, the meadowlark looks chunky and shows white outer tail feathers. A series of shallow, stuttering wingbeats followed by a short glide (sometimes accompanied by a song or chatter) is the typical flight pattern.

Habitat & Range

Eastern meadowlarks prefer grassy meadows, prairies, and pastures with good grass cover. They can also be found along golf courses, in hay fields, and in the grassy margins of airports. Found year-round across most of the eastern United States, this species is declining slowly across its range, especially in areas with growing urbanization and heavy agricultural use. As abandoned farm fields grow up into shrubby woodland, they become less suitable habitats for meadowlarks.

Feeding

The meadowlark is a ground feeder that searches vegetation in spring and summer for insects, such as crickets, grasshoppers, grubs, and caterpillars. In winter, the diet shifts to seeds, grains, and some fruits. In fall and winter, eastern meadowlarks often form large flocks, with dozens of birds foraging together in the same field.

Nesting

Meadowlarks nest on the ground in thick grass. The nest is well concealed in a depression on the ground and is woven out of dried grasses. Two to six eggs are laid and incubated for about 14 days. Youngsters fledge about 10 days later. Both parents feed the young. For nesting, meadowlarks seem to prefer grasslands that are cut only once every three to five years. Even so, many meadowlark nests are lost to agricultural activity, to predation, and to pesticides.

Backyard & Beyond

To find a meadowlark, you must locate a suitable habitat, which usually means locating a rural spot with hayfields and pastures. During spring and summer, meadowlarks sing throughout the day, but do so most actively early in the morning. Listen for the slurring whistled song and the sputtering blackbirdlike calls. Scan the wires, treetops, and fenceposts for the singing adult bird.

Brown-headed Cowbird

Molothrus ater

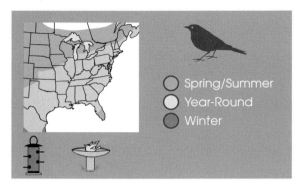

Spring/Summer
Year-Round
Winter

The cowbird's habit of laying its eggs in the nests of other, smaller songbirds makes the brown-headed cowbird a nest parasite. Cowbirds learned this behavior over centuries of following roaming herds of buffalo. The buffalo stirred up insects, the cowbird's main food. But all the movement made it impossible to stop, build a nest, and wait for the young to grow. So the cowbirds did the most convenient thing—laid their eggs in any nest they could find along the way.

All About

The cowbird is a small (7$1/2$ inches long) blackbird. Males have a glossy black body and a dark brown head, while females are a dull gray-brown overall. The short, conical bill and pointed wings help to distinguish the brown-headed cowbird from larger blackbirds. The cowbird's song is a series of liquid gurgles followed by a high, thin whistle.

Habitat & Range

Cowbirds are found in a variety of habitats, but they prefer woodland edges, brushy fields, and old pastures, though they are equally at home in city parks and suburban backyards. Forest fragmentation has allowed the cowbird to parasitize the nests of woodland species, such as thrushes and vireos. In winter cowbirds often join flocks of other blackbirds—red-winged blackbirds, grackles, and European starlings—foraging in fields and grasslands and roosting en masse in large woodlots.

Feeding

The diet of the cowbird consists of weed and grass seeds, along with insects, especially grasshoppers and beetles. Nearly all food is taken from the ground.

Nesting

Male cowbirds court females with a variety of songs, bows, and sky-pointing displays. When she is ready to lay an egg, she finds a nest that often already contains the eggs of the nest's owner. This "host" nest is most frequently that of a smaller songbird—yellow warblers, song sparrows, red-eyed vireos, and chipping sparrows seem to be frequent victims—and the female cowbird may even remove one of the host's eggs before depositing her own. Hatchling cowbirds are almost always larger than their nest mates, and are able to out-compete them for food, enhancing the cowbird's chances of survival. Some bird species have evolved to recognize cowbird eggs and will build a new nest on top of the old one or will remove the cowbird egg.

Backyard & Beyond

Finding cowbirds is almost never a problem, but limiting their impact on our songbirds can be problematic. One way to discourage cowbirds is to stop offering mixed seed and cracked corn during spring when they show up at bird feeders before many migratory songbirds return. If you see a songbird feeding a fledgling that is larger than itself, the fledgling is likely a cowbird.

Red-winged Blackbird
Agelaius phoeniceus

- ○ Spring/Summer
- ○ Year-Round
- ○ Winter

The red-winged blackbird's name succinctly describes the male's handsome plumage; yet, the females of this ubiquitous species have baffled many a bird watcher. Their streaky brown plumage is confusingly sparrowlike. Studies have shown that one dominant male red-winged blackbird may have many adult females nesting on his territory.

All About

The *conk-a-ree* call of the male red-winged blackbird fills the air over marshes and fields all across North America. As he gives this call, announcing himself loudly to rivals and potential mates alike, he spreads his shoulders just so, showing bright red and yellow epaulets against his black wings. Redwings are medium-sized ($8^3/4$ inches long) blackbirds with an all-black body, an orange-red and yellow patch on the shoulder, and a nearly conical black bill. Females are streaky brown overall, but their longer bill helps separate them from the sparrows (which have stouter bills).

Habitat & Range

Wet meadows, cattail marshes, upland grasslands, and pastures are all breeding habitat for red-winged blackbirds. In fall and winter, they may join with other blackbird species to form huge flocks. Northern nesting redwings migrate (starting in September and October) to the southern U.S., while southern nesting birds are nonmigratory. Fall blackbird flocks move during the day in oblong, loose clouds of birds. These flocks forage by day in agricultural fields and are often perse-cuted as a nuisance species for the crop damage they inflict. Spring migration begins in mid-February and continues through mid-May.

Feeding

The red-winged blackbird's diet is mostly plant matter—weed seeds, grain, sunflower seeds, and tree seeds—along with some insects, all of which are gleaned from the ground. They will also visit feeding stations for sunflower seeds, cracked corn, peanuts, and suet. Surprisingly, they are able to use a variety of feeder types.

Nesting

Nesting starts early for the red-winged blackbird, with males singing from an exposed perch on their territories as early as February in the South, later in the North. Females choose a nest site on a male's territory and build cup-shaped grass nests that are suspended from vertical supporting vegetation. Mud forms the foundation of the nest and soft grasses are the inner lining. Clutch size is three to four eggs, and the female alone incubates them for 10 to 13 days. Both parents care for the nestlings for about two weeks, until they are ready to leave the nest.

Backyard & Beyond

Red-winged blackbirds are present continent-wide for most of the year. Wet meadows, swamps, and salt marshes are common habitats for these birds, especially in spring and summer. Listen for the male's loud *conk-a-ree* song.

Common Grackle

Quiscalus quiscula

○ Spring/Summer
○ Year-Round
○ Winter

Grackles are large, conspicuous, and noisy birds that are equally at home in a town or country setting. This species benefited greatly from the European settlement of North America as forests were turned into farm fields and new feeding and nesting opportunities emerged for the common grackle. Residential areas and farmland are particularly attractive to grackles.

All About

Nearly half of the common grackle's 12½-inch length is its tail. The grackle's black plumage is glossy and can show bright purple, bronze, or green highlights, especially on the head. Adult common grackles show a pale yellow eye, contrasting sharply with the dark head. The powerful bill is long and sharply pointed. In flight, grackles hold their long tails in a "V", much like the keel of a boat. Males and females are very similar in appearance. Grackles utter a variety of harsh, metallic tones.

Habitat & Range

Common grackles are found in almost every habitat in eastern North America; though, in winter the population is more concentrated in the eastern and southern United States. Grackles prefer edge habitat and open areas with scattered trees or shrubs. From late summer to early spring, grackles gather in large roosts with other blackbirds. These roosts can contain as many as half a million birds, and are notable both for their noise and their droppings.

Spring migrants may reach breeding territories as early as mid-February. Fall migration begins in September and peaks in October.

Feeding

During breeding season, grackles eat mostly insects, but they are opportunists and will take nestling birds or eggs, small fish, mice, and frogs. In winter the diet shifts to seeds and grain. The impact of foraging winter flocks on crops has earned the common grackle a reputation as an agricultural pest. Most of the grackle's foraging is done on the ground, where the birds toss aside leaves and rubbish to uncover their food.

Nesting

Grackles prefer to nest in dense conifers, close to rich foraging habitat. The large, open, cup nest is built by the female from grass, twigs, and mud and is lined with soft grass. She incubates the four to five eggs for about two weeks. The male joins her in feeding the nestlings an all-insect diet until fledging time arrives about 20 days later.

Backyard & Beyond

Look for long dark lines of migrating common grackles during the day, especially in fall. Migrating flocks can contain thousands of birds and may stretch from horizon to horizon. At feeders grackles relish cracked corn and sunflower seeds most of all. Grackles are also known to take hard, stale pieces of bread and dunk them in a birdbath to soften them up.

Orchard Oriole

Icterus spurius

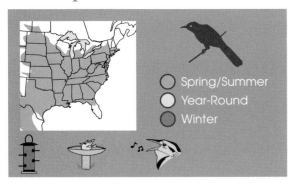

*T*he smallest oriole in North America is also the darkest, with a designer color scheme of chestnut and black that is rarely seen in songbirds. Look for it along watercourses, on farmsteads, and in orchards. In suitable habitats, the orchard oriole may nest semicolonially, with several nests to a tree. This raises interesting and as yet unanswered questions about its mating system and social behavior.

All About

The male's deep orange-chestnut underparts are set off by a black hood, back, and tail. The female is an even olive-yellow overall, with whitish wing bars. She is small enough to sometimes be mistaken for a warbler. Newly fledged young are olive-yellow, and males in their second spring are similar, but for a striking black "beard." This plumage can confuse the beginning bird watcher. The orchard oriole's song is rich, fast, and varied, with chatters and metallic notes pouring out in a jumble. The alarm call is a dry *check!*

Habitat & Range

The orchard oriole is strongly associated with watercourses and inhabits areas with smaller, denser trees than does its larger cousin, the Baltimore oriole. Farmyards and gardens and some yards with scattered trees are graced with its dynamic presence. Orchard orioles spend a relatively short time on the breeding grounds, often departing for Central America as early as July, after raising a single brood.

Feeding

This oriole eats primarily insects, but it is fond of nectar and fruits as well, taking whatever is available. Blooming black locust trees, rich with sweet nectar, are irresistible, and it will slit the sides of trumpet vine flowers to access the nectar. Orchard orioles glean tree leaves for insects and sometimes hunt grasshoppers near the ground in agricultural fields.

Nesting

A master weaver, the orchard oriole makes a neat, round basket of green grass leaves that slowly dries and shrinks to a pale, densely woven ball. Though it is similarly suspended, its nest is not long-necked or pendulous like the Baltimore oriole's; instead, it is a deep cup. Four to six eggs are incubated by the female. Young fledge about 11 to 14 days later. They are fed by both the male and female until the male departs for the wintering grounds.

Backyard & Beyond

This oriole is not particularly attracted to feeders; however, fruit or nectar feeders might lure the occasional patron. Orchard orioles migrate in segregated flocks, with adult males departing suddenly in late July. Females and similarly plumaged fledglings flock together and forage for another four to six weeks before starting south.

House Finch

Carpodacus mexicanus

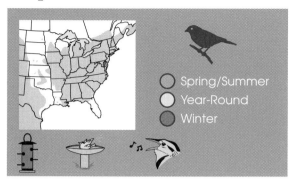

○ Spring/Summer
○ Year-Round
○ Winter

Bird watchers who rely on an eastern field guide that is more than thirty years old may be forgiven for some confusion. This bird won't be in it! The house finch, native to the West, is a well-established, but recently arrived resident of the eastern United States. Released upon the passage of protective legislation forbidding trade in native wild birds, a small population of the so-called "Hollywood linnets" began breeding on Long Island in 1940, and they have now blanketed the eastern United States with their progeny.

All About

People who feed birds are familiar with the house finches that sometimes cover feeders with fluttering, tweeting flocks. It's easy to see why they were kept as cage birds; the male's cheery, rich song, marked by a few harsh notes, tumbles brightly down the scale. Females are streaky, pale brown birds with white undersides; males have a rich pinkish-red rump, head, and upper breast. By comparison, male purple finches have an overall "dipped in wine" look, with a reddish suffusion to their back and wings, while female purple finches are much more boldly streaked with brown and white than are female house finches.

Habitat & Range

As its name suggests, the house finch prefers nesting and feeding near homes. It's a thoroughly suburban bird in the East, but in its native West, it is found in undisturbed desert habitats as well. This species appears to be developing migratory behavior in the East, with a general movement toward the South in winter.

Feeding

Most of the house finch's diet is vegetarian, and it spends a great deal of time feeding on the ground. Weed seeds, buds, and fruits are its mainstays away from feeding stations.

Nesting

House finch nests are shallow twig platforms with a finely woven inner cup composed of rootlets, grass, feathers, and string. They are tucked into dense ornamental evergreens, hanging baskets, ledges, ivy-covered walls, and other nooks where there is an overhanging structure. Two to five eggs are incubated by the female, while the male feeds her. Young are fed regurgitated seeds and fledge from 12 to 16 days later.

Backyard & Beyond

For most feeding station proprietors, the question is not how to attract house finches, but how to discourage them. Even attractive birds with pleasant songs wear out their welcome when they descend in dozens, monopolizing feeders. Black-oil sunflower seeds are a favorite, closely followed by Niger and mixed seeds. Some people resort to removing perches from tube feeders, thus discouraging house finches, which are poor clingers.

American Goldfinch
Carduelis tristis

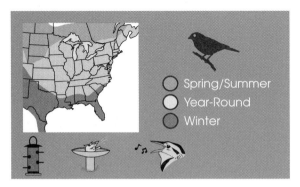

- ○ Spring/Summer
- ○ Year-Round
- ○ Winter

The bright canary-yellow and black plumage of the breeding male American goldfinch has earned this species the nickname "wild canary." It is a familiar visitor to bird feeders at all seasons, especially in winter. The goldfinch's undulating flight is accompanied by a twittering call of perchickoree or potato chip!

All About

American goldfinches appear very different in summer and winter. The male's brilliant yellow body and black cap in summer give way to a drab, olive-brown plumage in winter. Female goldfinches, though never bright yellow, also lose most of their color. Both sexes retain their black wings and tail year-round. The sweet, high-pitched, warbling song of the male is often given in early spring, just as these small (5 inches long) birds are beginning to show their first bright yellow feathers.

Habitat & Range

Weedy fields, brushy woodland edges, and open habitats with scattered shrubs are the American goldfinch's normal habitats. In the breeding season, they prefer weedy fields with thistles and other seed-producing plants. In winter, goldfinches roam in noisy flocks, seeking food in fields, gardens, and at feeding stations.

Feeding

Goldfinches are seedeaters in all seasons, consuming a huge variety of weed, grass, and plant seeds as well as tree buds. In goldfinch nests par-asitized by brown-headed cowbirds, young cowbirds are unable to survive the all-seed diet fed to nestling goldfinches. Goldfinches are agile birds, able to exploit seed sources that other finches cannot, by hanging upside down from seedheads, plant stalks, and bird feeders.

Nesting

Goldfinches' nesting season begins late, an adaptation to time so that nesting occurs when there is the greatest natural abundance of seeds, as well as the soft thistle down that goldfinches use to line their nests. Late June is the earliest nesting time, but peak nesting season is late July, though some nesting occurs as late as September. The site is in a shaded spot in a sapling or shrub and is selected by the pair. The female builds the open cup nest from twigs (attached with spider web), rootlets, and plant stems, and she lines it with soft thistle down or a similarly soft material. Four to six eggs are incubated by the female for about two weeks, with the male bringing food to her on the nest. Both parents tend the nestlings for 12 to 17 days before they fledge.

Backyard & Beyond

The twittering calls of goldfinches will alert you to the presence of these energetic songbirds. At bird feeders, goldfinches especially like thistle seeds (sometimes called Niger seeds), sunflower seeds and bits, and peanut bits. Goldfinches love to drink and bathe in shallow birdbaths and are especially attracted to moving water.

House Sparrow

Passer domesticus

- Spring/Summer
- Year-Round
- Winter

Introduced to North America in the early 1850s from England to help control wireworms, the house sparrow population spread across the continent in just 50 years. The house sparrow enjoys a close association with humans, almost always nesting and living in proximity to our settlements. It is one of the world's most successful and widespread species.

All About

The chunky little house sparrow is known for its constant *cha-deep, cha-deep* calls and for the male's black bib in breeding plumage. Breeding males have a black bill and a contrasting black, gray, and brown head and face pattern. Winter males are a muted version of the breeding plumage. Females are drab gray-brown overall and lack the bib. House sparrows are constantly chirping and are aggressive competitors at feeders and nest sites.

Habitat & Range

House sparrows are year-round residents. It's easier to describe where you *won't* find house sparrows because they are utterly ubiquitous. Pristine natural habitats—forest, grassland, or desert—that are lacking human development will also lack house sparrows. Historically, the house sparrow associated with horses (and the seeds and insects in their droppings) and other livestock. Today, house sparrows are found in the most urban of habitats, living on food scraps and nesting in building crevices—though they are still a common inhabitant of horse barns, farmyards, and feedlots.

Feeding

Seeds and grains will be on the house sparrow's normal menu throughout the year. In spring and summer, they take advantage of bountiful insect populations. At any time, house sparrows are quick to take food at bird feeders or scraps of food offered directly or indirectly by humans in parks, picnic areas, fast food restaurants, and strip malls. Cracked corn, sunflower seeds, peanut bits, and bread products are favorite foods.

Nesting

Males choose a cavity and sing by it to attract the female. Both build the messy nest of grass, weed stems, feathers, paper, and string. House sparrows will appropriate nest boxes from bluebirds, swallows, and purple martins (forcing many nest box landlords to use controls and special housing to discourage house sparrows), and they may even kill nest box competitors. The female lays between three and six eggs, which are incubated by both parents for 10 or more days. The parents share feeding duties until the nestlings are ready to fledge at about two weeks.

Backyard & Beyond

House sparrows are feeding station regulars, especially in towns and cities. To discourage house sparrows from dominating nest boxes, use boxes with interiors less than 5 inches deep, remove their nesting material regularly, and place nest boxes far from buildings and thick shrubbery.

Lack of Birds

- During spring and summer, the diet of many of our seed-eating feeder visitors shifts to a greater reliance on insects, fruits, and other natural, abundant food sources. Even during the traditional fall and winter bird-feeding seasons, birds may not immediately find a feeding station. Once the first chickadee, goldfinch, or titmouse "tunes in" to your feeders, the word will spread quickly and other birds will show up. Temporary loss of birds at a feeder can be caused by the presence of a hawk, a cat, or stale birdseed.

Discouraging Squirrels

- It is a battle that has been going on for nearly a century: humans trying to keep squirrels from getting to bird feeders. There are many squirrel-proof feeders available, but squirrels figure out many of these after a time. Placing your feeders on baffled poles far from any tree, deck railing, or other potential launching pad that a squirrel could use seems to be the most successful strategy. Alternatively, offer the furry menaces some cracked corn (or ears of field corn) far away from your feeders. Keep squirrels happy elsewhere, and you may keep them off your feeders.

Blackbirds, Pigeons, Jays, and Sparrows

- Certain birds can hog all the space and food at your feeders to the exclusion of the smaller, less aggressive species. You can limit the impact of these "feeder hogs" by removing their preferred food from the menu. For blackbirds, pigeons, and doves, limit the cracked corn and mixed seed; for jays and crows, limit the suet, peanuts, cracked corn, and table scraps; for sparrows, limit the cracked corn and do not feed bread. Larger birds (such as grackles, rock pigeons, and blue jays) can also be discouraged through the use of small tube feeders with short perches—small birds can use 'em, but big birds can't.

Hawk at Feeders

- Cooper's hawks and sharp-shinned hawks are songbird specialists that can be attracted to the bird activity at your feeders. Their tactic is a quick surprise attack, scattering the feeder visitors and perhaps catching a slow, sick, or unwary individual. As unpleasant as it may seem, it is perfectly natural and is an important aspect of nature's balance.

Cat at Feeders

- Place your feeders a short distance away from thick cover where hunting cats might lurk. Mount your feeders high enough (above 4 feet) that a leaping cat cannot reach feeding birds. A circle of short (1-foot) wire fencing can make it more difficult for charging cats to catch birds.

Night Marauders

- If your feeders empty out overnight, you probably have a mammal making nocturnal visits to your feeder. This furry critter could be a raccoon, an opossum, a flying squirrel, deer, or even a bear! Feed only as much seed as can be eaten by your birds during a single day, and you'll discourage these late-night diners.

Sick Bird at Feeders

- Sick birds often show up at feeders, desperate for an easy meal, and they usually succumb to their illness within a short while. Although most bird illnesses are not transferable to humans, it pays to be cautious. Contact your local wildlife officials about any sick birds you see at your feeders—they often monitor wildlife health trends. If you find a dead bird, avoid making direct contact with it (wear gloves or use a plastic bag to pick it up), and bury it or discard it in the trash. Clean your feeders thoroughly and consider halting your feeding for a few days to allow the healthy birds to disperse temporarily.

Food and Feeder Chart

Species	Food
Quail, pheasants	Cracked corn, millet, wheat, milo
Pigeons, doves	Millet, cracked corn, wheat, milo, Niger (thistle seed), buckwheat, sunflower, baked goods
Roadrunners	Meat scraps, hamburger, suet
Hummingbirds	Plant nectar, small insects, sugar solution
Woodpeckers	Suet, meat scraps, sunflower hearts/seed, cracked corn, peanuts, fruits, sugar solution, mealworms
Jays	Peanuts, sunflower, suet, meat scraps, cracked corn, baked goods
Crows, magpies, nutcrackers	Meat scraps, suet, cracked corn, peanuts, baked goods, leftovers, dog food
Titmice, chickadees	Peanut kernels, sunflower, suet, peanut butter, mealworms
Nuthatches	Suet, suet mixes, sunflower hearts and seed, peanut kernels, peanut butter, mealworms
Wrens, creepers	Suet, suet mixes, peanut butter, peanut kernels, bread, fruit, millet (wrens), mealworms
Mockingbirds, thrashers, catbirds	Halved apples, chopped fruit, mealworms, suet, nutmeats, millet (thrashers), soaked raisins, currants, sunflower hearts
Robins, bluebirds, other thrushes	Suet, suet mixes, mealworms, berries, baked goods, chopped fruit, soaked raisins, currants, nutmeats, sunflower hearts
Kinglets	Suet, suet mixes, baked goods, mealworms
Waxwings	Berries, chopped fruit, canned peas, currants, dry raisins
Warblers	Suet, suet mixes, fruit, baked goods, sugar solution, chopped nutmeats
Tanagers	Suet, fruit, sugar solution, mealworms, baked goods
Cardinals, grosbeaks, pyrrhuloxias	Sunflower, safflower, cracked corn, millet, fruit
Towhees, juncos	Millet, sunflower, cracked corn, peanuts, baked goods, nutmeats, mealworms
Sparrows, buntings	Millet, sunflower hearts, black-oil sunflower, cracked corn, baked goods
Blackbirds, starlings	Cracked corn, milo, wheat, table scraps, baked goods, suet
Orioles	Halved oranges, apples, berries, sugar solution, grape jelly, suet mixes, soaked raisins, dry mealworms, currants
Finches, siskins	Thistle (Niger), sunflower hearts, black-oil sunflower seed, millet, Canary seed, fruit, peanut kernels, suet mixes

Nest Box Chart

Species	Interior Floor Size of Box (inches)	Interior Height of Box (inches)	Entrance Hole Diameter (inches)	Box Mounting Height (feet)	Habitat for Box Placement
Chickadees	4x4	9–12	$1^1/8 - 1^1/2$	5–15	Open woods and edges
Prothonotary Warbler	4x4	12	$1^1/4$	5–12	Wooded areas, swamps and streams
Titmice	4x4	12	$1^1/2$	5–12	Wooded areas and edge habitat
White-breasted Nuthatch	4x4	12	$1^1/2$	5–12	Wooded areas and edge habitat
Carolina Wren	4x4	9–12	$1-1^1/2$	5–10	Old fields and thickets
Eastern Bluebird	4x4	12	$1^1/2$	5–6	Open land with scattered trees
Tree Swallow	5x5	10–12	$1^1/2$	5–10	Open land near pond or lake
Purple Martin	6x6	6	$2^1/8$	15–25	Open country near water
Great-crested Flycatcher	6x6	12	$1^3/4 - 2$	6–20	Open woods and edges
House Finch	5x5	10	$1^1/2$	5–10	Backyards and porches
Downy Woodpecker	4x4	12	$1^1/2$	5–20	Forest openings and edges
Hairy Woodpecker	6x6	14	$1^1/2$	8–20	Forest openings and edges
Red-bellied Woodpecker	6x6	14	2	8–20	Forest openings and edges

Nest Box Chart

Species	Interior Floor Size of Box (inches)	Interior Height of Box (inches)	Entrance Hole Diameter (inches)	Box Mounting Height (feet)	Habitat for Box Placement
Red-headed Woodpecker	6x6	14	2	8–20	Forest openings and edges
Northern Flicker	7x7	16–24	$2^1/_2$	10–20	Farmland, open country
Pileated Woodpecker	12x12	24	4	15–25	Mature forest
Bufflehead	7x7	17	3	5–15	Wooded lakeshores, swamps
Wood Duck	12x12	24	3x4 oval	5–20	Wooded swamps, bottomland
Hooded Merganser	12x12	24	3x4 oval	5–30	Wooded swamps, bottomland
Goldeneyes	12x12	24	$3^1/_4$ x $4^1/_4$ oval	15–20	Wooded lakeshores, swamps
Common Merganser	12x12	24	5x6 oval	8–20	Wooded lakeshores, swamps
Saw-whet Owl	7x7	12	$2^1/_2$	8–20	Forest clearings and edges
Screech-owls	8x8	18	3	8–30	Farmland, orchards, woods
Barred Owl	14x14	28	8	15–30	Mature bottom-land forest
Barn Owl	12x36	16	6x7 oval	15–30	Open farmland, marshes
American Kestrel	9x9	16–18	3	12–30	Farmland

A Glossary of Common Bird Terms

- **Avifauna:** The community of birds found in a given region or habitat type.

- **Cavity nester:** A bird that nests inside an enclosed area such as a hollow tree, an old woodpecker hole, or a bird house.

- **Crown:** The top of a bird's head.

- **Diurnal:** Active during daylight hours.

- **Edge habitat:** A place where two or more habitats come together, such as where woodland meets an old meadow. Edge habitat typically offers a rich diversity of birds.

- **Endemic:** A breeding species that is unique to a given geographical region.

- **Extinct:** A bird that no longer exists in the wild. The Carolina parakeet is an example of an extinct species.

- **Extirpated:** A bird that once was present in a given area but no longer is. It does exist in other areas, however. For example, the red-cockaded woodpecker has been extirpated from much of its original range throughout the South, but remains in small pockets of its former range.

- **Eyeline:** Refers to a line of contrasting colored feathers over or through a bird's eye, often used as a field mark for identification.

- **Field mark:** An obvious visual clue to a bird's identification. Field guides are based on describing field marks of birds.

- **Fledgling:** A bird that has left the nest, but may still be receiving care and feeding from a parent.

- **Hotspot:** A location or habitat that is particularly good for bird watching on a regular basis.

- **Juvenile/Juvenal:** *Juvenile* (noun) refers to a bird that has not yet reached breeding age. *Juvenal* is an adjective, referring to the plumage that a juvenile bird wears.

- **Life bird:** A bird seen by a bird watcher for the first time is a life bird. Life birds are usually recorded on a birder's life list, a record of all the birds he or she has seen at least once.

- **Lores:** The area between a bird's bill and its eyes.

- **Migrant:** A bird that travels from one region to another in response to changes of season, breeding cycles, food availability, or extreme weather. Many of our warbler species that spend the spring and summer in North America *migrate* to Central or South America for the winter.

- **Mimic:** A term used to describe birds that imitate other sounds and songs. Three common bird species are mimics: the northern mockingbird, gray catbird, and brown thrasher.

- **Nape:** The back of a bird's neck, often referred to in reference to a field mark for identification.

- **Neotropical migrant:** Refers to migratory birds of the New World, primarily those that travel seasonally between North, Central, and South America.

- **Nestling:** A bird that is still being cared for in the nest.

A Glossary of Common Bird Terms

Peeps: A generic term for groups of confusingly similar small sandpipers.

Pishing (or spishing): A sound made by bird watchers to attract curious birds into the open. Most often made by repeating the sounds *spshhh* or *pshhh* through clenched teeth.

Plumage: Collective reference to a bird's feathers, which can change both color and shape through the process of seasonal molt. During a molt, a bird loses some or most of its old worn-out feathers and grows new healthy feathers to replace them. Breeding plumage is worn by birds during the breeding season and this is often when a bird is at its most colorful. Non-breeding or winter plumage is worn during fall and winter, generally, and is often less colorful than breeding plumage.

Primary feathers (primaries): The long flight feathers originating from the "hand," or end, of a bird's wing.

Raptor: A term used to refer to a bird of prey, including hawks, owls, osprey, and vultures.

Resident: A non-migratory species—one that is present in the same region all year.

Spotting scope: A single tube optical device mounted on a tripod and used to look at distant birds. Most birding scopes are between 15x and 60x in magnification power.

Suet: The large chunks of hard, white fat that form around the kidneys of beef cattle. Suet is used by bird watchers as a high-energy winter food for birds.

Tail spot: Spots, usually white, on a bird's tail, often used as a field mark for identification.

Underparts: A term referring to the lower half of a bird (breast, belly, undertail), often used in relation to a field mark.

Upperparts: A term referring to the upper half of a bird (crown, back, top of tail), often used in relation to a field mark.

Vagrant: A bird that wanders far from its normal range.

Wing bars: Obvious areas of contrasting color, usually whitish, across the outer surface of a bird's wings.

Frequently Asked Questions

General

Q. There is a bird in my backyard that not only sings throughout the day, but also *all night long!* This particular bird has many, many songs. Do you have any idea what kind of bird this is?

A. Your bird is most likely a northern mockingbird. Don't worry, male mockingbirds only perform this nocturnal singing in the spring and summer, during the time of the full moon. Try running an electric fan (to create a buffer of sound) or using your earplugs on those nights when the male mockingbird is singing. Having a mocker around is a good thing—some would even consider you lucky!

Q. A female robin recently built a nest in a tree on my patio. On May 10, she started laying her eggs—four in total. How long before they hatch, and how long after that do they still need the nest?

A. Robins incubate their eggs for 12 to 14 days. Once hatched, the nestlings remain in the nest for another 14 to 16 days before fledging. Two weeks is normally the incubation period for most songbirds. Another two weeks is an average time before the young leave the nest.

Q. Many times I have seen hawks being mobbed by American crows or other blackbirds. Is this a common phenomenon, and why does it occur?

A. Mobbing behavior by crows is common. The crows are reacting to the potential threat that the hawk poses as a predator to the adult crows and their offspring. The mobbing often serves to harass the hawk into leaving the area. Occasionally, a mobbed hawk will turn the tables and attack and kill a crow.

Q. A woodpecker is pecking holes in my house siding. Is there anything I can do to get it to stop?

A. A woodpecker drilling on your wooden house is only doing what comes naturally—drilling into wood in search of shelter or food. Most house-wrecking woodpeckers do their damage in fall, which is when they begin making their winter roost holes. Try mounting a nest box with an appropriately sized hole over the drilled area. Fill the house with wood chips, and you may divert the bird's attention and gain a tenant.

Woodpeckers also use wood and sometimes metal parts of houses as drumming sites. They drill their bills against the surface in a rapid staccato beat. This drumming noise is a territorial announcement and a method for attracting a mate. Drumming happens most regularly in spring. There are several things you can try; one of them may work.

1. Place some sheet metal or heavy aluminum foil over the area the bird is using.

2. Hang some aluminum pie plates around the affected area. Make sure they move in the wind (to scare the bird away).

3. Place a rubber snake near the drilling area (to scare the bird away).

4. Repeatedly scare the bird when it lands on your house.

5. If nothing else works, call your local wildlife official to see if someone can come to your house to remove the offending bird.

Frequently Asked Questions

Q. Is seeing a robin a true sign of spring's arrival? Where do they go in winter?

A. American robins are surprisingly hardy as long as they have access to their winter food sources: fruits. They switch over in winter from their mostly insect-based summer diet. As such, robins are *facultative migrants*. This means that they will migrate only as far south as they need to or are forced to by bad weather or food shortages. During ice storms, when fruits are covered in a thick coating of ice, many robins flock together and move south. In the same way, if a robin spends the winter in your region, it's probably because there's enough food to see it through.

The idea that robins are the first true sign of spring is somewhat mythical. In much of northern North America, a few robins overwinter, but they stick to woods and thickets where they can find fruit. Most backyard bird watchers do notice the robins' return when these birds appear on lawns with the onset of warm weather, seeking their warm-weather food: earthworms, grubs, caterpillars, and other insects.

Q. Do all birds mate for life?

A. No. Some species have unusually strong pair bonds between mated birds. These species include some eagles, cranes, swans, geese, and ravens. Being mated "for life" means, really, for as long as both birds are alive. When one of the pair dies, the other will take a new mate. Most North American bird species pair up primarily to reproduce, and then go their separate ways soon after they have nested. In some species, the pair bond is brief. In the case of ruby-throated hummingbirds, the pair bond lasts only as long as courtship and copulation. The male has nothing to do with the incubation or raising of the young birds.

Q. Do all birds migrate?

A. Not all bird species migrate, but most do. Migration in North America is defined as the seasonal movement of birds, northward in spring from the wintering grounds, and southward in fall from the breeding grounds. Among the birds that are *resident*, or that do not migrate, are many grouse, ptarmigan, and quail species; many owl species; pileated, red-bellied, downy, and hairy woodpeckers along with white-breasted nuthatch, Carolina wren, northern cardinal, wrentit, ring-necked pheasant, Townsend's solitaire, common raven, gray jay, and northern mockingbird.

Bird Care

Q. Is it true that if you find a baby bird out of the nest, you should not touch it because the parent birds will detect your scent and abandon the nest?

A. No, most birds do not have a well-developed sense of smell. However, most mammalian predators (skunks, foxes, raccoons, weasels, and so forth) do have a good sense of smell and may follow your scent trail to a bird's nest. If you are going to handle a baby bird be sure to place it out of harm's way, back in the nest or in an open-topped cardboard box propped in a tree. Many bird species are equipped to survive outside the nest at a very young age. These species include many shorebirds, gamebirds, and birds such as robins and wrens.

Q. If I find a baby bird that has fallen from a nest, what should I do?

A. Try to place the nestling back in its nest if at all possible. This will be the baby bird's best chance at a normal life. If you can't find the nest or a place to put the nestling out of harm's way, you will need to get the bird to a licensed rehabilitator as soon as possible.

Baby birds are unable to *thermoregulate* (regulate their body temperature), and so must be kept in a protected area with a heat source. A soft nest made of tissues inside a small cardboard box, placed on a heating pad set on LOW temperature, is a good example of a temporary home. A moist sponge placed in the box will add a touch of desired humidity. This will warm the bird.

Try to contact a wildlife rehabilitator as soon as possible. Your state fish and wildlife officers are responsible for licensing and regulating the activities of rehabilitators and have listings for those in your region. Make sure anyone else giving you advice is familiar and current with the specialized needs of wildlife.

Q. I found an injured bird. What should I do with it?

A. A person must have special permits from the federal, state, or provincial government to handle injured or dead non-game bird species. While your first instinct may be to call your local veterinarian, many vets are unwilling to care for "wildlife cases." In many situations, the best thing to do is to let nature take its course. Birds and other creatures are part of nature's natural cycle of life and death. An injured or dead bird may be a meal for another animal. If you feel you *must* do something to help an injured bird, call your local wildlife office, department of the environment, fish and game, or extension office. Your local vet may take rehabilitation cases—or may know of a licensed rehabilitator in your area.

Window Strikes

Q. A bird is flying from window to window, butting its head against the glass while looking into the house. Can you explain this behavior?

A. Your bird is fighting its reflection in the windows, thinking that the reflection is a rival bird. The behavior will last through the breeding season. One solution is to place screens over the outside of the window. Plastic wrap stuck to the outside will also work—anything that will break up the reflection will do. You may also offer your bluebirds places to perch, such as snags and posts, far from windows. Bluebirds love a perch in the middle of a lawn or field. This has worked to distract the birds from windows.

Q. How can I keep birds from flying into my windows?

A. Silhouettes of flying hawks or falcons do work, but they perform best when applied on the outside of the glass. Hanging ornaments such as wind chimes, wind socks, and potted plants also helps. Misting the outside of the window with a very weak detergent or soda solution will eliminate the reflection, but will also impair visibility for you. Awnings, eave extensions, and window screens will eliminate reflection and stop the collision problem. Plastic cling wrap applied to the inside or outside of the window can also be effective. One of the most effective solutions we have found is FeatherGuard, a series of bright-colored feathers strung on fishing line and hung over the outside surface of the glass.

Bird Feeding

Q. What is the best seed to offer birds?

A. Black-oil sunflower seed is the most universally eaten seed at bird feeders. But there are many other seeds and foods to offer birds. What is most popular with your birds depends on where you live and what birds are present.

Q. What is the best feeder for bird feeding?

A. There is no single best feeder for bird feeding. A well-rounded feeding operation will include a platform feeder, a tube feeder, a hopper feeder, a suet feeder, and a peanut feeder. And don't forget the birdbath!

Q. I recently purchased a bird feeder, but have yet to see any birds. What am I doing wrong?

A. You're not doing anything wrong. It takes time for birds to locate a new feeding source. A spell of bad weather always drives birds to concentrate at feeders. Try putting your feeder in a new location far from your house and the portion of your yard where you are active. Put the feeder in or near a tree that the birds regularly use.

Q. Do birds that eat at feeders lose their ability to find food naturally? If I stop feeding them, will they starve?

A. No. Birds are not totally reliant on the food offered at your feeding station. Birds are programmed by instinct to forage for food, and they have evolved over millions of years to be very mobile in their food-finding habits. Because they can fly, birds are efficient at going to where the food is. Though feeding stations have been linked to slightly improved survival rates for birds in harsh weather conditions, overall bird feeding does not drastically affect the birds' survival. Also, when warmer weather comes, many of the seed-eating birds that frequented your feeders during winter switch to an insect-based diet in spring.

Q. How do I keep squirrels away from my bird feeders?

A. Baffling your feeders (preventing squirrels from gaining access to the feeders) is the best way. Feeders can be strung from a thin wire, far from any object from which the squirrels can leap. String the wire with empty 35mm film canisters (with the lids on), which will spin and dump the squirrels off. There are many squirrel-proof feeders on the market. These may give the squirrels a small electric shock, may prevent them from reaching the seed, or may rotate or bounce to dump the squirrels off. But be forewarned: Squirrels have been known to outsmart the most ingenious of the squirrel-proof inventions.

And if you can't beat 'em, join 'em! Feed squirrels ears of dried corn, but place the corn away from your bird feeders. Given the choice, squirrels will always go for the easiest food, and they *love* corn.

Q. What can I do to protect the birds in my yard from cats?

A. Hang feeders at least 5 feet above the ground. For ground-feeding birds, arrange ornamental border fencing in two or three concentric circles about 16 inches to 2 feet apart, to disrupt a cat's ability to leap at feeders or to spring on birds. Harass offending cats with a spray of water to train them to avoid your yard. If all else fails, use a live trap to catch the cats and take them to the local animal shelter. If the cats belong to your neighbors, ask them to restrain their pets from accessing your yard.

Hummingbirds

Q. What is the best ratio of water to sugar to use for feeding hummingbirds?

A. Four parts water to one part sugar (a 4:1 ratio) has been shown to be the closest to the sucrose content of natural flower nectar. Concentrations stronger than this (such as a 3:1 ratio or stronger) are readily consumed by hummers, but no scientific evidence exists regarding the potential helpful or harmful effects on hummingbirds.

Q. Can I use molasses or honey instead of sugar to make my hummingbird nectar?

A. No. White table sugar is the only human-made sweetener that, when mixed with the right amount of water, closely resembles natural flower nectar. Resist the urge to use other sweeteners, which spoil quickly and may not be good for hummingbirds to consume.

Q. Is the red dye found in premixed solutions bad for hummingbirds?

A. Though no conclusive scientific evidence exists showing harmful effects of red food dye on hummingbirds, this chemical additive is certainly not a necessary ingredient in hummingbird solution.

Many commercially available brands of hummingbird solution contain red food coloring that is meant to be attractive both to hummingbirds and to shopping bird watchers. Brightly colored flowers are nature's way of attracting the eye of a foraging hummingbird, so the red solution in feeders is aimed at attracting hummingbirds. Bright red feeder parts (which most hummer feeders have) or a bright red ribbon hung near the feeder can be just as attractive as red-dyed solution. Red dye or food coloring may or may not be harmful to hummingbirds, but it is completely unnecessary.

Q. How do I foil a "bully" hummer?

A. Many hummingbird species defend feeding territories, and assemblages at feeders usually develop hierarchies. The behavior exemplifies natural selection at work, and you should do nothing except enjoy it.

If you're worried about hungry hummers, put up several more feeders near your original one. The bully will be overwhelmed by the sheer numbers of other birds and will quit being so territorial.

Q. Do hummingbirds migrate on the backs of Canada geese?

A. No. This is either a Native American myth or just an old wives' tale. Hummingbirds are excellent, strong-flying migrants. A healthy ruby-throated hummingbird can easily handle the 500-mile flight across the Gulf of Mexico.

Q. Is it true that hummingbirds at my feeder will not migrate if I leave my feeder up in the fall?

A. No. This is another in a long line of bird myths. Birds are genetically programmed to migrate when their internal "clocks" tell them to do so. They will depart when the time is right—whether your feeders are up or not. However, leaving your feeders up in fall, and getting them up early in spring may help early or late migrants that are passing through your area.

How to Build a Simple Birdhouse

These plans are designed to help you build a simple birdhouse—one that is easy to put together and will attract a number of species. The $1^1/2$-inch entrance hole will allow birds as large as bluebirds to enter the house, but even tiny house wrens and chickadees will find this house appealing.

Before you begin the building process, read through this entire plan. This will make the building go more smoothly and should prevent costly, frustrating errors. Study the instructions and drawings together. The letters in the instructions refer to the drawing that illustrates a particular section of directions.

Now, let's look at materials. Cedar will last, but it can be expensive. Pound for pound, cedar is the most durable, weather resistant, and provides the best insulation—so if your budget permits it, cedar is the best wood to use for birdhouses. After years of weather, nails in cedar can become loose, so I suggest using screws in place of nails for cedar construction. Pine is easy to nail and does not split easily, but it will decay unless preservatives are used (on the outside of the box only).

An excellent alternative material is $5/8$-inch thick exterior plywood. It is tough, weathers well, and will not split along the edge if you use nails of the proper size, usually four-penny galvanized box nails. Called T 1-11, this wood has vertical grooves to resemble boards and is often used for exterior siding on homes. Most lumber yards and home centers sell T 1-11 in large 4-x-8-foot sheets. When assembling a birdhouse using exterior plywood, always remember to keep the weather surface of the wood on the outside of the birdhouse. It is an obvious point, but one that is easily forgotten in the midst of the building process.

Unless otherwise instructed, use four-penny galvanized box nails for nailing house parts together. Remember to use screws when using cedar or pine or when you feel extra strong binding is necessary.

It's impossible to predict which bird species is most apt to settle in your new birdhouse. Half a dozen cavity-nesting birds prefer a box with a single slant roof and a $1^1/2$-inch-diameter entrance. Depending on your location, it could be tree swallows, hairy or downy woodpeckers, or perhaps titmice, chickadees, Carolina or house wrens, or even bluebirds.

Good luck with your building—and with being a landlord to the birds!

Materials:

western red cedar, exterior plywood, or T 1-11 siding scraps ($5/8$ inch thick, 31×14 inches), which will be cut into the following pieces:

bottom: 5×5 inches
sides (cut 2): each $10 \times 9 \times 5$ inches
back: $12 \times 6^1/4$ inches
front: $9^1/2 \times 6^1/4$ inches
roof: $8^1/4 \times 8^1/4$ inches
four-penny galvanized box nails
right-angle screw hook, about $1^1/2$ inches long
caulking compound
sixteen-penny galvanized framing nails
2 galvanized siding nails (or wood screws), $1^3/4$ inches long

Tools:

square	2 C clamps (optional)
ruler	rasp
pencil	hammer
saw	wood blocks of
plane	various sizes
brace, with $1^1/2$-inch	drill, with assorted
expansion bit and	small bits
$1/2$-inch diameter	
bit	

How to Build a Simple Birdhouse

Instructions:

A

1. On the weather surface of the plywood, measure and mark with a pencil the exact outlines of each piece. Be sure the grain of the wood runs vertically on the two side pieces, the back, and the front. The T 1-11 siding has a vertical groove running down it. This won't hurt anything—but when laying out the parts, keep the groove away from the edge of each piece to avoid problems with nailing later on.

2. Lay out the two side pieces with a common line along the 9-inch dimension so that the tops angle toward the center line, making a shallow V. In this way, when you assemble the house, the weather surface will end up on the outside.

3. After checking the measurements once more, carefully saw or cut out all the parts. Trim the rough edges with a plane to knock off splinters. You won't need to sand anything—this is going to be rustic!

4. Lay the parts on the workbench and mark them, just to keep track. There are six parts—two sides, a roof, a bottom, a front, and a back.

5. To accommodate the roof slant, you will need to bevel the top edges of the front and back panels with a plane. Set the two pieces in front of you, just as they will be when assembled. On the weather surface of the front panel and on the inside surface of the back, draw a horizontal line 1/8 inch down from the top. Then bevel off 1/8 inch from each piece individually.

6. On the front panel, center a vertical line running 3 inches down from the top. Put a cross

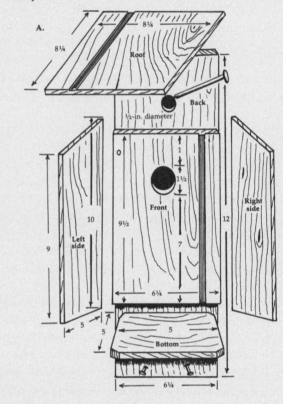

A Simple Birdhouse

A.

Note: Dimensions are in inches

mark on the line, 1 3/4 inches from the top. Open the expansion bit to precisely 1 1/2 inches, then test it on a scrap board and measure the hole. Now, to ensure a clean cut, clamp the panel tightly to a board. Center the bit on the cross mark and drill the hole. (If you have no C clamps, lay the panel on a board and drill halfway. Turn it over and drill through the other side.) Round off the sharp edges with a rasp.

7. On the bottom piece, measure 3/8 inch in on each side of each corner and mark. Place a ruler diagonally across each corner and connect the two marks. Saw off the four corners at these points. The resultant openings in the finished house will allow adequate drainage and air circulation for the birds.

8. On the back panel, with the weather side up, center a vertical line—2 inches long—down from the top. At the bottom of the line, drill a 1/2-inch hole.

9. Mark a line across the weather surface of both side panels, 1 inch up from the bottom. On the right panel, extend the bottom line across the edges. Mark a line across the face of the front panel, 1 inch up from the bottom. It, too, should extend across the edges.

10. Now, mark a line across the weather surface on the back panel, 2 1/2 inches up from the bottom, and extend it across the edges.

B

1. You are now ready to start putting things together. Lay the right-hand side panel (the one on the right when the entrance of the completed birdhouse faces you), weather surface up, on the bench. Start two nails, each 1 1/2 inches in from the edge and 1/4 inch below the bottom line. Drive them in until they barely peek through the other side. Be sure they are straight.

2. Place the bottom panel (weather side toward you) on edge and at a right angle to the bench, against a flat wall or solid surface. (When the corners are cut off, it is easier to get the side and bottom flush when both are pressed against a flat wall.) Lay the right side panel (weather side out) across the upper edge of the bottom piece, matching the line on the side panel with the interior surface of the bottom. (Place a block under the other end of the right panel.) Drive the nails in part way—just enough to hold.

C

1. Turn the assembled pieces over so the right side faces you. Place two nails in the weather surface of the back panel, 1/4 inch below the line you marked earlier and 1 1/2 inches from the ends of the bottom panel. Drive them in until they begin to show on the other side.

2. Put the back piece on the two pieces that you assembled. Make sure that the lines marked on the bottom match, and that the edges are flush with the outside of the side panel.

B.

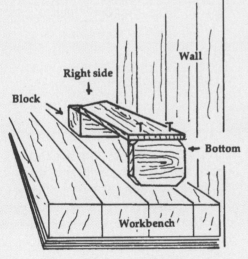

C.

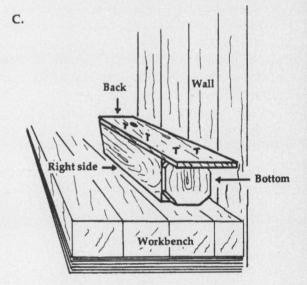

How to Build a Simple Birdhouse

D.

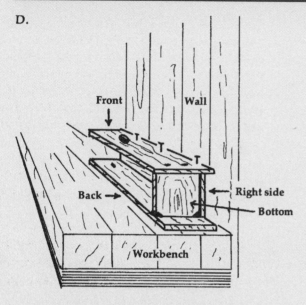

2. Put the front in place, matching the lines marked at the bottom with the interior surface of the bottom panel. There should be about a 1/2-inch gap at the top of the right side when the roof is on.

3. Drive the nail into the bottom, nearest the enclosed side, until the nail holds. Then start a nail 2 inches down from the top of the front panel and 1/4 inch in from the edge. Make sure that the front panel edge and the side are flush. Drive the nail in part way. Spring the bottom corner into alignment, and drive the nail near the open edge part way into the bottom. Start another, 2 inches up from the bottom, and drive it in part way. If everything looks good, pound in all the nails.

E.

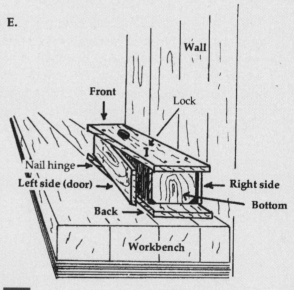

3. Drive the nail into the bottom, nearest the side panel, enough to hold. Start another nail along the edge of the back panel, 2 inches down from the top and about 1/4 inch from the edge. Check to see that the back panel edge and the side are flush. Drive the nail in part way.

4. Now check the bottom. Its outer corner may be sprung slightly. Press it into alignment with the back panel marks, hold, and drive the other bottom nail in part way. Check it over to see if the bottom is lined up. If so, place one more nail along the edge, 4 inches up from the bottom of the back panel, and drive in all the nails.

D

1. Turn the unit on its back. Lay out the front panel, weather side up—racing stripe dazzling your eyes—and start two nails 1/4 inch below the bottom line and 1 1/2 inches in from each edge. Be sure the points have just come through the other side.

E

1. Fit the left-hand side panel into position. If it is tight, plane down the edge for a looser fit. You want this "door" to open easily even when the wood swells in wet weather, so you can inspect the nest and clean out the house at the season's end.

160

2. Check for about a ¹/₂-inch gap at the top. Drive two nails—one into the bottom and one into the front, halfway up—part way in to hold temporarily. (They will be removed later.)

3. On the left edge of the front panel, make a mark 1 inch from the top. Using a square, draw a horizontal line across the left side panel on the mark. At one end of this line, drive a nail through the front panel into the edge of the left panel. At the other end of the line, drive a nail through the back panel into the edge of the left panel. These nail hinges will allow the "door" to be opened.

4. Put a mark on the front panel 2 inches up from the bottom and centered over the edge of the door. Drill a small hole, about 2 inches deep, at the mark. Use a right-angle screw hook twisted into place as a lock nail. It is not likely to fall out of the hole, as a nail might, when the box is tipped forward. Remove the temporary nails and test the door.

F

1. On the roof, start two nails, each ¹/₄ inch in from the back or top edge of the roof, and about 2 inches in from the left and right sides. Remember that the roof slants, and you want the nail angled so it goes straight into the edge of the back panel. Stand the box upright with a block under the front. Run a strip of caulking compound along the top edge of the back panel. Place the top on, with the wood grain running down the slant, not across it.

2. Adjust the roof for equal overhang on each side. It should be flush with the back. Drive the nail in part way.

3. Sight along the front and drive two more nails—gingerly—into the top edge of the front panel until they hold. If it looks right, hammer them in.

G

1. Now for hanging the birdhouse. If there are predators in your area, resist the temptation to hang your house on a tree or fencepost. If your area is predator-free (and not many areas are in North America), trees or fenceposts may be acceptable. To be safe, I suggest baffling all of your bird houses.

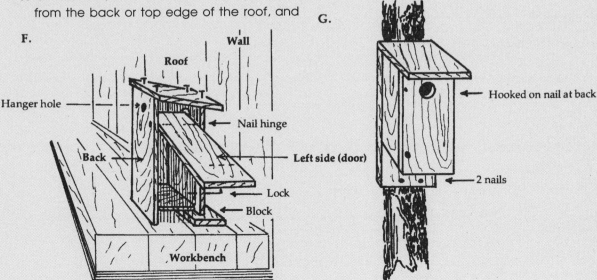

F. Wall / Roof / Hanger hole / Nail hinge / Back / Left side (door) / Lock / Block / Workbench

G. Hooked on nail at back / 2 nails

Bird-Friendly Plants for Your Yard

TREES

Common Name	Latin Name	Good For/Other Notes
Apples	*Malus* spp.	Fruit, insects, cavities
Ashes	*Fraxinus* spp.	Seeds, insects, cover
Aspens	*Populus* spp.	Seeds, insects, cover, cavities
Birches	*Betula* spp.	Seeds, insects, cover
Cedars	*Juniperus* spp.	Fruit, year-round cover
Cherries	*Prunus* spp.	Fruit
Chokecherry, common	*Prunus virginiana*	Fruit
Cottonwoods	*Populus* spp.	Cavities, shelter
Crabapples	*Malus* spp.	Fruit, insects
Dogwoods	*Cornus* spp.	Fruit
Firs	*Abies* spp.	Year-round cover
Hackberries	*Celtis* spp.	Fruit, cover
Hawthorns	*Crataegus* spp.	Fruit, cover, nesting
Hemlocks	*Tsuga* spp.	Seeds, insects, shelter
Hollies	*Ilex* spp.	Fruit, year-round cover
Junipers	*Juniperus* spp.	Year-round cover
Larches	*Larix* spp.	Seeds
Madrones	*Arbutus* spp.	Fruit
Maples	*Acer* spp.	Seeds, cover
Mesquites	*Prosopis* spp.	Shelter
Mountain ashes	*Sorbus* spp.	Fruit
Mulberry, red	*Morus rubra*	Fruit
Oaks	*Quercus* spp.	Acorns, cover, insects
Pines	*Pinus* spp.	Year-round cover, insects
Poplars	*Populus* spp.	Cavities, shelter
Sassafras	*Sassafras albidum*	Fruit, cover, cavities
Shadbush, or serviceberry	*Amelanchier laevis*	Fruit, flowers
Spruces	*Picea* spp.	Year-round cover
Sycamores	*Platanus* spp.	Cavities, shelter, insects
Willows	*Salix* spp.	Cavities, shelter, insects

Bird-Friendly Plants for Your Yard

SHRUBS

Common Name	Latin Name	Good For/Other Notes
Arrowwood viburnum/ Viburnums	*Viburnum dentatum/ Viburnum* spp.	Fall fruit. Tolerates shade
Bayberry, northern	*Myrica pensylvanica*	Fruit. Male & female plants needed for fruit
Blackberry, American	*Rubus allegheniensis*	Fruit, dense cover, nesting
Blueberry, highbush	*Vaccinium corymbosum*	Fruit, flowers, cover. Needs acid soil
Chokeberry, red	*Aronia arbutifolia*	Fruit. Moist soil preferred
Cranberry, highbush	*Viburnum trilobum*	Fruit. Shade tolerant
Dogwoods	*Cornus* spp.	Fall fruit, dense cover
Elderberry, American	*Sambucus canadensis*	Fruit, dense cover
Hercules' club	*Aralia spinosa*	Fruit
Hobblebush	*Viburnum alnifolium*	Fruit. Shade tolerant
Hollies, deciduous	*Ilex decidua, Ilex* spp.	Winter fruit. Male & female plants needed for fruit
Huckleberry, black	*Gaylussacia baccata*	Fruit. Sandy soil preferred
Inkberry	*Ilex glabra*	Fruit. Thicket-forming. Needs acid soil
Mahonia	*Mahonia aquifolium*	Fruit, year-round cover
Manzanitas	*Arctostaphylos* spp.	Early fruit, thick cover
Nannyberry	*Viburnum lentago*	Fruit. Shade-tolerant
Pokeweed	*Phytolacca americana*	Fall fruit.
Roses	*Rosa* spp.	Winter fruit. Summer flowers
Shadbushes	*Amelanchier* spp.	Early fruit
Spicebush	*Lindera benzoin*	Fruit. Needs moist soil
Sumacs	*Rhus* spp.	Fruit available all winter
Winterberry, common	*Ilex verticillata*	Fruit. Male & female plants needed for fruit
Yews	*Taxus* spp.	Year-round cover. Some fruit

VINES

Common Name	Latin Name	Good For/Other Notes
Ampelopsis, heartleaf	*Ampelopsis cordata*	Fruit. Resembles a grape vine
Bittersweet, American	*Celastrus scandens*	Fruit. Avoid Asian species.
Grapes, wild	*Vitis* spp.	Fruit attracts 100 species, cover

Bird-Friendly Plants for Your Yard

VINES

Common Name	Latin Name	Good For/Other Notes
Greenbriars	*Smilax* spp.	Fruit, thick cover
Trumpet honeysuckle	*Lonicera sempervirens*	Nectar, fruit, cover. Avoid Asian species
Trumpet vine	*Campsis radicans*	Nectar, summer cover
Virginia creeper	*Parthenocissus quinquefolia*	Fruit attracts 40 species

FLOWERS

Common Name	Latin Name	Good For/Other Notes
Asters	*Aster* spp.	Flowers attract butterlies, seed
Bachelor's button	*Centaurea cyanus*	Seed
Black-eyed Susan	*Rudbeckia serotina*	Seed
Blazing star	*Liatris* spp.	Seed, flowers attract butterflies
California poppy	*Eschscholzia californica*	Seed
Coneflower, purple	*Echinacea purpurea*	Seed, flowers attract butterflies
Coreopsis	*Coreopsis* spp.	Seed, flowers attract butterflies
Cornflower	*Centaurea cyanus*	Seed
Cosmos	*Cosmos* spp.	Seed
Daisy, gloriosa	*Rudbeckia* cv.	Seed
Goldenrods	*Solidago* spp.	Flowers for butterflies, winter cover
Joe-Pye weeds	*Eupaorium* spp.	Flowers for butterflies, winter cover
Marigolds	*Tagetes* spp.	Seed
Penstemons	*Penstemon* spp.	Nectar, seed
Poppies	*Papaver* spp.	Flowers attract butterflies, seed
Primroses	*Oenothera* spp.	Seed
Sedums	*Sedum* spp.	Flowers attract butterflies, seed
Sunflowers	*Helianthus* spp.	Seed
Thistles, globe	*Echinops* spp.	Flowers, seed, nesting material
Zinnias	*Zinnnia elegans*	Seed, flowers attract butterflies

Bibliography

American Bird Conservancy. 2003. *Guide to the 500 Most Important Bird Areas in the United States.* New York: Random House.

American Ornithologists' Union. 1998. *Check-List of North American Birds.* 7th edition. Washington, DC: American Ornithologists' Union.

Choate, E. A. 1985. *The Dictionary of American Bird Names, Revised Edition.* Boston: Harvard Common Press.

Ehrlich, P. R.; Dobkin, D. S.; and Wheye, D. 1988. *The Birder's Handbook.* New York: Fireside Books.

Kaufman, K. 1996. *Lives of North American Birds.* Boston: Houghton Mifflin Co.

Kaufman, K. 2000. *Birds of North America, A Kaufman Focus Guide.* Boston: Houghton Mifflin Co.

National Geographic Society. 1999. *Field Guide to the Birds of North America.* 3rd edition. Washington, D.C.: National Geographic Society.

Peterson, R. T. 1996. *A Field Guide to the Birds* (Eastern). Boston: Houghton Mifflin Co.

Poole, A., and Gill, F., eds. 1992–2002. *The Birds of North America.* Philadelphia, PA: American Ornithologists' Union/Birds of North American, Inc.,

Sibley, D. A. 2000. *The Sibley Guide to the Birds.* New York: Alfred A. Knopf, Inc.

Stokes, D., and Stokes, L. 1996. *Stokes Field Guide to Birds: Eastern Region.* Boston: Little, Brown and Co.

Terres, J. K. 1995. *The Audubon Encyclopedia of North American Birds.* New York: Wings Books.

Thompson III, B. 1995. *An Identification Guide to Common Backyard Birds.* Marietta, OH: Bird Watcher's Digest Press.

Thompson III, B. 1997. *Bird Watching For Dummies.* New York: John Wiley & Sons.

Thompson III, B. 2003. *The Backyard Bird Watcher's Answer Guide.* Marietta, OH: Bird Watcher's Digest Press.

Zickefoose, J. 1995. *Enjoying Bird Feeding More.* Marietta, OH: Bird Watcher's Digest Press.

Zickefoose, J. 2001. *Natural Gardening for Birds.* Emmaus, PA: Rodale Organic Living Books.

National Organizations for Bird Watchers

National Organizations

American Bird Conservancy
P.O. Box 249
The Plains, VA 20198
(540) 253-5780
www.abcbirds.org

American Birding Association
P.O. Box 6599
Colorado Springs, CO 80934-6599
800-850-2473
www.americanbirding.org

Cornell Laboratory of Ornithology
Attn: Communications
159 Sapsucker Woods Road
Ithaca, NY 14850
800-843-2473
www.birds.cornell.edu

National Audubon Society
700 Broadway
New York, NY 10003
(212) 979-3000
www.audubon.org

National Wildlife Federation
11100 Wildlife Center Drive
Reston, VA 20190-5362
800-822-9919
www.nwf.org

The Nature Conservancy
4245 North Fairfax Drive, Suite 100
Arlington, VA 22203-1606
800-628-6860
www.tnc.org

Field Guides to Birds

Griggs, J. L. 1997. *All the Birds of North America*. New York: Harper Collins.

Kaufman, K. 2001. *Birds of North America (Kaufman Focus Guides)*. Boston: Houghton Mifflin Co.

National Geographic Society. 1999. *National Geographic Field Guide to the Birds of North America, 3rd edition*. Washington, D.C.: National Geographic Society.

Peterson, R. T. 2002. *A Field Guide to the Birds of Eastern and Central North America (Peterson Series)*. 5th ed. Boston: Houghton Mifflin Co.

Robbins, C. S., et al. 1983. *Birds of North America: A Guide to Field Identification (Golden Field Guide Series)*. Revised edition. New York: Golden Press.

Sibley, D. A. 2000. *The Sibley Guide to the Birds*. New York: Alfred A. Knopf, Inc.

Stokes, D., and Stokes, L. 1996. *Field Guide to the Birds of North America*. Boston: Little, Brown and Co.

Audio Guides to Birds

Elliott, L. 2004. *Know Your Bird Sounds, volumes 1 and 2.* Mechanicsburg, PA: Stackpole Books.

Elliott, L.; Stokes, D.; and Stokes, L. 1997. *Stokes Field Guide to Bird Songs: Eastern Region (Stokes Field Guide to Bird Songs).* New York: Time Warner Audio Books.

Peterson, R. T. 2002. *A Field Guide to Bird Songs of Eastern and Central North America. Revised edition.* Boston: Houghton Mifflin Co.

Walton, R. K., and Lawson, R. W. 1989. *Birding By Ear, Eastern and Central North America (Peterson Field Guide Series).* Boston: Houghton Mifflin Co.

Walton, R. K., and Lawson, R. W. 1994. *More Birding By Ear (Peterson Field Guide Series).* Boston, MA: Houghton Mifflin Co.

Periodicals for Bird Watchers

The Backyard Bird Newsletter
P. O. Box 110
Marietta, OH 45750
800-879-2473
www.birdwatchersdigest.com

Bird Watcher's Digest
P. O. Box 110
Marietta, OH 45750
800-879-2473
www.birdwatchersdigest.com

Living Bird
Cornell Laboratory of Ornithology
159 Sapsucker Woods Road
Ithaca, NY 14850
800-843-2473
www.birds.cornell.edu

Photography Credits

Arthur Morris/Birds as Art: Pages 35, 46, 47, 48, 49, 50, 51, 52, 53, 54, 55, 56, 57, 58, 59, 60, 61, 63, 64, 65, 66, 67, 68, 69, 70, 71, 72, 73, 74, 75, 76, 77, 78, 79, 80, 81, 82, 83, 84, 85, 86, 87, 89, 92, 95, 96, 97, 98, 100, 102, 103, 104, 105, 106, 107, 108, 109, 110, 111, 113, 115, 116, 118, 119, 120, 121, 122, 123, 124, 125, 126, 127, 128, 131, 133, 134, 135, 136, 137, 138, 139, 140, 141, 142, 143, 144, 145

Bird Watcher's Digest: Pages 34, 37, 38 (both photos), 39 (both photos), 40, 41

Tom Vezo: Pages 62, 90, 91, 99

Maslowski Photography: Pages 88, 94, 114

Brian Henry: Pages 101, 117

Barth Schorre: Pages 129, 130

Ron Austing: Page 93

Cliff Beittel: Page 112

Bill Bevington: Page 132

Randall Ennis: Page 33

Charles Melton: Page 42

Julie Zickefoose: Page 43

Index

Sighting Notes

Date	Species/Description	Location

Sighting Notes

Date	Species/Description	Location

Sighting Notes

Date	Species/Description	Location

Meet Bill Thompson, III

Bill Thompson, III is the Editor of Bird Watcher's Digest, *the popular bimonthly magazine devoted to birds and bird watching. From an early age, Bill knew his life would be intertwined with birds and bird watching. One of his first words was "junco" and one of his early memories is of seeing a male cardinal in a tree. In 1978, his parents, Bill and Elsa Thompson,* founded Bird Watcher's Digest *in their living room, fulfilling their dream. It has been published continuously since its inception.*

In addition to this book for Cool Springs Press, Bill Thompson is the author of the best-selling book, *Bird Watching for Dummies.* He is also the author of many booklets published by *Bird Watcher's Digest.* His articles on bird watching have appeared in numerous books and magazines, including *National Gardening.* Bill is a frequent guest lecturer and speaker for many events. In addition, he is a longtime member of The American Birding Association and is a Director of the Ohio Ornithological Society.

Bill, his wife Julie Zickefoose (an acclaimed artist and nature writer), and their two children enjoy life on an 80-acre farm in Whipple, Ohio. One of their life dreams became a reality when they added a 50-foot-tall bird-watching observation tower to their home. To date, they have recorded sightings of more than 180 bird species. When he's not serving as an editor, traveling, lecturing, or writing books, Bill enjoys playing guitar in his band, *The Swinging Orangutangs*, with his wife and brother, Andy.